THE CRIME OF IMPUNITY

THE CRIME OF PUNISHMENT

JOE KAYE

To order additional copies of this book,
Visit: www.createspace.com/4270547

DEDICATED

To my beloved Sarah E. Wright,
whose searing novel
This Child's Gonna Live
is an imperishable tribute
to a field-working Black woman,
one of the most remarkable
figures in American fiction.
Tribute, as well, to the heroism
and gritty beauty of
Depression-time Black folk
on the Eastern Shore of Maryland
in a losing battle for their land
but a triumphant one
for their dignity.

AND DEDICATED

to the time
when the Inquisition's
instruments of torture
will be joined
as museum curiosities
by great stone buildings
with empty cages.

ACKNOWLEDGMENTS

If I were to acknowledge here my profound gratitude to the Women's Press Collective, and especially Lisa Daniell and Courtney Francis, for their placing at my disposal their entire resources, they would take umbrage, protesting that theirs were simple acts of solidarity and, in fact, the type of thing that is the reason for their being. So I will refrain from thanking them here.

I must, however, thank Edward Davis, Olya Lipina and, above all, Saida Bain, who created the jacket design and with exceptional patience and skill labored with me to get the book publisher-ready.

WHAT "EVERYONE" KNOWS

Everyone is fed up with crime. Everyone knows who's doing it. And everyone knows what's got to be done about it – everyone except those soft-headed, bleeding-heart liberals, ivory tower intellectuals, politicians fishing for votes of "certain" constituencies, judges playing sociologist, and so-called civil liberties groups more concerned with the rights of criminals than with those of their victims. Everyone knows about criminals being coddled, about country club prisons with revolving doors, and the bad joke called rehabilitation.

Everyone knows that Blacks and Hispanics are the criminals, especially the Blacks, and if they're not in prison it's only because they haven't been caught yet. And everyone knows that those who fill the prisons are lowlifes, animals, vermin, the dregs, raised by rotten mothers and not raised by shiftless and violent fathers.

So it's time to stop biting one's tongue for the sake of political correctness and let the chips fall where they may. It's "zero tolerance" time, "Three strikes and you're out" time, lock-the-cell-door-and-throw-away-the-key time, time to rid the world of those on Death Row trying to game the system, time to clean up the streets, put away the gang-bangers, and let the criminal element know who's in charge.

1

INTRODUCTION

When people talk about crime, it's almost always *street* crime they have in mind. This is true not only of the general public but of politicians, the media, college professors, criminologists, law-enforcement professionals, right-wingers, liberals, and even radical advocates of prisoners' rights. When the politicians or the media insist on "getting tough on crime," it is not white collar or corporate crime they are referring to. When a clamor is raised about the rights of victims, it is not about the rights of victims of corporate crime. When the now fashionable victim impact statements are given in court, they are not those of corporate crime victims. When such crime is mentioned, it is usually treated as much less serious. And while the justice system metes out punishment for street crime with ever-greater harshness, corporate crime is usually punished, where it is punished at all, with a slap on the wrist. Both liberals and conservatives understand crime to be transgressions *against* property, ignoring the more devastating crimes that represent the transgressions *of* property.

The prisons are crammed with the "poor and vicious" classes, the "dangerous classes," as they were commonly called in 19th century America. No question that the poor are dangerous. They are dangerous, however, not because they are criminally inclined but because their condition is a permanent reproach to the status quo. They are dangerous and must be held under tight control because they pose a threat to one day overturn the political and economic arrangements upon which the *rich and dangerous classes*

3

base their power and from which they siphon off their ill-gotten gain.

The purpose of this book is to challenge what "everyone knows," the conventional wisdom about crime and the criminal justice system. To this end, a few writers have made important contributions. They have done a good job of exposing "crime in the suites," corporate malfeasance, the corruption of politicians, the lies and distortions of the commercial media, and the inequities and cruelty of the criminal justice system. We are indebted to them for their valuable information as well as important insights, from which we have heavily borrowed. But analysis needs to go further. For it is our contention that it is the *elite*, the *plutocracy*, the wielders of social power, who are the primary criminals in our society. Moreover, that the source of the crimes of the elite is not greed or other defects of character, any more than character defects are the source of the crimes of the poor. Rather, the criminal acts of the rich and powerful, as well as those who serve them, are *required* of people in their position. Too terrible would be the consequences of honesty and moral conduct, not only for themselves personally, but for the institutions they serve. Yet while the crimes of the elite are not *caused* by greed, greed is a necessary *condition* for such crimes, the psychological expression of the implacable laws of an immoral system.

Beyond the misdeeds of the elite which are *officially* recognized as criminal, the fact is that the majority of the elite's sleazy acts are not considered crimes. Some of their criminal behavior is judged as "only" unethical, "only" unjust. Much of it in fact is considered perfectly legitimate. Not surprising. *For it is the elite who make and enforce the laws, make and enforce the rules of society, and therefore sit on judgment on themselves.*

Now, since we will be making moral comparisons, it should be noted that the crimes of our corporate, political and media elite, along with those of their hired hands, are not one-shot occurrences, not crimes of passion nor of desperation driven by elemental survival needs. They are continual, methodical, and ruthless. Moreover, they are carried out with a clear conscience. For the philosophy of the elite divides the world into the handful of worthies and the masses of slobs. It is the elite who are the true career criminals – career not only in the sense that their criminal deeds are performed throughout their work life, but also because their careers *require* criminality, in fact, are *equivalent* to criminality. While this may seem preposterous to the many whom the elite have safely brainwashed, we hope to show that this conclusion is quite sober. And so we contend that the vast majority of the "scum," "vermin," "animals," "lowlifes," languishing behind bars, and particularly the demonized African-Americans, are in no way morally inferior to the "pillars" of our society. In fact, quite the reverse.

CORPORATE VERSUS STREET CRIME

While there are a few who focus on corporate crime, when crime is discussed generally, corporate crime falls below the radar. Christopher Jencks, an influential academic, writing some years ago for the liberal *New York Review of Books*, seems to be an exception. He not only acknowledges the existence of white-collar crime, but even concedes that there is a street crime/white collar crime double-standard, a double-standard, however, which he then proceeds to justify. Millions annually defraud the IRS, says Jencks, "yet very few Americans view tax fraud as a serious threat to themselves or to the public." And he goes on, "Unlike robbery, tax evasion has no individual victims, does not create the same kind of fear or the same sense of personal violation as being raped or having your house burgled."[1]

In fact, the public *does* become outraged when it learns, although it is rare that it is allowed to learn, about the extraordinary degree of tax evasion by the super-rich and the corporations, as the Occupy Wall Street Movement dramatically attests. Moreover, Jencks apparently forgets about the enormous brouhaha raised against "welfare cheats," and "welfare queens" that were part of the push-back against the expansion of the social safety net. Yet in those rare cases, always well publicized, where some on state assistance have indeed chiseled the system a bit (the state cheats them infinitely more), one cannot claim that public anger is motivated by fear or "a sense of personal violation." Jencks also forgets about drug offenses which, again, do not entail any sense of personal violation. And yet media-generated hysteria about drug crime has resulted, especially since the 1980s, in a surge of incarcerations that are filling the prisons to bursting point.

Jencks continues: "We react to most other white-collar crime with equal indifference. Given a choice almost everyone would rather be robbed by computer than at gunpoint. This does not make white collar crime morally preferable to blue collar crime, but it does explain why white collar crime is not a major political issue."[2] Thus, Jencks blames public opinion for the double-standard, which he treats as if it were formed independently, as if it were not created and manipulated by the politicians and the media.

Indeed, as Professor Jencks asserts, we would all prefer to be robbed by computer than at gunpoint. But being robbed at gunpoint is a rare occurrence and the amounts involved are relatively trivial, even in the case of bankrobbery. On the other hand, being robbed by computer as well as other nonviolent means is commonplace and far more costly. And this has always been true. In the *1960s*, for example, the price-fixing conspiracy of the electrical industry alone cost $2 billion more than all the burglaries in that same period combined, and during that time a presidential commission task force concluded that, "The economic losses from various white-collar crimes such as consumer fraud, price-fixing, and tax evasion are many times greater than all street crimes combined."[3] In the *1980s*, according to the calculations of a California professor of Criminology, Henry Pontell, an expert on white collar crime, estimates that bailing out just one corrupt savings and loan institution (and there were many such bailouts) cost more than the total losses from all the robberies in history. In the *1990s*, employee theft exploded. Between 1994 and 1998, expense account abuse rose by 600 percent. Credit card fraud tripled. Lest this and other white-collar crime be attributed to the low-level workforce, it was found that owners and executives stole 16 times more than their employees. As of *2000*, white collar crime was estimated at $400 billion annually, compared to about $50 billion for street crime. And *today*, the cost of the Wall Street frauds, which have plunged the country and the world into unprecedented crisis, now runs into the *trillions*.

The mugger or armed robber would be more than happy to abandon his trade and exchange it for embezzlement, consumer fraud, price-fixing, insider trading, money laundering, and the countless swindles associated with the Wall St. operatives and other "respectable" business people. Such criminal activities are infinitely more lucrative and far less dangerous to the perpetrators. That such a choice is not made is due solely to the fact that the street criminal lacks the practical means. The methods used by the criminal are a function of his social class, not moral compass.

Having touched on the existence of white-collar crime, Jencks forgets about it immediately. The rest of his discussion refers only to street crime, and particularly to violent street crime, which he attributes in large measure to bad genes, throwing in bad parenting, for good measure. About such explanations, more later. And so while initially stating that the white-collar criminal is not morally superior to the street criminal, it becomes clear that Jencks thinks otherwise.

Similarly, in his large tome, *Crime and Punishment in American History*, Lawrence Friedman begins by referring to white collar crime. But as with Jencks, it rapidly disappears from view. There must be something in the water – or in the ideology.

Let us note at this juncture that we are not primarily concerned with the perpetrators of white collar crime who are merely self-serving. We are not concerned with bookkeepers and accountants who embezzle from their bosses, executives who steal from their own companies or politicians who take bribes under the table, widespread as all this is. We will ignore the crimes committed by the "law-abiding" middle class: the routine evasion of income taxes by small entrepreneurs, the cheating on sales taxes by mom-and-pop shopkeepers, the fleecing of their customers by used car salesmen, or the commonplace fraud of automobile repair shops (which alone totals $40 billion a year). We put aside income earned or paid "off the books," the theft of office supplies, expense account padding, the filing of false accident claims, small-time bribe-taking and bribe-giving, etc. Our focus is on our eminent business leaders and politicians, held up as role models by admiring biographers and even more admiring autobiographers. What we are mainly interested in are the crimes which are an *essential* part of the institutions of our society, the crimes that make the system work, crimes unreported or under-reported by the media, or if covered, most often tucked away in the pages of a business section.

Beyond the monetary cost of elite crime, there is the toll of ruined lives, of needless death, sickness and injury. Thus, tobacco sales account for over 400,000 deaths yearly, 20 times more than those defined in the penal codes as murder and manslaughter. At least 100,000 die annually because of exposure to deadly chemicals, while other dangerous products cause approximately 20,000 deaths and 130,000 serious injuries. Each year there are six million on-the-job casualties, half of which result in permanent disabilities. Tens of thousands die of illnesses each year related to occupational hazards. Over a million workers have been killed on the job since the 1920s. This carnage is not only tragic but criminal because for the most part easily avoidable, requiring only that companies take reasonable measures to protect the health and safety of their workers and the public, which they do not.

All this would seem to be dramatic enough to attract the scrutiny of the media. But as an integral part of the elite themselves, the media has an interest in suppressing awareness of corporate crime's devastating consequences. Still, in the last few years there has been a flood of corporate scandals too huge to be swept under the rug, some involving executives simply enriching themselves personally, but most committed for the benefit of their corporations. The main driving force behind this crime wave has been the relentless demand by Wall Street to increase stock prices by any means necessary. Success in this, in turn, is supposed to justify the top executives plundering their corporations with a combination of outrageously excessive salaries, bonuses, stock options, inflated expense accounts, and severance packages. This we skip over. We intend to concentrate on the vast conspiracy of corporate perpetrators, in collusion with investment banks, accounting firms, insurance companies, stock rating services, and regulatory agencies, including even a former CEO charged with the proper functioning of the New York Stock Exchange.

Public and investor confidence in Corporate America and especially Wall Street has been shaken, so the government makes a show of getting on the job with hearings and legislation supposedly designed to curb future abuses, legislation riddled with loopholes sufficient to render regulations innocuous. For the moment, Wall Street has scaled back its operations to a more restrained level of larceny. It is a measure of its unprecedented economic and political power that the government has failed to carry out even token prosecutions to mollify an outraged public opinion, which was standard operating procedure following past scandals. We are speaking here of Wall Street insiders and not a few freelancers such as Bernie Madoff. Already a chorus of protests is rising from the bankers, speculators, and the always obliging media claque, complaining that the virtually meaningless new regulations are hurting Wall Street's ability to compete on the global market. But what does this mean? One of two things: either the financial elite are lying and it is possible to compete without engaging in swindling, or else it is telling the truth, in which case corporate globalization is based on worldwide swindling or, in other words, the financial world and criminality are everywhere synonymous.

Gradually, as night follows the day, whatever limited restrictions are imposed will be relaxed and the financial reptiles will crawl out from under their rocks, returning to their old predatory ways – that is, until society is swamped in the next, even larger wave of looting, again causing public outrage, whereupon the guardians of our economic system will bestir themselves once more and we will go through still another charade of governmental righteous indignation, accompanied by the appropriate wrist-slapping. Yet there is reason to believe that we will not be waiting for long for the next cycle, for the crisis which we exported to Europe threatens to boomerang back to us and drive us into a 1930's style Great Depression, or worse.

There is another aspect of the crime double-standard. The prisons are not only stuffed with the poor, they have become ever more disproportionately filled with people of color, and especially African-Americans. Crime in the streets has been given a black face, savage and menacing. Crime in the suites, on the other hand, is white and polite.

Jencks, like almost all other "experts" in the field, is convinced that Blacks commit crime far in excess of their percentage of the population, citing arrest figures which prove, he claims, that, "We cannot blame these statistics on police prejudice...The conclusion that blacks are five to ten times as likely as whites to commit most violent crimes is almost inescapable. This means that the genes determining skin color are as closely correlated with criminal violence in the United States as the genes determining gender."[4]

Jencks admits he can't figure out exactly how those

genes work, and agrees that nobody else seems to know, either. But he is confident that the answers will be found. That was over 20 years ago and we are still waiting. But Jencks was sure of this: That gains made by the civil rights movement were accompanied by a dramatic rise in Black crime, supposedly disproving liberal notions linking crime and social injustice. Friedman, the historian on crime, also attributes the increase in crime in the 1950s and 1960s to the rise of the Black freedom movement and its accompanying climate of "permissiveness," simply echoing in academic language the old saying, "Give a nigger an inch and he'll take a mile."

We cite these two liberals only to show how far to the right the discussion on crime has moved, how complete the ideological triumph of the Reagan counter-revolution. Later, we shall be examining the real reasons for the huge racial disparities in the prisons, which we hope will shed light not only on the nature of the criminal justice system, but also of U.S. society as a whole. *For we contend that the criminal justice system is racist, cruel and inhuman, and it is so because it exists to protect a social system that is racist, cruel and inhuman.*

THE CRIME OF IMPUNITY

ELITE CRIME

WHEN IS A CRIME NOT A CRIME?

In examining the criminal acts of the elite, it is striking how many of them are categorized as mere infractions of civil law or bureaucratic regulations and therefore not warranting criminal punishment. Actually, the greatest number and most serious of their criminal acts often are not even considered violations of civil law. Those who commit wholesale murder, for example, when they perpetrate it under color of war, not only are not punished but are showered with honors. At the same time, the retail murderer is considered the lowest form of human life. Nothing original about these observations. Similarly, larceny, when it is committed on the street level, receives heavier punishment with each repetition. But the uninterrupted corporate looting of the people here and abroad, when punished at all, is at most subject to penalties which neither land top executives in prison nor put the corporations out of business. In fact, the fines that are occasionally imposed are factored in as simply the cost of doing business.

One could compile an encyclopedia of the criminal acts of the leaders of every sector of industry and finance, every branch of government, and every type of media venture, proving that any serious probe of elite economic and political behavior should be classified as a criminal investigation.

We should dearly love to present comprehensive statistics on elite crime. But, unsurprisingly, there is no government agency that compiles, correlates and makes public such crime statistics. So we shall be setting forth just a few representative samples, just the tip of the iceberg but sufficient to demonstrate the elite's utter lawlessness, a mere glimpse into our real underworld, an underworld perched in our upside-down society at the top of our social pyramid.

BOARDROOM BANDITS

Let us begin with the pirates of finance and industry, or the "business community" as they are reverentially called. The unprecedented scale of recent corporate crime, until the explosion of the current sub-prime scandal, was epitomized by the Enron fraud, perpetrated not only by its top executives, but by the company's associated banks, led by Citigroup, as well as by Arthur Andersen, Enron's "independent" accounting firm without whose machinations the scheme could never have been put over. Part of the fallout for Arthur Andersen resulted in its having to close its doors, a rare punishment which the courts later found to be totally unjust. Unjust because none of its executives were ever sent to prison for collaborating in the theft of billions of dollars? No, unjust because Arthur Andersen was deprived of the ability to engage in future rip-offs of the public, which the courts consider every company's birthright.

Skimming over some other prominent corporate felonies of recent date -- the $11 billion WorldCom fraud, the $3 billion Tyco conglomerate fraud, the frauds by Time-Warner, Adelphia, Xerox, Office Max, and a slew of others -- we note that WalMart, the world's largest retailer, was cited by Human Rights Watch for its illegal union-busting activities, child labor violations, and payment of sub-poverty wages -- this last, according to our statute books, not constituting a crime.

The New York Times reports "a parade of substantial terms imposed on former chief executives convicted of white-collar crimes."[5] These "substantial terms," handed out only to calm an outraged public, are much lighter, however, than the sentences of many street criminals charged with far less.

Hundreds of corporations have scurried to "amend" fraudulent financial statements in the face of looming government audits. Hundreds of others are similarly amending illegally backdated stock options given to their top executives.

Let us look at the record of some specific industries:

TOBACCO

We have already noted the US death toll from smoking. Far more Americans have died at the hands of tobacco companies than have been killed in all our wars combined – deaths, moreover, accompanied by prolonged agony. In other words, we are dealing here not only with murder but with torture. Yet for over a century, the tobacco companies swore to the public and the government that their products were perfectly safe, even though it has now been learned that their own documents revealed they knew otherwise.

As people became increasingly concerned about the hazards of smoking, the tobacco companies created a dizzying array of products meant to be reassuring: filtered, "low tar," "lite," and mentholated cigarettes (the latter pitched particularly to the African-American community). For the sake of maximum profits, nothing has been too loathsome, whether it be deliberately engineering their products to be still more addictive or targeting children. By contrast, peddling to children is something at which many "low-life" drug pushers draw the line.

While smoking kills 400,000 Americans annually, 5 1/2 million people die worldwide, most at the hands of US tobacco companies.

As we mentioned, the financial cost of street crime is estimated at about $50 billion annually. The financial damage caused by smoking is double that. In a humane society, one would think that the government would ban the manufacture and sale of such weapons of mass destruction.

One would think that a state which has created so many categories of crime carrying the death penalty would seek it also for the top tobacco executives, or at least life without parole. Yet never have they served a single day, much less done hard time. In fact, Washington actually compels other countries to import American tobacco products, especially the underdeveloped countries.

In fact, a federal judge blasted the tobacco companies for a "decades-old conspiracy to deceive the public about the dangers of smoking."[6] Yet despite ever-greater restrictions on advertising, despite the increasing numbers of localities that ban smoking in public spaces, despite ever-greater cigarette taxes, and despite the billions of dollars paid by the tobacco companies to settle litigation, *The New York Times* reports that "the future of cigarettes appears to be brighter than ever."[7] Two billion cigarettes were shipped abroad last year. Certainly the tobacco companies may congratulate themselves on their success in targeting women. "You've come a long way, Baby!" gushes the manufacturer of Doral cigarettes. And indeed, women have broken through the glass ceiling, and in lung cancer rates are vaulting toward equality.

HEALTH CARE

The Pharmaceutical Industry

It would seem that pharmaceutical companies, producing life-saving and health-restoring medicines, would be worlds apart in their business ethics from tobacco companies. But it turns out that these two industries are like peas in a pod. The drug companies lie just as baldly about the safety of their products. They knowingly peddle products whose dangers outweigh any possible benefit. Blood pressure medications, anti-depressants, and anti-psychotic drugs, their most lucrative profit generators, are notorious in this respect.

The pharmaceutical companies are constantly churning out new and ever more expensive drugs that have little or no value, or little advantage over older and less expensive ones. Such is the case with recently patented heart drugs. Niacin, the cheap B vitamin, is about as effective as these in preventing heart attacks. But Niacin "just never caught on," said Dr. B. Greg Brown, Professor of Medicine at Washington University. "It's a mystery to me. But if you're a drug company, I guess you can't make money on a vitamin."[8]

The public is bombarded with direct marketing, calculated to pressure physicians through their patients, an unethical practice not permitted anywhere else in the world.

Almost a million cancer patients take drugs for anemia, which have been shown to cause heart problems, to make a cancer condition worse and even to hasten death. But they are enormously lucrative. In doing the cost/benefit analysis, it wasn't even close. Lucrative wins every time. The May 1987 *New England Journal of Medicine* reported that a diabetes drug, Avandia, substantially increased the risk of heart attack and caused at least hundreds of deaths.[9] Both the pharmaceutical company responsible for marketing the drug, and the Food and Drug Administration ignored that risk and in fact the company tried to silence scientists who raised the alarm.

One of the most recent scandals involves the cholesterol-lowering drugs Zetia and Vytorin, manufactured by Merck and Schering-Plough. Clinical studies that have now been made public reveal that these drugs are no better than a placebo. Meanwhile, they have been prescribed to over three million patients worldwide. The companies have raked in billions of dollars, and in the case of Schering-Plough, its worthless product accounted for 70 percent of its earnings.

Here are but a few more examples of crimes committed by a veritable Who's Who of the pharmaceutical industry:

Johnson & Johnson has marketed a heart drug which caused kidney problems that were hidden from the FDA. **Glaxo-Smith-Kline** marketed a drug for high blood pressure which caused liver damage, a problem, again, hidden from the FDA. This resulted in one of the few cases where company executives were actually prosecuted criminally. Needless to say, they were not sentenced to prison time. The same company also hid the results of clinical trials showing its anti-depressant medication increased suicidal thoughts among children and teenagers. **Eli-Lilly** gave almost $2 million in bribes to a group of scientists and hospital directors in return for favorable opinions on its products. **Novo Nordisk** bribed doctors' assistants to switch prescriptions to its own products. **Astra-Zeneca** likewise bribed doctors and was forced to pay $185 million in fines. **Bristol-Myers-Squibb** made false statements to the government involving its anti-clotting and huge money-making drug Plavix. **Abbott Labs** jacked up the price of its established AIDS drug in order to drive patients to one of its newer AIDS products. And many companies have suddenly increased their prescription drug prices 100-fold, even 1000-fold, for the treatment of rare diseases on which patients depend to remain alive. **Perdue Pharma**, the maker of the pain-killer OxyContin, which brought in $3 billion in revenues, had to pay $600 million in restitution for denying to doctors and patients that it was addictive. Though OxyContin caused soaring rates of teenage addiction, crime, and death, and though corporate executives were guilty of a felony, they were allowed to take a plea to a misdemeanor with no incarceration. When the judge inquired of the prosecutor why he was being so lenient, the prosecutor replied, "Each corporate official will bear the stigma of being a convicted criminal." Thus, the executives have been spared sharing a cell with those whose crimes stemmed from addiction to their product, and for whom the stigma was evidently not punishment enough.

Drug company bribery of physicians takes place

on a truly colossal scale, not a crass bribery, of course, but befitting the dignity of professionals. A Minnesota study a decade ago undertook to measure the corruption of the medical industry in that state. It found that during 2005 alone, drug makers gave $57 million to about 5,500 doctors, nurses, and other health care workers. From 2000 to 2005, drug-maker payments to Minnesota psychiatrists rose more than six-fold to $1.6 million while during the same year prescriptions of anti-psychotic drugs for children under state insurance programs rose more than nine-fold. Pfizer secretly paid hundreds of thousands of dollars to a researcher at the National Institute of Health, and several dozen others at the Institute were found to be on biotechnology and drug company payrolls.

Medical journals "have devolved into information-laundering operations for the pharmaceutical industry,"[10] former editor Richard Horton wrote in the March 2004 British medical journal *Lancet*, explaining how the journals rely on revenues from industry advertisements and orders for articles. But it is worse than that. Just now, a widespread industry practice has been uncovered of the ghostwriting of medical research articles that appear in academic journals under the names of seemingly reputable physicians. *The Journal of the American Medical Association*, for example, in 2008 exposed Merck's manipulation of dozens of publications to promote Vioxx, a drug found to cause fatal heart attacks.[11] But Merck is far from the only company guilty of such corrupt practices, which raises questions about the validity of much of the published medical research. Speaking of Vioxx, another dangerous drug in that family was manufactured by Pfizer, which has now agreed to pay almost a billion dollars to compensate for the devastation caused to thousands of victims of its drug Celebrex.

Companies bribe doctors to report favorably on their drugs, as well as to prescribe them to their own patients. The pharmaceutical industry largely finances and controls continuing education programs in medical schools. The National Kidney Foundation, for one, receives multi-million-dollar donations from drug companies, which may explain why it has recommended a drug to treat kidney disease found by heart specialists to carry an unacceptable risk of heart failure.

Those who blow the whistle about the dangers of certain medications or devices have had their careers destroyed. Such was the case, for example, of Dr. Eric Topol at the Cleveland Clinic's Medical College when he exposed the unethical manipulation of data involving a Merck-formulated product.

Pharmaceutical companies engage in lies and deceptions regarding clinical tests and suppress vital information when it is harmful to their interest. And so drugs are put on the market which are either useless or so dangerous as to be responsible for thousands of deaths, organ damage, or other morbid effects. For example, the results of clinical trials of certain anti-depressants, withheld for years by the drug companies, have finally been released, thanks to independent researchers who have had to resort to the Freedom of Information Act. The trials showed that the popular (and very expensive) anti-depressants

Prozac and Paxil, made by Eli-Lilly and Glaxo-Smith-Kline, worked only for the very seriously depressed, while for the great majority they were no more effective than a placebo – in other words, were virtually useless. An Eli-Lilly anti-psychotic drug, Zyprexa, has proved to be either dangerous or useless in many cases. 23 million potential victims have taken it since it was introduced, including those for whom it was aggressivly marketed for off-label treatment, including elderly victims of dementia, and childrren with disruptive behavior. Zyprexa earned almost $5 billion in one year alone. The company was found to have systematically hidden the risks of side effects, including diabetes, and while it has been forced to pay large fines and restitution, this constitutes for the company only a minor annoyance. And the beat goes on. Aware that its drug for rheumatoid arthritis had dangerous risks, including death, Eli-Lilly, once again, kept the information secret.

The practice of suppressing the results of clinical trials is widespread and justified on the grounds that they are the property of the companies which have paid for them, and therefore they are free to do with them as they please, the public be damned. Further, the Inspector General of the Department of Health and Human Services has charged the FDA with negligence in ensuring the safety of the millions of people who *participate* in clinical trials. And Arthur L. Caplan, chairman of the department of medical ethics at the University of Pennsylvania has noted that "rats and mice get greater protection as research subjects...than do humans."[12]

The latest word, based on *voluntary* reporting to the

FDA, shows that the number of deaths and serious injuries associated with prescription drugs has risen to record levels. In the first three months of 2008, there were reports of almost 5,000 deaths and 21,000 injuries, and it is estimated that these represented only 10 percent of the actual adverse effects. Extrapolating from these figures for the entire year we get 200,000 deaths and almost a million injuries.

Since health care is based on the profit motive, is it any surprise that vital areas of public health that are unprofitable to drug companies are not deemed worthy of attention? Thus, there is little effort to find vaccines for a range of diseases that annually kill millions around the world. Some suspect that the pharmaceutical industry aim is not to *cure* but to *manage* illness. For a lifetime dependency on drugs represents a horn-of-plenty, while curing illness only kills the goose that lays the golden eggs.

Back before the Civil War, as Gustavus Myers informs us in his *History of the Great American Fortunes,* a congressional committee found that "there was scarcely a wholesale or retail druggist who was not conciously selling spurious drugs which were a menace to human life," sold, moreover, at exorbitant prices. "There is not a single record of any criminal action pressed against those who profited from selling this poisonous stuff."[13] While the actors may have changed over the years, it's the same old script. The Federal Drug Administration, charged with protecting our health, works hand-in-glove with those endangering it. In general, the FDA is little more than a lapdog for the industry. Many FDA advisers, serving on industry committees, earn handsome fees from the companies whose products they are reviewing. The FDA has known for *over a quarter of a century* that for those on chemotherapy, anti-nausea suppositories are worthless. But during that same time millions of dollars were pocketed by their manufacturers. Only now, under political pressure, has the agency withdrawn its approval.

The pro-industry bias of the FDA can be traced, among other things, to lavish lobbying. In 2004 alone, $87 million of pharmaceutical company money went into the coffers of political candidates and parties, and the political influence it has purchased ensures a health care system that is an overwhelming failure. And while President Obama's health care plan will do little to improve the health of the nation, it will greatly improve the health insurance industry's bottom line.

Among the most heinous crimes of the pharmaceutical companies is their refusal to make drugs available to impoverished victims of HIV/AIDS in underdeveloped countries, especially Africa. Not only do they charge prices well out of the people's reach, but they bar other companies or governments from making them more cheaply. Thus, the pharmaceutical companies are guilty of depraved indifference to human life. But according to the dominant ethical standards of society, it is criminal only to be found guilty of indifference to corporate profits.

A striking illustration of the morally degenerate character of the drug companies is the scandal concerning cough and cold medications for infants and children. Recently, in-house safety experts for the Food and Drug Administration recommended their outright ban for children under 6, reporting that there was no evidence of their effectiveness. Further, a panel of FDA experts found that a significant number of children died after taking decongestants or antihistamines. That panel also criticized the companies for "inaccurate, inadequate and dangerous labeling of their products." Medical groups such as the American College of Chest Physicians and the American Academy of Pediatrics urged the total ban of the products, a ban which the manufacturers vowed to fight. After all, there are some 800 cold remedy products for children, almost 4 billion doses sold, ringing up $500 million annually.

Johnson & Johnson has settled with Justice Department claims totaling over $2 billion for abusive marketing practices involving the anti-psychotic drug Risperdal, which has generated global sales of over $24 billion, as well as other prescription drugs. The company has agreed to enter a misdemeanor plea. Need I add that no prison time will be imposed? In 2009, Pfizer settled with the government for another $2 billion and keeps on operating without missing a beat.

The latest scandal involves, once again, Glaxo-Smith-Kline, who has given $3 billion to the government to make its investigation into fraudulent practices go away, the largest such settlement in history, which hasn't affected its stock price in the slightest.

And so, summing up, we place on one side of the scale the seven-figure-salaried, sophisticated and well-educated drug company executive who for the sake of profits deliberately puts in jeopardy the lives and health of millions; and on the other, the functionally illiterate slum-dweller, peddling other kinds of drugs for the sake of survival, some considerably more benign than those sold over drugstore counters, who sooner or later winds up in a prison cell. So here's the question: By what rational standard is not the first man infinitely more cell-worthy than the second?

Now drug companies are in a race to seize the little remaining of what has been left to native peoples, their traditional medicine. Company representatives are swarming over their communities, taking samples from the bark of trees, roots, and grasses, the curative power of which has been long known to the indigenous peoples. After removing these and putting them in a pure chemical form, the traditional medicines are converted through the magic of the U.S. Patent Office into the exclusive property of the drug companies. It may be anticipated that soon the indigenous peoples will be sued in U.S. federal court for patent infringement. And now drug and medical companies are *claiming the right to patent life itself!* They are all racing to stake their claim to all the genes or parts of genes of human and animal tissues. There is no limit to what the public perceives as madness, but which corporations and a government which is their instrument deem eminently sane and reasonable.

Physicians and Surgeons

It is not alone the pharmaceutical companies but the entire health care business which is riddled with criminality. As the *New York Times* editorialized, "New evidence keeps emerging that the medical profession has sold its soul in exchange for what can only be described as bribes from the manufacturers of drugs and medical devices."[14] Thus, Medtronics paid surgeons millions of dollars to use and recommend medical devices which sometimes proved to be defective, sometimes even causing deaths which it covered up.

Still another form of bribery involves the formation of companies through which doctors are hired to give "investment advice" on drugs and medical devices. Then there are the millions of dollars' worth of free lunches delivered daily by the drug companies to physicians and their staff, along with millions of dollars' worth of free samples.

We should surely expect a higher ethical standard from doctors and scientists, most of whom were probably initially attracted to their profession out of a genuine desire to serve humanity. But it is hard to stand up to the tempting opportunities of our time in this "free-market" society.

Surgeons routinely perform great numbers of unnecessary but lucrative operations, especially hysterectomies, mastectomies, and prostectomies. Surgeons enrolled with Tenet Health Care performed unnecessary heart surgery on hundreds of patients. About half-a-million

Americans underwent spinal fusions last year generating billions of dollars for doctors and hospitals despite serious doubts as to whether back pain is actually alleviated by such surgery. Surgeons are often investors in companies that make the hardware they install, a fact about which their patients are kept in the dark.

Countless unnecessary procedures are performed in medical offices to pay off expensive equipment. Thousands of urologists have invested in multi-million dollar radiation equipment to treat prostate cancer. Reimbursements for this procedure is many times greater than that earned for other types of treatment, so the temptation is great to use such equipment, whatever its efficacy. Oncologists make money by providing chemotherapy even where there is little prospect of success. Dr. Robert Geller, a leading oncologist, has stated, "It's clear that physicians stopped making decisions based on what made scientific or clinical sense in favor of what made better business sense."[15] And another oncologist, Dr. Brian Moran, concluded, "It's all money-driven, and it's a shame medicine has come to this."[16] Seems like cancer is not a curse but a cash cow.

In a *New York Times* article, cardiologist Sandeep Jauhar pointed to what he considered the most important contributing factor to growing corruption: "As reimbursement rates have declined in recent years, most doctors have adapted by increasing the quantity of services... to grab patients and generate volume." Jauhar quotes one cardiologist as saying, "I tried to practice ethical medicine, but it didn't help. It didn't pay, both from a financial and a reputation standpoint." And so Dr. Jauhar concluded: "In our health care system, where doctors are paid piecework for their services...almost any sort of terrible excess can occur."[17] Evidently, the Hippocratic Oath has been amended to "Do no harm...to your bottom line."

From 1997 through 2005, more than a third of Minnesota's licensed psychiatrists, including the last eight presidents of the Minnesota Psychiatric Society, took money from drug makers. Dr. Steven Sharfstein, the immediate past president of the American Psychiatric Association, has complained about this kind of cozy relationship which has resulted, it would seem, in the widespread prescribing of the antidepressant Lexapro, despite the fact that there are both cheaper and at least as effective alternatives. The great frequency of the controversial bipolar diagnosis in children has gone hand in hand with a shift from inexpensive antidepressants to far more expensive, and for the psychiatrist far more lucrative, antipsychotic drugs. Under Congressional prodding, it has been revealed that three prominent psychiatrists at the Harvard Medical School, whose writings have contributed to the explosion of anti-psychotic drugs for children, received over a million dollars in "consulting fees" from the drug industry.

Hospitals

Our Good Samaritans, the private hospitals, are not to be outdone in their venality. **Beth Israel**, one of

New York's most prestigious medical institutions, had to reimburse the government $540 million for just *one year's worth* of fraudulent Medicare billing, a practice engaged in by other hospitals, as well. **Columbia University** was forced to reimburse $5 million to Medicaid for billing for services it did not perform. And that same hallowed institution, charge with training our future political and moral leaders, has been caught using defenseless foster children as guinea pigs for AIDS drug experiments. **Health South** has been guilty of enormous accounting fraud. **Health Care of America**, one of the fastest-growing hospital chains, defrauded the government of hundreds of millions of dollars through such practices as overbilling, billing for services not performed, and paying kickbacks to doctors. **St. Barnabus Health Care Systems**, a chain of New Jersey hospitals, was made to reimburse $265 million to the Government for fraudulent Medicare charges following a patient class action suit. **Catholic Health Care West**, the largest non-profit hospital system in California, had to make refunds to hundreds of thousands of patients following a price-gauging lawsuit.

One of the latest scandals, costing the taxpayer tens of millions of dollars, involved a number of Los Angeles hospitals which drummed up business by scooping up the homeless and then dumping them back on Skid Row after claiming, sometimes fraudulently, to have treated them under state insurance programs.

The health care industry as a whole is involved in Medicare and Medicaid fraud totaling anywhere from $200 to $400 *billion* annually, a practice testified to by a whistle-blower, formerly employed in a key procurement position for a pharmaceutical company, who asserted that no less than 7,000 health care institutions were guilty of such fraud.

Added to the indictment against hospitals should be the charges of union busting, of underpaying and overworking nursing staff, and of generally operating according to the philosophy that the demand for adequate patient care is an unwarranted infringement of its business model. The tragic results of such a philosophy are seen in the 100,000 patients who die each year from hospital infections caused in large measure by the gross negligence of hospital administrations and staff. The majority of such deaths are easily avoidable if the hospitals would put into place hygienic measures that are simple and inexpensive. Evidently, inexpensive is still too expensive.

Health Maintenance Organizations

Not doctors, not hospitals, but the HMO's are the ones calling the shots, determining what constitutes appropriate medical treatment and demanding that the standard of care be reduced in the interest of maximizing profit. In that connection, not too long ago two New York hospitals sued one of the largest of the HMO's, **United Health Group**, whose business plan boils down to routinely denying payment of patients' legitimate medical bills. Not mincing words, the hospitals called such practices a "racket." HMO's are also increasingly selective in accepting or retaining members, refusing those with prior medical problems, steadily raising deductibles and premiums, and engaging in a host of practices which make medical insurance less a patient protection than a nightmare. The recent legislation passed on the initiative of President Obama, after extensive "consultation" with the HMO's, does little to reduce health care costs but a great deal to expand the HMO customer base. Not surprising, given the huge amount of money spent by HMO's on lobbying, some $54 million -- to be fair, not so huge in comparison to the $108 million spent by the hospitals, which in turn is dwarfed by the $265 million poured out by the drug and health products industry.

We have spent perhaps an inordinate amount of time on the health care industry because it is here that the contradictions are most glaring between the needs of the people and private profit, so glaring and so unacceptable to society that the governments of all the advanced capitalist countries have long ago abolished or sharply curtailed profit-making in their health care systems – all except the leader of the free world.

LAWYERS

Having dealt with physicians, surgeons and psychiatrists, let us quickly pass by another branch of the learned professions: the legal fraternity. We skip over the "rabble" of the profession, the so-called ambulance chasers, clamping on their clients the obligatory neck brace and creating fabricated scenarios in negligence cases. We shall likewise skip over the shenanigans around

Surrogate Court, where judges tap their lawyer buddies and others politically connected for the lucrative assignments of administering, or should we say milking, the estates of the deceased.

Sworn to uphold the law, lawyers more often than not are hired to get around it. Wherever crooked deeds are performed – by corporations, politicians, by anyone who can pay the going fees – you will find "legal talent" figuring the angles. Lawyers are well known for selling out the interests of their small clients to large corporations, or for needlessly stringing out cases and running up fees to line their own pockets. It is lawyers who are responsible for making statutes, rules and regulations virtually incomprehensible to the public, including the federal tax code, insurance policies, stockholder reports, consumer credit card agreements, and mortgages. Legalese is an important weapon in keeping the public ignorant, powerless, and under the lawyer's thumb. The lack of scruples on the part of many in the legal profession makes them excellent material as politicians, an occupation which, of course, they dominate.

ACCOUNTANTS

The last person anyone wants to hire is an accountant with scruples. The careers and remuneration of accountants rise in tandem with the ingenuity of their manipulation of inconvenient numbers. In the endless string of corporate scandals of recent years, the top accounting firms have almost invariably been implicated. We have mentioned Arthur Andersen's role in the Enron swindle. Another example is the prominent accounting firm KPMG, which helped perpetrate the huge frauds of the Quellos hedge fund with its phony leases, fake loans, and offshore tax dodges. But none of the big firms have a clean record. While they are supposed to act as watchdogs for investors and the general public, in the real world they are often the corporate criminals' indispensable aiders and abettors. And this is only natural, for it makes a lot more business sense to play ball with one's clients than be whistle-blowers. While Arthur Andersen was forced out of business, other equally crooked accounting firms continue to prosper while busily contriving shady means of enriching their corporate clients.

OUR BUSINESS LEADERS OF TOMORROW

As for the ethical and legal behavior that may be expected of our professionals and business executives of tomorrow, the signs are not encouraging. National surveys conducted in the years 2002-2004 reveal that more than half of the business and engineering students admitted to cheating, along with almost half of the students in education and in law school. A majority of college students now feel that cheating is a perfectly legitimate method for achieving their career goals. So it is only natural that when they enter the business world, they are morally equipped to lie, cheat and steal, as is required of those who take the helm of corporations and of other institutions which serve corporate needs. We will, perhaps, be accused of being naïve. After all, business is about making money, not serving humankind. Except that corporations spend a lot of money trying to convince us otherwise, insisting they are truly public-spirited, anxious to create jobs, to protect the worker (especially against predatory unions), are concerned about the well-being of the communities in which they operate. In sum, we are told that the mission of the corporation is to make life better for us all. Thus, the slogan of the pharmaceutical company Merck is "Where the patient comes first"; of the manufacturer of Tylenol, "Your child's safety is our No. 1 priority; of Lockheed-Martin (with visuals of a cross-section of the American people) "We Know Who We're Serving"; of the insurance companies of Hurricane Katrina notoriety, "Nationwide Is On Your Side" and "Like a Good Neighbor, State Farm is there." Merrill-Lynch, one of those responsible for the financial manipulations leading to this country's economic collapse, assures its customers it is not in the brokerage but the "wealth management" business, whose employees are not brokers but "consultants," employed by the company not to sell but to "help," and to be an "advocate in your corner." So if corporations oppose raising the minimum wage, as they always do, it is not because it will cut into their profits but, as they explain, because it will cause more unemployment. Likewise, if they oppose a tax on dividends, it is not out of self-interest, but because it will hurt widows and orphans. And if they oppose environmental regulations, it is only because they are concerned about the impact on local communities if they, in order to remain competitive, are thereby "forced" to move their operations offshore.

THE ENERGY INDUSTRY

The largest corporate scandal in recent years, before the so-called sub-prime debacle, involved the now infamous energy company Enron, bankroller of George W. Bush, a company which engaged in a vast pyramid scheme that ripped off consumers and investors, and conned their employees out of their life savings.

The energy companies were the darlings of the Bush Administration. And the passion was reciprocated. In 2000 alone, they coughed up $58 million for Bush's presidential campaign, and in return received huge tax breaks, suspension of regulations protecting the environment, and other measures furthering power, oil, coal and gas company interests. Such contributions to the White House and Congress are huge bargains, pennies on the dollar, compared to the billions raked in in return. While the energy corporations are usually more generous toward Republicans, the Democrats are never left out in the cold. Yet despite the legal protection offered by the government, the greed of the industry occasionally generates such public outrage that Washington is forced to take some action. For instance, the Williams Companies, one of the largest suppliers of electricity and natural gas, had to cough up $100 million in fines and restitution as a result of a conspiracy to overcharge customers during California's artificially-created energy shortage. Similarly, the El Paso Corporation was finally punished for engaging in the same conspiracy, which the Federal Energy Regulatory Commission had for a long time ignored. Nevertheless, the people of California will for generations to come be paying for energy company price-gouging.

We should not fail to mention the crimes of the nuclear power industry, which routinely covers up its breakdowns, including the escape of radioactivity into the atmosphere and water, cover-ups which are routinely abetted by the federal Nuclear Regulatory Commission.

An environmental catastrophe is looming, threatening the very existence of human life on earth, for which oil, coal and energy companies bear major responsibility. Not only have they saturated the atmosphere with their poisons, causing tens of thousands of premature deaths annually, but they fiercely oppose even the most modest pollution restrictions. Huge sums are spent trying to convince the public that global warming is either a leftist fantasy or a natural phenomenon for which human (corporate) activity is in no way responsible. Or the public is told that global warming, like spinach, may be unpleasant but is actually good for you. In this propaganda effort, the energy corporations finance right-wing "think tanks" whose "thinkers" think mostly about which side their bread is buttered on.

OIL

In 1978, the government granted permission for a chemical to be added to gasoline that enabled the oil companies to make some extra profit. It wasn't long before that additive, not biodegradable, was leaking out of underground gasoline storage tanks and poisoning groundwater and wells, and could not be removed with conventional treatments. And yet, the industry successfully lobbied the government to allow its continued use, knowing full well the environmental and health damage it was causing.

In 1989, the tanker EXXON VALDEZ spilled 11 million gallons of oil off the Alaskan coast, causing one of the worst man-made environmental disasters in history. Exxon is also responsible for another oil spill in Brooklyn, which took place some 50 years ago, another horrendous environmental disaster. Its clean-up has only recently begun after stubborn company resistance, and is moving along at a pace comfortable for snails but agonizing for the people that have been for half a century living in a poisoned environment.

For decades, the oil companies avoided taxes through, for example, the rip-off known as the oil depletion allowance. As a result of this and other government-sanctioned rackets, oil companies have paid a far smaller percentage of their enormous profits than small businesses, and even less than the vast majority of working people. How comforting to our friend Professor Jencks that such robbery of our taxpayers has not been committed at gunpoint.

Not content with their legal tax evasion, the oil companies are currently cheating the government out of billions of dollars of royalties due and unpaid from offshore drilling operations. In fact, the Department of the Interior is actually working with the companies to defraud itself. In this connection, a further scandal has emerged. It seems that government officials in charge of the oil royalties have for years been plied with booze, dope and prostitutes at oil industry functions, all paid for by the oil companies – and us. Exposed by the Interior Department's Inspector-General, the Bush Justice Department decided that there was nothing criminal about the oil companies stealing billions from the government and the American people, nothing criminal about government employees accepting bribes, bribes moreover, in the form of schedule 2 narcotics and hookers. Meanwhile, for smoking a joint on their stoops, thousands of poor Black kids are daily herded into prison, which we shall discuss later.

As soaring gasoline prices have bitten into the average family budget, the oil companies have raked in unprecedented profits. To counter rising anger, the oil industry, and especially ExxonMobil, launched a public relations campaign, (tax deductible, of course). Rather than cleaning up the environment they are largely responsible for poisoning, they spend tens of millions trying to clean up their image, with endless commercials portraying themselves as being in the vanguard of the environmental movement, leaders in the effort to develop clean energy, and careful stewards of the earth's ecology. So to their criminal robbery they add criminal deception.

The street criminal violently mugs a relatively small number of individuals; the big oil companies loot the entire nation. According to Jencks the public doesn't mind a bit because the oil companies engage in price-gouging, not eye-gouging. Their profits hover around $100 billion annually. But they never laid a hand on us.

THE OIL INDUSTRY: A BIT OF HISTORY

The history of the oil industry is one of criminal monopoly. It was formed with ruthless efficiency by the pious John D. Rockefeller who, when he wasn't driving his competitors out of business through means both legal and illegal, could be found teaching Baptist Sunday school. Responding to public outrage that reached its height at the turn of the 20th century, the courts broke up the Standard Oil trust into a number of "independent" units. But, lo and behold, after World War II the Federal Trade Commission confirmed that Standard Oil stood at the heart of an international oil cartel that was, through secret agreements, divvying up the world market and keeping prices artificially high. When some wet-behind-the-ears government officials wanted to prosecute the companies, they were ordered to lay off. The American companies, they were told, were instruments of US foreign policy in the Middle East. Actually, it's been the other way around. US foreign policy has always been an instrument of the American oil companies.

BP may take pride in far surpassing Exxon in its

ravaging of the environment. Its 2010 Gulf of Mexico disaster dwarfs that of the EXXON VALDEZ. Thus, while half a million barrels of oil were spilled with the sinking of the VALDEZ in Alaska waters, the oil rig explosion in the Gulf of Mexico off the Louisiana coast caused the spill of ten times more.

Upon investigation it turns out, as it almost always does, that the "accident" was bound to happen sooner or later since it was the fruit of gross negligence by all the parties charged with operational safety. And, as it turns out, as it almost always does, the government was well aware of that negligence and chose to look the other way. Moreover, even as the tragedy was unfolding, the Obama Administration, through the Coast Guard, was actively assisting in minimizing to the public the extent of the disaster, simply parroting BP's propaganda, and preventing on behalf of BP any independent efforts to get at the truth.

So hundreds of thousands lost their livelihood, most of whom have become impoverished, and a vast area has been poisoned for generations to come with incalculable consequences, even as the government and BP have falsely assured the public that everything is now back to normal. BP is known for its long history of recklessness. This is only the most devastating of a series of its disasters. That it has paid to victims some billions of dollars, which it will not take long for it to recoup, has been hailed as conscientious restitution. What it really represented was BP's ticket to admission for further offshore drilling, which the Obama Administration has now punched.

Theodore Roosevelt called the oil interests the "Invisible Government," while Woodrow Wilson referred to them as the "Invisible Empire."

The huge Teapot Dome Scandal of the 1920s reached right into the Harding Administration, as oil company executives conspired with government officials to steal US oil reserves. In 1947, the chairman of the Texas Democratic Committee revealed that "The oil industry today is in complete control of state politics and state government,"[18] while in 1955, Texas Governor Price Daniel, running for the Senate, said he did not see how anyone could get elected in Texas without the backing of oil money. During the 1950s and '60s the leaders of both the US Senate and the House of Representatives just happened to be from oil-rich Texas. It was Robert Taft, "Mr. Republican," who stated publicly that for three decades the Rockefeller oil company bank, Chase Manhattan, had named every Republican Presidential nominee.

Oil has lubricated the careers of many Secretaries of State, from Charles Evans Hughes under Woodrow Wilson, who became chief counsel to the American Petroleum Institute, to President Truman's Secretary of State Dean Acheson and President Eisenhower's Secretary of State John Foster Dulles, both of whom came from law firms representing the oil interests. Under-Secretary of State George Ball became a director of Standard Oil of California, as did John McCone, who served as the head of the CIA. Another prominent CIA director, Allen Dulles, brother of John Foster Dulles, also worked for an oil company before entering government.

45

Texas representatives of the major oil interests have disproportionately chaired powerful congressional committees. Lyndon Johnson, performing a lifetime of service for Texas oil, assumed the presidency with the assassination of John Kennedy, whose policies had earned Big Oil's enmity, an assassination that took place, significantly, in Dallas. Food for thought: The leading Dallas newspaper framed Kennedy's portrait in black on its front page hours *before* his assassination.

Since World War II, the central focus of US policy in the Mideast has been to ensure control over the region's oil wealth. In 1953, a democratically elected Iranian government dared to nationalize its oil, the lion's share of which was owned by the British, with US oil companies as junior partners. Too weak to accomplish the deed itself, the British asked Washington to organize a coup, which it did. The Shah was then installed as dictator, and in gratitude restored the oil to their previous owners, except that now the British were the junior and the Americans the senior partner. After all, fair's fair. As part of the deal, Iran agreed to serve, along with Israel, as regional gendarme for Washington and London against Arab nationalism. With the popular revolution of 1979 and the Shah's overthrow, the oil once again became the property of the Iranian people. The alliance between the West and Iran came to an end. So, once again, under the pretense of fear of the Iranians developing nuclear weapons (although we have them by the thousands and Israel by the hundreds), Washington is once again preparing regime change.

The somewhat similar story of Iraq picks up when

its British puppet king was overthrown in 1958, Britain having been the colonial power. As in Iran, the oil was nationalized. So the British parachuted into Jordan while the Americans invaded Lebanon. Under world pressure they were, however, forced to quickly withdraw. But a golden opportunity presented itself after the September 11th attack on the World Trade Center. Bringing Iraqi oil under the control of mainly US oil companies was much of what lay behind Washington's aggression, supported by our touchingly loyal British ally, loyal both to Washington and to British Petroleum. After getting rid of Sadam Hussein in the name of preventing his use of weapons of mass destruction that the CIA swore were in the dictator's hands (Didn't find any? Well, nobody's perfect), oil contracts have been signed with Exxon, BP, Shell, the French-owned Total, among others, who will be feasting on the largest oil reserves in the world.

Meanwhile, while Washington blithely ignored the millions of Iraqis who died as a result of both the US invasion and its previous sanctions, it is absolutely "outraged" at the Syrian government's shooting of civilians (a little less outraged at the death-dealing brutal dictatorships of Bahrein and Yemen, who are Washington's allies).

Just to put things in perspective: *In just the 15-year period immediately following World War II, the US oil companies extracted more wealth out of the Middle East than the British had managed to do from the whole of their vast empire in the entire 19th century.*

It is worthy of note that the 2003 invasion of Iraq was secretly planned and organized by President Dick

Cheney (some mistakenly believed he was Vice President), who moved to the White House from the position of CEO of the oil services giant Halliburton, taking with him a $32 million severance package. Meanwhile, George W. Bush, whose father has close business ties with the oil-bloated Saudi royal family, was assigned the role of Iraqi war pitch man. Also facilitating the criminal enterprise was then head of the National Security Council, later Secretary of State, Condoleeza Rice, a former director of Chevron Oil.

COAL

The coal industry, too, is doing its bit to demonstrate it is part of the green movement, touting the idea of "clean coal" when in fact it has all but abandoned efforts to capture deadly carbon dioxide emissions from dirty coal-burning power plants.

Over the years, the lives of more than 100,000 coal miners have been claimed by Black Lung disease, while 265,000 more lingered on, suffering its ravages. From 1900 to 1968, 100,000 workers were killed mostly in mine explosions. Between 1930 and 1968 such accidents were responsible for a million-and-a-half injuries. The term "accident" requires qualification, however, because many lives would have been saved if only the industry had been willing to spend relatively trifling amounts on mine safety, just as so many Black lung victims could have been spared had the industry spent a little more on protecting their health.

The history of the coal and other mining industries is one of extraordinarily violent and bloody wars, even by the standards of US labor history, as sheriffs, deputized goons, and even the National Guard, shot down strikers and busted heads. Strikers and their families were evicted from company-owned shacks and starved out when company stores cut off credit, all because of miners' outrageous demands for the right to organize and a living wage.

TEXTILE AND CLOTHING

Moving from coal mines to textile mills means moving from Black to Brown Lung, byssinosis, a disease caused by prolonged exposure to cotton dust. Until recently, cotton mill owners steadfastly denied its very existence despite its being known by medical authorities for over 250 years. A textile industry journal actually called it "a thing thought up by venal doctors" which, if it did exist, was a disease of "inferior races."[19] Finally, thanks to the changed political climate of the 1960s, a newly-created Occupational Safety and Health Administration (OSHA) tried to enforce minimal health and safety standards. But the textile mills remained defiant, refusing to pay even the ludicrously low fines assessed against them. Not willing to spend a few dollars to protect their workers' health, they were most generous in their contributions to the politicians.

For many years, J.P. Stevens, the industry's second-largest corporation, fired anyone suspected of engaging in union organizing or even of being a union sympathizer, illegal acts which the government likewise illegally ignored. J.P. Stevens became the model for many other corporations which copied its tactics of flouting labor laws and illegally keeping unions out of their factories, again with government complicity.

The textile industry was one of the first to discover the charm of offshore operations, leaving hundreds of thousands of workers stranded and entire communities in a state of permanent economic and psychological depression.

The National Labor Committee has for years been documenting the horrific conditions of clothing sweatshop workers in Latin America and Asia – the use of child labor, the unconscionable hours, the sexual abuse of young women who make up the vast majority of the workforce – conditions of virtual enslavement, all for the benefit of Liz Claiborne and other prestigious labels, as well as retailers like WalMart and GAP. When the harsh truth is periodically exposed, these companies invariably plead ignorance and profess shock. If they cannot be sent to prison, the corporate executives should at least be sentenced to doing time in their own sweatshops.

ASBESTOS

To the tobacco companies we owe lung cancer, to the coal companies Black Lung, to the textile companies Brown Lung, and to the asbestos manufacturers such as Johns Manville, we are indebted for the killer diseases of asbestosis and mesothelioma.

From the 1930s on, asbestos producers, as well as the successive administrations in Washington catering to them, knew that asbestos caused fatal lung disease, knew that asbestos workers died prematurely. But again, damning information was suppressed. So thanks to the profit lust of the manufacturers and the companies using asbestos products, 7,000 people will die annually for decades to come.

CHEMICALS

In 1984, the most deadly chemical company crime in history took place in Bhopal, India, where because of the negligence of Union Carbide, a devastating explosion caused 20,000 deaths outright, with 200,000 injuries, half of which were permanent, along with thousands of miscarriages. A federal judge in the United States obligingly tied up the case brought by the victims, giving the company time to liquidate much of its assets and protect it from huge civil claims. Indian officials have been trying for years to bring Union Carbide's former CEO Warren Anderson to justice on the charge of manslaughter, but he is too busy here living the life of luxury to go back and face trial. And the US government protects him from extradition.

Exposure to a wide variety of deadly chemicals causes tens of thousands of workplace-related deaths in the US each year. The people are also being bombarded in their homes with hazardous chemicals. Although in the 1970s a law was passed requiring the government to conduct chemical testing and to set new health and safety standards, it exempted all chemicals then being produced. So thirty years later, many of those chemicals continue to be manufactured and used in household and other products. No surprise that recent studies have detected over 100 chemicals in our bodies compromising our immune system, including carcinogens and other toxic agents.

Chemical plants have left a trail of abandoned hazardous waste sites. As a result of popular pressure, a Superfund was created to clean up those sites, to which the corporations were forced to contribute. But now, through the failure of Congress to renew the environmental tax on the oil and chemical companies, the fund has been allowed to become depleted.

The chemical companies share responsibility for the manufacture of some of mankind's most terrible weapons. The defoliation chemical Agent Orange, containing dioxin, the most lethal molecule known to man, was dumped on a million acres of Vietnam. Agent Orange's legacy was an extraordinary rate of cancer, birth deformities, and genetic damage passed from generation to generation. But profits from Agent Orange were too tempting to pass up. A herd of chemical companies rushed to cash in, including Dow, Monsanto, Diamond Shamrock, Hercules, and Uniroyal. Vast areas of the Vietnamese countryside remain a wasteland to this day. Those companies, particularly Dow, were also the proud producers of napalm, a kind of jellied gasoline which when used in bombs clings to its victims and incinerates them in an agonizing death. International law has since outlawed it.

But it was not the Vietnamese alone who suffered from Agent Orange's effects. In another example of blowback, tens of thousands of US veterans were also stricken, many terminally. And 2,000 of their children were born deformed. But as the war was raging, Dow's president assured the public that Agent Orange produced at worst only a mild rash. Finally, after many years, the government agreed to compensate our veterans. Yet to this day it refuses to make restitution to the Vietnamese.

It is still little known that the raw materials used by Saddam Hussein to gas tens of thousands of Kurds, and cited as one of the barbaric acts that justified US aggression against Iraq, was provided by American chemical companies, among others.

Companies such as Monsanto are busily engineering genetically modified foods, about whose long-term safety the world still worries, despite bland assurances. A study just released reveals that the ingestion of genetically modified corn produced tumours in mice. The beauty of genetically modified seeds, from the point of view of the companies, is that they have been engineered to not reproduce, so that each year farmers

53

must continually repurchase them. Monsanto and other companies hope that ultimately this will give them a stranglehold over the world food supply, for the great majority of the world's farmers cannot compete with this new technology. Moreover, they have been further ruined by the dumping on the world market of subsidized US and European agricultural products, revealing the hypocrisy of the West's championing of free trade. The latest UN report highlights the catastrophic effects of the domination of Western agribusiness — US chemical companies being an integral component — which are causing food shortages, skyrocketing prices, the exacerbation of world hunger, the degradation of land and natural resources, and looming ecological disaster.

RAILROADS

The railroads were once this country's most important industry, and its history reveals everything that is most corrupt and predatory about the "free enterprise" system. In its heyday, railroad chiefs such as Jay Gould were among the greatest of the "robber barons." Gould's criminal manipulations, imitated by his fellow magnates, included collusion in price-fixing, under-the-table rebates to favored big business customers, price-gouging the masses of poor farmers, charging for trackwork never completed, watering stock, meaning selling stocks to duped investors at hugely inflated values, to name but a few of his sleazy business practices. Gould and his colleagues went to

Washington as well as the state capitals with suitcases full of greenbacks. They also arranged to have friendly Congressmen inside the sacred legislative halls handing out shares of railroad stock to their colleagues. As a case in point, after one particularly liberal distribution of bribe money, the government granted Northern Pacific Railroad, headed by Jay Cooke, (Jay Crook) a million-and-a-half acres. The Vice President and Chief Justice of the Supreme Court were presented free shares of stock, as was Horace Greeley, the editor of the *New York Tribune*, one of the nation's most influential newspapers, as was the nation's leading evangelical preacher, Henry Ward Beecher. Both became Cooke's shills. Not to be outdone, in the course of smoothing the way for a takeover of the Southern Railway in 1893, J.P. Morgan, king of the hill, handed out $100 million worth of stock to government and media figures. Free railroad passes to politicians, of course, became standard.

The record of the railroads was unsurpassed in its indifference to human life, especially that of its workers. Through the 19th century, hundreds of thousands of railroad workers lost their lives and hundreds of thousands more were injured through accidents on the job, most quite avoidable, again, because of company refusal to take the necessary safety precautions. But in fairness, spending money to save the lives of their workers would have been quite foolish, given that most were Chinese, Irish and Black.

During the great general strike of 1877 led by the railroad workers, the railroad barons had no problem convincing the government to send in troops, drowning the strike in a river of blood. Though certain industries such as coal and the railroads are notorious for their particularly brutal history of repression against labor, violence against the worker is "as American as cherry pie." The United States has the bloodiest labor history of any industrialized nation on earth, attested to, among other things, by the armories set up in major cities to crush labor militancy wherever it reared its ugly head. One need only list the names of various episodes of labor strife to get the flavor: the Herrin Massacre, Bayview Massacre, Haymarket Massacre, Ludlow Massacre, Memorial Day Massacre, Matewan Massacre, Centralia Massacre, Latimer Massacre. To picket, march or demonstrate in the cause of labor has been during most of American history, and even occasionally to this day, to invite police or vigilante violence and/or a jail cell, to be branded as a criminal conspirator, an insurrectionist, held in contempt of court, in contempt of the American Way of Life.

In the space of 20 years, the government gave the railroads a staggering 130 million acres of prime agricultural land, rich in timber and mineral resources, extending from Wisconsin through parts of Minnesota, the Dakotas, Montana, Iowa, Oregon and Washington State, equaling in area all of New England, plus New York and a large part of Pennsylvania. Not only did they give away the land, but they gave huge sums to the railroads in the form of subsidies, and made loans which, despite the generosity of their terms, were often not repaid. The railroads were even permitted to take from the public land the materials needed for construction. And with all that, many a promised railroad line for which land and money were given were never completed. Thus, the main cost of building railroads was political bribes. Later on, Congress passed laws permitting the railroads to grab 30 million acres of coal fields, obtained, even by the admission of government investigators, through "fraud, perjury and violence," registering phony "settlers" and driving out genuine ones.

Still more. The federal government handed over millions of acres to the states, which they in turn distributed to land companies, speculators and, of course, the railroads. Not content with this booty, the railroads extorted more from cities and towns, threatening not to run track through their municipalities at a time when a railroad line meant the difference between thriving metropolis and ghost town. Texas alone granted 32 million acres to a dozen companies, an area larger than the State of Indiana. To be sure, it was not a one-sided deal, for while the railroads got the land, the politicians got the kickbacks. Meanwhile, Washington reneged on its promise to give each Black freedman 40 acres and a mule, small compensation, one would think, for the horrors of slavery and over 200 years of backbreaking labor. In fact, the federal government would not even *sell* land to the former slaves, preferring instead to make it available to foreign speculators.

OTHER CORPORATE GIVEAWAYS

On the subject of corporate giveaways, mention should be made of the lucrative city franchises awarded over the years to transportation companies and utilities, monopolies which generated enormous profits for the companies and, of course, enormous graft for the politicians. We have already noted government giveaways in connection with non-payment of royalties by the oil companies. Even when paid, they have been considerably undervalued, representing in effect a substantial subsidy. The nuclear power industry has received vast subsidies, of which the public is generally unaware. Payments by lumber companies for timber taken from our national parks do not begin to cover government costs. Grazing and mineral interests receive similar sweetheart deals. One of the worst of these goes back to 1872 when legislation allowed mining companies to claim lands for $50 an acre from which they have since extracted billions of dollars' worth of gold, silver and other minerals. The automobile industry was built on government subsidies, primarily in the form of a vast program of federally-funded highway building. Then there were the huge subsidies to "defense" contractors. 40 percent of government investment in research and development has been given to corporations gratis.

For a century-and-a-half the manufacturing, extractive and agricultural interests have gorged themselves on subsidies and tariffs to protect them from world competition, making goods more expensive for the mass of consumers. The big sugar producers continue to enjoy huge subsidies. Agribusiness in general loots the US taxpayer, at the same time as mentioned previously, impoverishing the farmers of the Third World.

In 2004, Congress passed another giveaway, called the American Jobs Creation Act. This allowed corporations to repatriate, almost tax-free, profits earned abroad, a measure supposedly intended to encourage them to hire more workers at home. Drug companies were among the chief beneficiaries of this giveaway, putting in corporate coffers about $100 billion in untaxed profits. But instead of hiring workers, they actually *laid off* tens of thousands. A similar program was adopted in New York State with equally dismal results.

The greatest example of corporate welfare is the Pentagon budget, the sacred cow of both political parties. And to the extent it is not a pure boondoggle, it serves a foreign policy solely aimed at assisting foreign plunder by the country's grasping commercial, industrial and financial interests, especially the oil interests. For the sake of the Pentagon budget, the people are bombarded with alarmist propaganda about foreign threats and never-ending crises, no matter how unchallengeable our strength and how suicidal for any country to attack us. Happily, a new "enemy" always conveniently arrives just in time to replace the previous one, to the enormous relief of the military-industrial complex.

So tax write-offs, tariffs, subsidies, off-shore leases, bailouts, etc., and especially the vast Pentagon budget, all add up to a grand rip-off, a plunder so vast with its string of zeros that it becomes too abstract to evoke the popular anger it deserves. "Stop Thief!" shouts the pickpocket as he makes his getaway. "Get the freeloaders!" shout the politicians and the media when it is a matter of throwing a few crumbs to the poor, as the real freeloaders push their snouts ever further into the nation's treasury. The biggest giveaway in history is now taking shape in the Federal Reserve's bailout of Wall Street.

AUTOMOBILE INDUSTRY

"What's good for General Motors is good for the country," said Charles Wilson, Eisenhower's Secretary of Defense and former GM head. But we can thank General Motors and the rest of the auto industry for the millions of deaths and injuries over the decades caused by the poor quality of their vehicles, a slaughter for which auto executives have never been held personally accountable. In 1982, the chair of the House Subcommittee on Transportation, after an exhaustive investigation, concluded General Motors manufactured and marketed 1.2 million unsafe Corvairs, knew about their inherent safety defects, and did nothing to correct them -- in fact, sought to conceal and suppress the evidence. Just one example.

Not to be outdone, the Ford Motor Company has consistently fought safety and pollution standards. It rigged safety tests and kept two sets of books or data -- the real one for itself and a phony one for the government. Ford was long aware that its transmissions were dangerous, as did the government, which allowed Ford to drag its feet in correcting the problem. Injuries mounted up while Ford assured the public there was nothing wrong with its cars. As late as 2006, Ford models were liable to catch fire upon impact. Ford recently settled a number of class-action suits involving its rollover-prone SUV's.

We are not saying that vehicles were deliberately made to crash, but they certainly were designed to fall apart -- planned obsolescence is the fancy name for it.

If US vehicles have become somewhat safer in recent years, it is no thanks to Congress, no thanks to the media, certainly no thanks to a new-found conscience among auto executives. American companies were forced to improve their products because of Japanese competition. But they are still picking the driver's pockets with their gas-guzzlers, still poisoning the atmosphere with their pollutants, still contributing to the epidemic of respiratory disease, still fighting auto emission and fuel efficiency standards, still contributing to global warming.

Clearly, an efficient mass transit system would have eased many environmental problems. But mass transit was precisely what the automobile and oil companies succeeded in destroying, especially in California, but elsewhere as well, by buying up and liquidating perfectly good mass transit facilities after World War II. As a result, the poor have for a long time been frozen out of an important portion of the country's economic life. Now it is clear that the vast majority of the people and the economy as a whole would benefit from Europe's excellent transit system, a system we lack, thanks above all to General Motors.

Henry Ford has gone down in our history books as the extraordinarily generous employer who paid his workers twice the going rate. What has been left out was his decades-long ruthless union-busting, his hiring of a horde of private Pinkerton goons and spies, his creation of at what was once the world's largest private army, and his one-man anti-Semitic crusade, more virulent than anything outside of Germany. Ford gangsterism did not end in the 1920s and '30s. Not too long ago the company set up an auto plant in Argentina, ruled at the time by a military dictatorship (which is the form of government that corporations find provides the most favorable "business climate"). Ford happily turned over to the regime the names of "trouble-makers," especially local union leaders, who were then duly imprisoned, tortured, or were "disappeared." Such cozy arrangements with foreign despotic governments are not unique to Ford. Chevron Oil in Nigeria, Coca-Cola, Drummond Coal, Chiquita, Dole and Del Monte in Colombia, are but a few other examples. In the case of Colombia, a very convenient arrangement of mutual assistance was worked out with the para-military, which within a ten-year period carried out the assassination of more than 1,500 union leaders and activists. Finally, with the recent economic crisis, the US auto companies received an unprecedented bailout from a public which for decades it has treated with utter contempt.

TIRES

It was only a few years ago that the Firestone and Bridgestone companies were churning out defective tires. Faithfully following the rules of our corporate culture, they too denied responsibility for the thousands of road casualties caused by their products. But they got their come-uppance. For example, in one huge class action lawsuit, Firestone was found guilty and fined the munificent sum of $50,000, amounting to about a buck per crushed skull or severed arm.

REAL ESTATE

There is no deeper cesspool of corruption than the real estate industry, teeming with landlords, developers, property managers, construction and finance companies, all of whom are major contributors to city and state politicians. The world of real estate is ruled by secret deals involving kickbacks, bid-rigging, tax breaks, zoning ordinances arranged to benefit developers at the expense of community residents, abuse of eminent domain, and the bribing of building inspectors. Added to this corruption are the vicious practices of racist red-lining, the targeting of people of color with usurious mortgages, and the steering of home buyers or tenants to their apartheid-designated places. While street crime receives "zero tolerance," the crime of racist housing practices is approached with the patience of Job. Rather than tossing the perpetrators of such crime behind bars, the agents of segregation are, in the tiny number of cases where such crime is addressed at all, called upon by the authorities to sit down and engage in protracted mediation and "conciliation." In the great majority of cases, the crime victims ultimately become exhausted, throw up their hands, and move into the segregated neighborhoods reserved for them.

The real estate industry is interested only in the development of luxury housing, commercial and office buildings. Not only do they refuse to erect housing for people of modest means, but they also work to prevent construction of desperately needed public housing, as well as lobby relentlessly to sabotage or prevent effective rent control.

There was a period in the 1970s when in the poorer neighborhoods of New York one would see block upon block of burned-out buildings. This was the work of systematic landlord arson, destroying buildings no longer profitable to maintain, to which municipal authorities turned a blind eye. "Urban renewal" drove millions of people from their homes, uprooting neighborhoods of color and the poor to make room for gentrification or highways to accommodate the needs of middle-class commuters and suburban commercial development.

One should not fail to mention Housing Court, where no self-respecting landlord's attorney will stoop to telling the truth and most self-respecting Housing Court judges pretend not to notice.

INSURANCE

The disaster of Hurricane Katrina should have been an eye-opener for those who believed in the goodness of government and the corporate world.

From President Bush down through the Louisiana governor and the New Orleans mayor, indifference to human suffering, especially that of the poor and Black community, was on full display. From the very beginning it was clear that New Orleans was viewed as a serendipitous opportunity for ethnic cleansing. As Representative Richard Baker of Baton Rouge gloated, "We finally cleaned up public housing in New Orleans. We couldn't do it, but God did."[20] It should be recalled that it was ethnic cleansing which supposedly motivated the United States and its NATO allies to rain down destruction on Serbia and drag its leaders to the International Criminal Court. But if it is a crime warranting an international tribunal, then consistency would dictate that George Bush and Bill Clinton, as well as officials down the line, should be sitting in the dock.

Of course, it was not politics alone that led to the ruin of the hundreds of thousands of people whose homes were destroyed. Simple commercial calculation was at work, as well. For most of the Katrina victims found their future blown away not by the hurricane but by the lawless refusal of insurance companies, including State Farm, to reimburse the losses of their policyholders. In fact, State Farm was caught destroying thousands of incriminating documents which substantiated their policy-holders' claims. Its greed is matched only by its shamelessness, as it continues to advertise that "With every policy comes the promise that we will be there when you need us."

Hit with a record number of natural disasters in the past few years, one would suppose the insurance industry to be in bad shape. Nothing could be further from the truth. The industry made record profits in 2005 and still more in 2006, even after Hurricane Katrina and the devastating Hurricane Rita. Premiums on home insurance over the past ten years have doubled, and in disaster-stricken areas have risen far more, while the amount of compensation has been so reduced that homeowners cannot afford to rebuild. Auto insurance companies also keep hiking their premiums while reducing claim payments. The Comptroller of the City of New York, William Thompson, in his December 2006 newsletter, has accused such companies of "driving many drivers into a financial ditch." It seems that the only thing insurance companies insure is their profits. Insurance companies have been investigated for making kickbacks to brokers. And the largest insurance brokerage company, Marsh & McLennon, has agreed to pay out almost a billion dollars in settlement of a bid-rigging scheme.

MERCHANTS OF DEATH

One of the closely guarded secrets kept from the American people by the politicians, the mainstream media, elementary school civics teachers and college professors, concerns the role of war contractors in fomenting and supporting militarism and wars of aggression. We have already touched on this. Nothing has been more profitable for corporations in the Fortune 500 than war and the threat of war. The bonanza endlessly flowing out of the Pentagon budget, moreover, is too great to be allowed to be interfered with by honest competition. So politically connected cliques of contractors connive with the Pentagon to get cost-plus, no-bid or rigged-bid contracts, are routinely permitted cost overruns, and are complicit with the government in other shady schemes to rip off the taxpayer in the name of national security. To keep the engines of their ill-gotten gain well lubricated, political contributions are lavished on both parties, ensuring that the Pentagon budget remains bountiful and US foreign policy belligerent.

Naturally, our patriotic "defense" contractors, the staunchest supporters of every war, have not hesitated to cheat the government even during times of national crisis, beginning with the American Revolution when merchants parlayed rancid food and defective equipment into extraordinary profits. A bitter George Washington was prompted to exclaim, "There is such a thirst for gain that it is enough to make one curse their own species for possessing so little virtue and patriotism."

There was the infamous conduct of government contractors during the Civil War when soldiers were given clothing and blankets that soon fell apart, were supplied food from diseased cattle and hogs, cavalry horses that had been doctored and soon broke down, and guns that could not hit their targets but were highly accurate in shooting the soldier's thumbs off.

In the 1890s, Andrew Carnegie, now known as a great philanthropist, knowingly sold defective armor plate to the US Navy.

Coca-Cola and Kodak closely collaborated with Hitler on the eve of World War II. Despite the threat to this country's survival posed by Nazi Germany, Standard Oil of New Jersey (now EXXON-Mobil) turned over synthetic rubber processes to the German Navy, withholding that same information from the US and British military. And US oil companies supplied the Japanese with fuel needed for their war machine. Right into the war, they did business with Nazi firms in occupied France, and assisted the Nazi war machine in the construction of an aviation fuel refinery. General Electric maintained its collaboration with Krupp, a major military supplier of Hitler, and IBM continued to lease its unique data machines that the Nazis found indispensable both in prosecuting the war and in most efficiently exterminating the Jews. The Justice Department charged scores of American companies with secretly capitalizing on business relationships with Nazi Germany. And a British Foreign Office memo concluded: "It is only too clear that where US trade interests are involved, these are being allowed to take precedence over hemispheric defense, over cooperation with us."[21] During the Second World War a major plane manufacturer, Curtiss-Wright, demonstrated its patriotism by not only selling the government defective engines but engaging in a criminal cover-up, as then Senator Harry Truman revealed in his investigation of war profiteering.

During the Cold War, such war profiteering was standard operating procedure. The. Pentagon was only too happy to pay $20 for plastic ice cube trays, $76 for 57 cent screws and, most famously, $640 for toilet seats. The scandals continue to this day. Auditors from the Government Accountability Office and others have identified dozens of companies that are repeatedly given government contracts despite shoddy work, cost overruns and fraud. It is rare that contractors with a record of poor and even dishonest performance are barred from feeding at the Pentagon trough, now in the $800 billion range. Lamented New York Congressperson Carolyn Maloney: "Fraudulent contractors are basically being given a green light to pillage the federal coffers."[22] And the *N.Y. Times* agreed: "Protecting the profit margins of major defense contractors still seems to count for more in the eyes of many legislators than protecting America's most vulnerable troops."[23] Boeing, for example, the No. 1 supplier of military aircraft, was found to have overbilled the Pentagon by over $2 billion, by no means the first time it has swindled the government. But nothing can alienate the affection of the Pentagon toward its suppliers. In the past decade, 80 percent of the top 50 government contractors have been assessed fines and penalties of over $12 billion for various forms of misconduct, which the companies simply factor into future bids.

The major source of Pentagon loyalty toward its contractors has been the "golden parachute," offered to high-ranking military officers who find lucrative jobs awaiting them upon retirement, working for the very companies with which they had previously been doing business. In their new careers, they lobby their military buddies who are still making procurement decisions.

The war contractors are guilty of two types of crime: On the one hand, through their political contributions they buy the necessary votes to ensure that the government spends stupendous sums on useless military hardware. As a result, the people are fastened with an ever-heavier and permanent debt burden. And to that degree the people are robbed of the money desperately required for genuine social needs. On the other hand, as mentioned before, they foment wars and a war psychosis to justify the huge military expenditures from which they handsomely benefit. The merchants of death set up and finance politicians, think tanks, and other manipulators of public opinion, whose job it is to proclaim how insecure the nation is, to alarm the people about one fabricated enemy or another, to demand that the country be kept on a permanent war footing, to question the patriotism of those who do not believe it is the mission of the United States to rule the world, to demonize those who call for cuts in the military budget, and to attack such people as being "soft on": soft on defense, soft on Communism, soft on terrorism.

Eisenhower referred to all this as the "military-industrial complex" and warned Americans about it in his presidential farewell address, which is maybe why he was kept on the golf links for most of his presidency.

But what is the record of the "super-patriots," not only the war contractors but the great majority of Corporate America who for a multitude of reasons support a bellicose US foreign policy? History shows that the elite has always placed its economic and political interests ahead of the country's security and welfare. Going back to 1812, John Jacob Astor, the richest man of his day, was accused by the government of treasonous collaboration with the British with whom we were at war, in order to prevent the interruption of his lucrative fur business. Later in the century, railroad king Jay Cooke would admit: "No one heartily loved their country better than their pockets."[24] Certainly, you will not find their patriotism going to the extreme of making personal sacrifices, sending their children to the battlefields of Iraq or Afghanistan, for example. Such prudence is part of a long and honorable tradition. During both the American Revolution and the Civil War, the law permitted the rich to pay poor men to serve in their place, a provision of which they took full advantage. James Mellon, founder of one of America's greatest industrial empires, wrote to his son forbidding him from joining the Union Army: "In time you will come to understand and believe that a man may be a patriot without risking his life or sacrificing his health. There are plenty of lives less valuable...."[25] Today, our "patriotic' corporations keep hundreds of billions of dollars earned overseas to escape US taxation.

THE FOOD INDUSTRY

From the merchants of death to the makers of infant formula. According to a UN report, a million infants died in 1986 because they were bottle- rather than breast-fed. Nestles and other companies push their products, especially in Third World countries, where bottle-feeding is particularly harmful because impoverished mothers are often forced to dilute the formula. Meanwhile, the manufacturers, using traveling nurses as hucksters, keep mothers ignorant of breast milk's immunological benefits.

Agribusiness is creating an environmental nightmare. Robert Kennedy in his book, *Crimes Against Nature*, describes how "industrial farms illegally dump millions of tons of untreated fecal and toxic waste onto the land and into the air and water. Factory farms have contaminated hundreds of miles of waterways, put tens of thousands of family farmers and fishermen out of work, killed billions of fish, sickened consumers, and subjected millions of farm animals to unspeakable cruelty."[26]

Missouri and Illinois, with the prodding of industry lobbyists who do not wish the public to witness the cruelty, have made it a crime to photograph factory farm animals. Thirteen states have libel laws forbidding criticism of food produced by factory farms, as well as other products of agribusiness. Just further examples of the collusion between government and industry against the public interest.

Cheaper food comes at a steep price, with the widespread use of pesticides, growth hormones, antibiotics, and genetically modified crops compromising both animal and

72

human health, as well as the environment.

As with the tobacco companies, the food processors strive to make their unhealthy products more addictive, injecting into them heavy doses of sugar and caffeine. And as with the tobacco companies, food processors target children, among other things flooding schools with junk food.

Engaging in the same deceptive practices as the pharmaceutical companies, the food and beverage industry finances fraudulent research studies. Dr. David Ludwig of Children's Hospital in Boston has concluded that: "Bias in nutrition studies may be more damaging than bias in drug studies because food affects everyone."[27]

Food companies widely engage in deceptive packaging and labeling, make false claims about the healthfulness of their products and finance front groups claiming to be independent to demonize people who urge a more healthy diet.

The food industry is irradiating and genetically modifying foods, now going so far as to clone animals, all done by stealth with the government's seal of approval so consumers have no idea what they're ingesting, and fighting labeling legislation that would allow consumers to avoid products that are potentially unsafe.

Fast food restaurants are having a catastrophic effect on both the people's health and the environment. High-end restaurants are not above a little larceny, now facing a record number of lawsuits from waiters, busboys and bartenders for stealing tips and cheating them on their wages.

Bottled water is a multi-billion-dollar industry dominated by Coca-Cola and Pepsi-Cola, whose products are simply elegant packaging of purified tap water. Aside from ripping off the consumer, the plastic bottles, which are not biodegradable, are contributing to environmental degradation and possible health risks to the consumer, including the leaching out of possibly hazardous chemicals. Coke and Pepsi were sued by the Indian government for lacing their products with poisons. Coca-Cola has also been implicated in the use of child labor in Latin America. Farm workers generally, mostly migrants, work in virtually slave-like conditions.

ADVERTISING/PUBLIC RELATIONS

For the right price, advertising agencies will sleep with anyone, and for its clients perform any act. "Madison Avenue" has no inhibition about putting lipstick on a pig, the only question being what shade? The advertising agency has come a long way from the carnival barker and has transformed the art of deception into a science. Today it lies about its client's products only when necessary, given the existence of somewhat inconvenient consumer protection laws, preferring to resort to its seemingly infinite palette of modest-to-wild exaggeration, half- and quarter-truths. Its goal is plausibility; truth is irrelevant.

Advertising's stock-in-trade is massaging the vanity of its target audience, pandering to its prejudices, making groundless anxiety seem reasonable, encouraging the snob in some, the mob in others. Advertisers are the midwives of the era's frantic consumerism, working round the clock to convince people that they are what they buy, and that if they're not "with it" they're "stepping in it."

Encouraging people to spend beyond their means and consume that which is either useless or positively harmful, Madison Avenue prostitutes the behavioral sciences to capitalize on the public's psychological weaknesses.

The advertising industry has now become indispensable to government and the politician, marketing not soap but dirt. In fact, the industry has become part and parcel of every institution: the university, philanthropies, scientific institutes, art establishments -- all of which have become increasingly marketing-dependent.

One wonders at the damage done to the American psyche and culture where the prevailing ethos is, as framed on the wall of an office in which I once worked, the inspirational message: "If nothing is being sold, nothing is happening." It is indeed both sad and criminal that vast amounts of our national resources are squandered on marketing, promotion and public relations, rather than being used to meet the people's real and urgent needs. Just another parasitic element of an increasingly parasitic, rather than productive system.

WALL STREET

Scot J. Paltrow, staff writer at the *Wall Street Journal*, has never lacked material in covering Wall Street scandals. Since the 1980s, there have been the junk bond scandals of Drexel Burnham Lambert; the sale of worthless limited-partnership interests to tens of thousands of small investors; the Nasdaq scandal in which dozens of brokerage firms colluded to fix prices; and the stock research scams involving deceptively rosy reports by stock analysts who had a conflict of interest.

Forced to return a billion-and-a-half dollars were the usual lions of Wall Street: Lehman Brothers, Salomon Smith Barney, Credit Suisse First Boston, Morgan Stanley, Goldman Sachs, Merrill Lynch, Citibank and Travelers. The latter two firms, having come to know each other during this fraud, fell in love and later merged to become Citigroup, making it at the time the world's largest financial institution.

The turn of the 21st century has brought with it an avalanche of scandals, breathtaking in scale, involving Enron, QualCom, WorldCom, Tyco and others. As a result, the regulatory authorities swore it would clean up the mess and that such things would never happen again. In 2003 and 2004, immediately following these assurances, every major US investment bank was found guilty of abetting fraud, including, again, Lehman Bros., Credit Suisse First Boston, Morgan Stanley, Goldman Sachs, Merrill-Lynch, Citigroup, UBS Warburg, and J.P. Morgan Chase. In that same year scandals exploded in connection with mutual funds fraud, considered up to that time the one area where Wall Street acted with integrity. Attorney-General Spitzer, in the thick of an investigation, reported that "Every time we turn over a rock in the mutual fund business, we find vermin crawling underneath it."[28]

Then there was the "late trading" scandal, something akin to the casino dealer playing with a marked deck, in which Goldman Sachs was heavily implicated, among others. The New York Stock Exchange itself was found to have turned a blind eye regarding this and other unlawful trading. Despite his repeated "failures," Richard Grasso, the CEO of the New York Stock Exchange, retired with a package of well over $100 million. Makes sense. He knew where all the bodies are buried.

Insider trading is rampant. In 2005, abnormal and unusually profitable trading was discovered in almost half of the companies shortly before merger deals were made public. In 2006, Bear Stearns was found guilty of fraud, not for the first time. Two years later it would pass into oblivion as a result of its reckless speculations

Wall Street is crawling with brokers, analysts, money managers, advisers, consultants, and personal wealth managers, whose large fees and commissions are based on steering their clients this way and that "Churning," it is called, when it reaches a point considered excessive even by the regulators, an extraordinarily tolerant lot. Mutual funds work out deals with brokers who act as shills, not hesitating to exaggerate or lie outright, for the right price. The third largest mutual fund received $100 million in kickbacks.

With dazzling ingenuity and monotonous regularity Wall Street's various players loot small investors, and some not so small. Not too long ago Wall Street firms coughed up $1 1/2 billion in restitution for fraudulent market research. In the end investors are no better off than if they had simply chosen funds that tracked stock averages, essentially eliminating the need for all the charts and "expertise" of the Wall Street hucksters.

Recently, we had the price-fixing scandal in the $35 billion federal bond auction market, in which the players are -- out loud, class -- Merrill-Lynch, Goldman Sachs, J.P. Morgan, Credit Suisse First Boston. There have been major investigations regarding municipal bonds amidst similar charges of large-scale bid-rigging. By the way, in this scandal Citigroup is also charged with illegally destroying documents.

Just as the legal profession has its ambulance chaser element, so Wall Street has salesmen running their scams in "chop houses," "boiler rooms," here and offshore, about which Gary Weiss a long-time investigative reporter for Business Week, wrote: "The boiler-room business model has been a mainstay...The concept is simple. Stocks in shaky companies, obtained at little or no cost, are sold to investors at huge profits. In the 1980s and 1990s, boiler rooms ripped off Americans for...perhaps $10 billion a year at their height....Domestic boiler rooms began to be replaced by the Internet in the late 1990s... But overseas boiler rooms have never slackened at all."[29] With the exception of an occasional lawsuit, the SEC has over the decades done very little to check this racket. At the very bottom in this crooked world are the penny stock traders.

Leading stockbrokers are repeatedly found guilty of an assortment of criminal practices. Five major trading firms were assessed $240 million for cheating their customers. Salomon Bros. entered fake bids for Treasury bonds. 20 stock grading firms were recently indicted for fraud. Computer Associates was found to have defrauded shareholders and the government for decades, for which it was fined $500 million. Before its unlamented demise, Bear Stearns repaid $160 million to investors for failing to properly monitor one of its hedge funds.

A short time ago, M.F. Global reported "it could not locate" $1 billion of money its clients had entrusted it with. Apparently, seeing an opportunity to make a killing on a speculation in Europe, and lacking its own funds to place its bet, it committed one of the gravest sins, and crimes, shocking even to Wall Street: M.F. Global "borrowed" its clients' money for its own gain. And winding up bankrupt, it could not put its clients' money back. Heading up M.F. Global was Jon Corzine, whose term as Governor of New Jersey was excellent preparation for his future career in larceny. That and being former CEO of Goldman Sachs.

And speaking of hedge funds, also known as private equity companies, these Wild West types of capital pools, unregulated, secretive, but often with huge financial resources, are currently responsible for half of all stock trading, The hedge fund Bayou defrauded investors of hundreds of millions of dollars. Another hedge fund, Milennium Partners, had to repay $180 million for its shady trading schemes. Hedge funds are currently under government investigation regarding their hidden relationship with the major banks which service them, and they are also under scrutiny for evading billions of dollars in taxes.

Credit rating agencies, such as Standard & Poor's, Moody's, and Fitch, on whom investors rely for accurate assessments of risk, have since the early 1970s been paid by the very companies whose creditworthiness they evaluate. This conflict of interest has resulted in situations such as the Enron debacle, Enron being given a clean bill of health up to a few days before it went bankrupt. The rating companies bear a major share of responsibility for the subprime mortgage crisis, having given their blessings to the tons of worthless paper known as collateralized debt obligations. In addition to contributing to the present financial chaos, the rating companies have helped push this country into a recession which may well have unprecedented consequences. The Connecticut Attorney-General is investigating Moody's for false assurances about securities, charging it with engaging in potential favoritism and abusive and illegal practices that involve dealings with the companies that they rate. And the *New York Times* called such practices not crooked but "flawed," a word never applied to the actions of the mugger or second-story man. Of course, street criminals with their lack of refinement do not deserve the delicacy of the *Times* in describing the crimes of gentlemen.

One of the amazing things about the reputation of Wall Street institutions is its teflon quality. The same firms commit fraud after fraud after fraud, are repeatedly cited by regulatory authorities and the courts, sometimes prosecuted, often fined, yet somehow the Wall Streeters continue to thrive. Merrill-Lynch is a case in point: In 1966, it was charged by the Securities and Exchange Commission with passing insider information to its clients; in 1986, one of its low-level brokers was arrested for fraud; in 1987, clients of Merrill-Lynch, thanks to its sleazy operations, lost almost $400 million in mortgage-backed securities; in 1994, Orange County, California was forced into bankruptcy when Merrill-Lynch sold it mortgage-backed securities which became worthless; in 1996 Merrill-Lynch was fined $25 million for a trading scam involving a Japanese corporation; in 2004, it assisted Enron in defrauding Enron's shareholders. Then, the Attorney-General of New York came after Merrill-Lynch and other Wall Street firms for giving favorable recommendations concerning corporations which they knew were failing. Merrill-Lynch was forced to pony up $100 million to settle a case involving sex discrimination charges. It was fined $2.5 million for mishandling emails during an SEC investigation, fined $14 million for overcharging clients on mutual funds, and lost a $6 million lawsuit in which it was shown that it took advantage of an elderly couple's deteriorating mental condition. Scandals may have hurt Merrill's clients, but they haven't done significant damage to the brokerage firm. In fact, they are making more money than ever. Now neck-deep in the sub-prime fiasco, Merrill-Lynch, this corporate offender, repeat offender, never-ending offender, has finally bitten the dust, having been taken over by Bank of America. And after presiding over his company's bankruptcy, Merrill-Lynch's CEO was duly punished with a $160 million exit package. What else is new?

While the government stood by and blew taps for Merrill-Lynch, it had no intention of letting Merrill-Lynch's partners-in-crime go under, pouring a trillion dollars of our money, and plenty more on the way, for the current Wall Street bailout. Whatever Lola wants, Lola gets. Meanwhile, Merrill-Lynch goes to court as the aggrieved party. True, they may have looted the public for decades, but they were no different than the other looters. How come the government didn't come to their rescue?

Prudential Securities has a similar history. It was caught selling worthless limited partnerships. Then in the 1980s, Prudential-Bache perpetrated to that date the biggest swindle in Wall Street history. Between 1993 and 1995, Prudential Insurance Co. of America paid $1.5 billion to settle a scandal involving its securities unit. It paid out another $2 billion for deceptive practices in its life insurance units. But none of this has prevented it from amassing assets today worth hundreds of billions. The question is where are the "three-strikes-and-you're out" laws for the corporate hoodlums?

Back in 1987, a federal prosecutor complained of rampant criminal conduct that had permeated the securities industry. Twenty years later, the situation has grown even worse. All the leading banks have been implicated in financial crimes, have swindled the government, the taxpayers, shareholders -- their own and others. They have not even been above cheating their fellow banks, which has resulted in what is now called a "liquidity crisis," that is, the banks refusing to lend money to one another because they're afraid of a double-cross.

Given this criminal history, one would think that Wall Street would be subject to the most stringent government regulation, especially since their machinations can cause the collapse of the whole economy, as we have seen in the sub-prime mess, about which more later. But just the opposite is the case. As Weiss points out, *the public is not protected from Wall Street; rather, Wall Street is protected from the public.* One example he cites is the system set up by the National Association of Securities Dealers which prevents brokerage firms from being sued by its clients, either individually and, more important, as a class. The complaining client must submit to "impartial" arbitration, which works out just fine for the brokers; not so fine for the defenseless clients. This practice of forced arbitration and removing victims of corporate malfeasance from the judgment of the courts has been spreading throughout the business world. The Securities and Exchange Commission, which is supposed to oversee Wall Street, turns out to be pure window dressing, existing mainly to gull the public into believing there is somebody watching its back.

Aside from its criminal behavior, the immorality of Wall Street manifests itself in other ways, as well. For example, Wall Street loves mergers and acquisitions, which bring in a lot of money in fees and commissions. And it is always good for a rise in the company's share price. That it also inevitably comes with worker layoffs, well, that's just nit-picking.

Today it is the transnational banks who "bestride the world like a colossus," gathering the threads of commercial and industrial activity in one hand and holding on its leash the most powerful politicians in the other. Corporations can only function with bank assistance, and corporate crime can only be perpetrated with bank complicity. For their role in the gigantic WorldCom fraud, J.P. Morgan and Citigroup were forced to make restitution to the tune of $2.5 billion, while Bank of America was assessed another half-a billion. J.P. Morgan was also found guilty of conniving with Enron, along with Credit Suisse and First Boston. Citigroup, Enron's leading banker-enabler, which helped to misrepresent the company's true financial condition, has recently settled with Enron stockholders for over $1.5 billion, on top of a previous settlement of $2 billion, with more lawsuits to come. The bank explained that in paying back $4 billion, it was in no way admitting to any wrongdoing, just trying to rid itself of the "uncertainties and expense" of protracted litigation. But of course it is just such protracted litigation for which it carries an army of lawyers in-house and on retainer. The *New York Times* informs us that this was only the latest in a series of Citigroup's troubles during the last decade-and-a-half "when the bank seemed to trip from scandal to scandal" paying billions to resolve various domestic cases as well as run-ins with regulators in other countries.

Back in 1994, Henry Gonzalez, chair of the House Banking Committee, reported that the overseas subsidiaries of multinational banking concerns such as Citibank did not regard themselves as bound by US laws on money laundering. The committee concluded that there were banks operating within banks as conduits for hot cash, primarily from narco-trafficking. The Bank of New York has recently admitted to money laundering to the tune of billions of dollars, as have others. It is clear that in the "War on Drugs" the banks have made a separate peace -- and a very profitable one. We will return to this.

A common swindle, strictly legal, involves non-interest-bearing accounts, such as, for example, most checking accounts. The banks earn almost 10 percent of their profits on such accounts and yet go on to charge service fees to "cover handling."

One of the richest sources of loot for the banking industry is the credit card business. With an ever-accommodating government deregulating credit card practices, the banks now engage in usury that puts loan sharks to shame. Egged on by the banks to become still more addicted to plastic, credit card holders sink into a quicksand of mounting fees, penalties, and ever higher, interest rates. While J.P. Morgan's revenue remained flat in 2006, its profits more than doubled thanks to its credit card division. When certain state governments have tried to protect their constituents from some particular credit card abuse, lo and behold, formerly dozing federal "bank supervisors" spring into action, claiming jurisdiction and demanding that the states lay off. In this they are backed by our ever-bank-loving Supreme Court.

Still not enough. Its wheels greased by generous payoffs, Congress pushed through a bankruptcy bill which ensures that credit card balances are given priority over child support and just about everything else. At the same time, corporate bankruptcy is treated with tender concern. Thus, companies are allowed through bankruptcy proceedings to renege on worker pensions, as well as environmental clean-up obligations, not infrequently their real motivation for declaring bankruptcy. But the ordinary working person seeking bankruptcy protection, half the time because of catastrophic medical expenses, must give the credit card issuers their pound of flesh. And, by the way, the name of this consumer rip-off law is the "Bankruptcy Abuse and Consumer Protection Act." Who says politicians have no sense of humor? And who says you can't squeeze blood out of a turnip?

Now that the banks have taken big hits, thanks to the sub-prime disaster, they are trying to make up for their losses by putting a further squeeze on credit card holders and jacking up interest rates. Incidentally, in a world where a contract represents a mutual obligation, the credit card contract is the only one where one party (the bank) may unilaterally change its terms.

One of the most spectacular banking scandals of the 1980s was the Savings and Loan fiasco, fruit of the Reagan Administration's philosophy of deregulation. After the way was paved for them by our upstanding political leaders, our upstanding business leaders set up savings and loans institutions which were no more than free-wheeling casinos that sucked in and then ruined tens of thousands of unsuspecting depositors and investors. When the banks finally went belly-up, the government hastened to arrange a bailout of $150 billion taxpayer dollars, confirming the old saying that the best way to rob a bank is to own one.

Since the government proved so generous in coming to the rescue of the S&L's, Wall Street naturally concluded that they should push bank deregulation still further. It got its buddies in Congress to repeal that firewall between commercial and investment banking, the Glass-Steagall Act. That law was enacted after the great 1929 stock market crash revealed the disastrous results of allowing one and the same bank to assume both the role of custodian of the people's savings and vehicle of wild speculation. Never mind, Wall Street's attitude, as it has been after every financial scandal and collapse, is simply, "That was then and this is now." The craving for the quick buck can only be held back for so long. So with Glass-Steagall out of the way, the commercial bank Citibank took over the investment bank Travelers, and a wave of financial services mergers followed, ultimately contributing to the present disaster.

Then there was the enormously corrupt $2 trillion municipal securities market, where Wall Street married local elected officials and they produced beautiful bouncing kickbacks, a sweet arrangement where everyone won except the public. Having been caught red-handed, the Bank of America threw its colleagues under the bus in a Justice Department investigation of municipal bond bids involving the financial institutions' widespread collusion.

Just now what may potentially be in the current wave of scandals the biggest scandal of all: Barclays Bank, London-based, has admitted to engaging in the rigging of LIBOR, which sets the interest rate for transactions around the world. So the amounts paid by untold numbers of borrowers, the majority just ordinary people for whom the interest they pay is of critical importance in their lives, has been affected by the crooked manipulation of one of England's mega-banks. Barclays has agreed to pay a fine of about a half-billion dollars, which is peanuts in comparison to the bank's profits as well as the trillions of dollars of corrupt transactions. Naturally, there is no question of criminal prosecution of this unprecedented criminal action. And there is clear evidence that other major banks, including major US banks, were involved with Barclays in interest rate manipulations. Now we're talking about trillions upon trillions of dollars impacting, directly or indirectly every man, woman and child on the globe And, as usual, those with responsibility for overseeing such matters, in this case the English government (probably US officials will soon likewise be implicated) somehow "missed the boat."

The all-too-familiar story would be tedious if it weren't so tragic.

ENVIRONMENTAL CRIME

We have already cited a number of the disastrous environmental crimes perpetrated by our "corporate citizens." They poison our atmosphere, pollute our streams and rivers -- even our drinking water -- contaminate our land, dump toxic chemicals, spray dangerous pesticides, and decimate our forests. Of course, in trashing nature the corporations are assaulting human life, and in this assault they are abetted by our "public servants" who, as in so many other matters, come down on the side of corporate profits against the public welfare. This is true irrespective of which party has been in power. Though the Republicans are generally more hostile to environmental protection, in this matter, as in every other, the Democrats likewise take care to serve the dominant economic interests.

But in furthering the program of the environmental criminals of Corporate America, the zeal of the second Bush Administration was unprecedented. Again, *Crimes Against Nature*: "Almost all the top positions at the agencies that protect our environment and oversee our resources have been filled by former lobbyists for the biggest polluters in the very businesses that these ministries oversee. These men and women seem to have entered government service with the express purpose of subverting the agencies they now command. The administration is systematically muzzling, purging and punishing scientists and other professionals whose work impedes corporate profit- taking. The immediate beneficiaries of this corrupt largesse have been the nation's most irresponsible mining, chemical, energy, agribusiness and automobile companies."[30]

The Bush Administration in many cases simply stopped enforcing environmental laws; dropped investigations into corporate violations previously under way, sharply reduced penalties and fines for environmental crime, and slashed agency enforcement positions. The results? Kennedy:

"The Environmental Protection Agency announced that for the first time since the Clean Water Act was passed 30 years ago, American waterways are getting dirtier... More sewage is flowing into our rivers, lakes, and streams as the White House throws out rules designed to end sewer-system overflows. Bush's policies promote greater use of dangerous pesticides, deadly chemicals, and greenhouse gases. The mercury and the pollutants that cause acid rain and provoke most asthma attacks come mainly from the smokestacks of one of the handful of outmoded coal-burning power plants. These discharges are illegal under the Clean Air Act. But President Bush recently sheltered these plants from civil and criminal prosecution, and then excused them from complying with the act."[31]

On his way out, Bush hastened to do away with the stroke of a pen as many environmental protections as he could manage before getting writer's cramp.

Still another of the innumerable effects of the ravaging of the environment is that 1 in 12 American women now have enough mercury in their system to cause neurological and other damage to their unborn, in part stemming from the consumption of contaminated fish.

While public pressure has managed to bar certain dangerous products from sale in this country, such as hazardous or untested pesticides and contaminated or expired pharmaceuticals, such products are routinely shipped to Third World countries where enforcement of health and safety regulations is even more negligent than it is here, with entirely foreseeable consequences. Even so, dangerous products marketed within the United States each year cause approximately 28,000 deaths and 130,000 serious illnesses.

Where are the exposés and alarms from the media about all this? And why is the Democratic Party so reticent about it, even during election campaigns? Where are the trials of corporate executives and their accomplices in government for causing the epidemic of asthma, from which 22 million Americans are now suffering, including 9 million children?

Obama has replaced Bush but not his fundamental policies, including his environmental policies. See, for example, the US role at the Doha conference on climate change, torpedoing any international agreement on significantly reducing greenhouse gases.

The world is hurtling into the "fiery furnace," and there is only a small chance of rescue, for unlike the biblical tale, it appears that the God of Mammon is much more powerful than any other.

Human life is now in jeopardy. The world is experiencing unprecedented hurricanes, droughts, floods, and wildfires. The desert is spreading while glaciers are melting at unprecedented rates. This is primarily the result of the corporations stubbornly resisting every effort to save the planet.

We are still on the subject of crime, and all this is criminal.

ELITE CRIME:
A SENTIMENTAL TRIP DOWN MEMORY LANE

Criminality in the business world is no recent phenomenon. It came into being a nanosecond after the Big Bang of the first private enterprise. The US elite began its thieving in so-called trade with the native peoples, a trade which laid the foundation for the fortune of America's first business tycoon, John Jacob Astor. Astor and his colleagues sold adulterated liquor to them in exchange for pelts which, moreover, were short-weighted. Fleecing them after getting them drunk, the good Christians charged outrageous prices for shoddy merchandise, and for good measure extended credit for its purchase at usurious rates.

Astor was but the first in a long line of cut-throats dubbed Robber Barons in the 19th century, a type that Balzac surely had in mind when he declared that "Behind every great fortune is a great crime."

The "Indians" were plied with alcohol not only to take advantage of them commercially, but to demoralize them, to destroy their capacity to resist European subjugation, just as 300 years later heroin and cocaine were injected into seething African-American ghettos.

The theft of the land of the indigeous proceeded through both violence and treachery. Hundreds of solemn and permanent treaties were entered into, intended by the Europeans to be broken from the very beginning. In 1830, Governor George Gilmer of Georgia, saw nothing wrong with this, for to him "treaties were expedients by which ignorant, intractable, and savage people were induced without bloodshed to yield up what civilized people had a right to possess,"[32] a belief shared by the elite in that day and to this day.

Those devout Christians brought to the Indians knowledge both of Our Savior and musket balls, the cross and carnage. With Jesus on their lips, the pious ones torched peaceful villages, slaughtered babies, and introduced methods of warfare that the "savages" rejected as barbaric. Later, the Americans would turn extermination of the buffalo into a tourist sport that had the beauty of both destroying the Indian's source of life and providing a diverting day trip for city dwellers. Indian leaders were assassinated after laying down their arms or as they were engaged in peace negotiations. In *Agents of Repression*, the outstanding intellectual Ward Churchill describes one by no means unique episode when women and children, attempting to run away from a scene of slaughter, were systematically exterminated. Finally, the few who remained in hiding were assured by the bearers of the Stars and Stripes that they had nothing to fear, whereupon "some small boys crept out and were surrounded by soldiers who butchered them."[33]

The genocide continued with "assimilation," as native children were torn from their parents and forced into boarding schools where their custodians proceeded to "beat the Indian out of them," the idea being "to kill the Indian and save the man." As Commissioner of Indian Affairs Price explained in 1892: "To domesticate and civilize wild Indians is a noble work. But to allow them to drag along, year after year, in their old superstition, laziness and filth instead of elevating them in the scale of humanity would be a lasting disgrace."[34] Then followed the General Allotment Act which, with all due legal niceties, separated the native peoples from another 100 million acres of their land.

To this day the swindling goes on as the Great White Father manages Indian wealth "in trust." Royalties assumed to have been collected for gas, timber and other natural resources on their lands were never disbursed. Finally, the Indians filed suit, claiming billions of dollars due. The judge hearing the case, Royce C. Lamberth, agreed with them, acknowledging practices "of a disgracefully racist and imperialist government that should have been buried a century ago." But it was the judge's honesty that was found to be disgraceful and he was promptly removed from the case, his replacement reducing the award to a pittance.

Having stolen native land, the colonists needed people to work it. Few were available abroad and none locally. And so for various reasons, Africa became the ideal hunting ground. To gather their labor supply, the Europeans launched raiding parties on the continent, exploited the animosities of rival African clans, provided weapons so that they might butcher one another, corrupted some African chiefs and intimidated others. Thus began the history of mass kidnapping and murder, the unparalleled horror of the Middle Passage, the depopulation of entire regions and the collapse of African economies. What the slave trade failed to destroy of formerly thriving societies was later finished by colonial conquest.

Scores of millions was the toll of this greatest of all holocausts, including those who died battling capture, those who perished in the coastal forts where they were assembled to be carried off to the Western Hemisphere, those who succumbed in the Middle Passage, and finally those who made it to the West Indian plantations only to die from European diseases and treatment of unspeakable cruelty.

As liquor was important in the dispossession of the native peoples, it became a cornerstone of the slave trade, building North American prosperity on the "triangular trade" – West Indian sugar converted to New England rum, exchanged for African slaves, sent to West Indian plantations to produce sugar. Later, whip-driven labor would not only lay the basis for the fortunes of the Southern plantation elite, but would stimulate New England manufactures and establish New York City's commercial and financial preeminance. In fact, without the foreign exchange produced by slave-produced cotton, the United States would be little more than a land of subsistence farming. Such was the glorious foundation upon which this country was built.

But, it will be said, slavery was perfectly legal in its day, not only legal but respectable. It will be asserted that to talk about the criminal nature of slaveholding is to judge one historical period by the standards of another, to be "ahistorical." Someone should have told the Black captives, the multitude who rose up, escaped, or engaged in a thousand forms of sabotage, that such resistance was ahistorical.

The Africans were not unique in their servitude. Europeans, pressured by economic distress, were forced to indenture themselves. And so in this "sweet land of liberty," for the first 150 years or so, three-quarters of the workforce consisted in one form or another of enslaved labor.

But getting back to the "Founding Fathers." Besides being slaveholders or in professions associated with slavery, they were also land speculators whose dealings did not always pass the smell test. Indeed, it was British interference with land speculation by North American colonists, including George Washington and his colleagues, which was one of the Patriot grievances that led to the American Revolution. For the British monarchy had committed the abominable crime of protecting the land rights of certain native tribes.

Shady land deals have ever since been a staple of the rich. In fact, fraudulent land grabs have been a central feature of our history. (See *History of the Great American Fortunes*) The railroads, as previously mentioned, received the lion's share of government giveaways, but other interests fed at the public trough, as well. Companies plundering the country's mineral resources received large tracts of land on the promise to build canals, promises never kept. No matter, the government let them keep the land anyhow. Sheep and cattle syndicates received huge areas set aside for homesteaders by copying the tricks of the railroad corporations and using thousands of names of sham settlers. Timber companies, too, feasted on government largesse. After the Civil War, 40 million acres of government land in the South were handed out for a song to groups of capitalists, including eight million acres rich in iron and coal deposits. Urban real estate was also bestowed to great moguls such as the railroad king Cornelius Vanderbilt. And everywhere these giveaways were accompanied by bribes of city councils, of state legislatures and, of course, of Congress. Such bribes were repeatedly exposed by investigating committees of those bodies themselves, and just as often ignored. Finally, when a few officials persisted in trying to recover some of the fraudulently obtained land, the matter ended up before the Supreme Court. The Court was faced with a conundrum: How could it let its corporate buddies keep their loot and at the same time uphold the law? It was a difficult delivery, but the baby came out just fine. The Court agreed that the land had been fraudulently conveyed. But fraudulent as the contracts were, it opined, they were still contracts, and contracts were the sacred foundation of Christian civilization.

In the beginning, open bribery was the usual technique used by the fat cats in getting their way. But with the growing sophistication of the political system and an increasingly indignant public, Myers informs us that the passing of money in direct form became less frequent and "a less crude, finer and more insidious system was generally substituted."[35] The elite "began to follow the advice of that Eastern magnate who declared that it was easier to elect, than to buy, a legislature." Hence began the enormous sums poured into political parties, into primaries and general elections, into "public relations" and lobbying, sucking the oxygen, limited as it was, out of the bloodstream of our democracy.

But let us not dwell on our history's sordid episodes. Let us move on to that glorious period in the latter part of the 19th century when a flood of immigrants gazed up hopefully as they sailed past the Statue of Liberty, that gift from France celebrating the Union victory and slave emancipation, whose original African features had to be recast before an offended nation would agree to accept it.

"Give me your huddled masses," reads the legend at its base. Translated into good American, this turned out to mean "Give me your sweated labor, you dagos, wops, spics and kikes, you polacks, micks and papist dogs – but don't send your chinks." Now the ships were carrying not slave but free labor, free, that is, to be ground down 12 hours a day, six or seven days a week, for destitution wages.

And so for decades, those huddled masses, insolent enough to organize or go out on strike, were starved out, shot, jailed, blacklisted, and beaten into submission. Only during the radical upsurge of the 1930s Great Depression did most workers finally win their rights, many of which were taken away again scarcely a dozen years later through the Taft-Hartley and Landrum-Griffin Acts, state "right-to-work laws, and the maneuvers of a National Labor Relations Board stacked with Right-wing appointees. (At one time a man had to slave away 70 hours a week to support his family. But we've come a long way since then. Now it takes a man and his working wife 80 hours between them.)

Stuffed in rural barracks or city tenements; sharing their hovels with rats and tuberculosis; shoved into factories of unbearable heat or unbearable stench; unsheathed blades slicing away fingers and limbs; thrust into shafts whose coal dust ravaged the lungs, surviving the day if he was lucky, often enough ripped apart in mine explosions.

No lash but that of hunger.

Nothing criminal here, that is, until someone whispered the word "union." There were laws, after all, against the huddled masses plagued with TB, Black Lung and Brown Lung, "yearning to breathe free." It was perfectly legal to pay workers starvation wages, but criminal for workers to go on strike to feed their families.

At least Lincoln freed the slaves, didn't he? The shackles were indeed removed, replaced by...chains. A moment of euphoria, after which the freedmen were left to face Southern white terror -- mob violence, lynchings, chain gangs, and the neo-slavery going by the name of share-cropping and peonage. Black men who dared to vote were shot clutching the sparkling new 15th Amendment. But since this was the "New South," disenfranchisement proceeded with delicacy, with poll taxes, literacy tests, and the white primary. And the Supreme Court looked at what had been wrought and proclaimed it good.

Still later, over the border came the "wet-backs," Mexicans summoned to do back-breaking field labor, not in chains but surrounded by shotguns.

Still, the country marches on. The term of contempt "wet-back" has given way to the polite and friendly "guest worker," meaning better not be in town after sundown or in the country after the harvests are in.

BUSINESS LEADERS AND MORAL QUALITIES

We are told that those in prison are moral degenerates. We will keep returning to this. But let us look at the moral qualities of our business leaders. In their world is not ruthlessness not only an asset but indispensable? Can one find anywhere in an annual report to the stockholders a section headed "Scruples"? Have banks ever withheld financing or have shareholders ever revolted because workers were being mercilessly exploited and abused, because consumers were being fleeced, or because the environment was being poisoned? How long would top executives last if they announced to their board of directors that henceforth they would be telling the truth about the corporation's business practices and would deal honestly and apply the Golden Rule?

Edwin Sutherland, in *White Collar Crime*, estimates that at least 60 percent of the leading corporations engage in habitually criminal behavior, a typical understatement of the careful scholar. Yet for the system to run smoothly, the public must continue to believe in the dog-and-pony show, must continue to believe that "crime does not pay," that we live in a just society.

Crime, indeed, does not pay for the lowly street criminal. But as Ferdinand Lundberg has concluded in his renowned study of elite history, *The Rich and the Super-Rich*, "Crime, carefully planned and executed, is demonstrably the royal high road to pecuniary success in the United States."[36]

We have examined the criminal activities of

101

various branches of business enterprise and have seen that whatever the differences in their products and services, they are identical in their criminal behavior. All operate under the one principle of being unprincipled. Since it is clear that their means are ruthless and corrupt, that their deeds are routinely covered up or falsified, one must question the legitimacy of ends that require such means. It would seem that the profit motive is itself criminal.

THE ELITE AND THE LAW

Having merely touched on a few but nevertheless representative crimes of the business elite, let us step back and examine their relationship to the law more generally.

While the law usually serves their interests, the political tide is sometimes so strong against them that they face the prospect of unwelcome legislation. In those cases the corporations use their influence to ensure that the laws they oppose are deliberately drafted to be vague and ambiguous, and thus subject to later legal challenge, or contain convenient. loopholes. Sometimes they simply flout laws even though they themselves have largely shaped them.

The agencies of governmental oversight have been captured by the very people they were designed to regulate. The creation of regulatory bodies began with fierce corporate opposition. Then that opposition turned to support as Big Business came to appreciate that not having a regulatory body was not as good as having one in its hip pocket, giving the appearance of oversight. Thus, every year or two, state Public Service Commissions convene public hearings to determine new telephone and electricity rates. In this ritual the utility companies, public interest groups, and individual consumers make their presentations. Invariably, the utilities request twice the rate increase they really desire, the public demands no increase or even a rollback, and the commissions take copious notes. Then, standing above the fray and proving they are mindful of the public interest, they "split the difference," grant half the raise the utilities asked for. The public utters a sigh of relief because the increase could have been greater, and the utilities "resign themselves" to the compromise. A similar farce is played out in New York City every two years by the Rent Guidelines Board.

Further, though infinitely more damaging to society than street crime, corporate crime is usually dealt with by "civil remedies," rather than criminal prosecutions. As Lundberg points out, "While the courts decreed in their wisdom that corporations are 'persons' and are entitled to all the protections of persons, it is one of the facts that one can't jail or execute one of the corporations...It is true that the legislation establishing the Sherman Act and the Federal Trade Commission did provide for prosecution of officers of offending corporations [but] such prosecutions have rarely been launched by business-minded public officials."[37]

Judge Thurman Arnold, who from 1938 to 1943 was in charge of the antitrust division of the Department of Justice, elaborated on corporate impunity:

"The operative function of the Sherman [Anti-Trust] Act is to make possible from time to time ceremonial observances of the American belief in competition. These ceremonial observances take the form of criminal prosecution so that one may believe the competitive situation is being defended...Meanwhile concentration and monopoly advance in rapid strides from decade to decade, as in Europe."[38]

In the half-century since Arnold wrote those lines, concentration and monopoly have in fact accelerated, and the merger or acquisition has become Wall Street's life-blood.

When caught violating the law, corporations are almost always allowed to avoid the criminal stigma. Most often its criminal behavior is resolved with court-ordered consent decrees negotiated behind closed doors where the corporation simply promises not to be bad again. Civil settlements are kept secret so that the public remains ignorant of the nature and extent of the corporation's wrongdoing. In the past, however, at least a few of the more egregious corporate offenses were prosecuted. But the Justice Department has changed its strategy. Instead of bringing criminal charges, the government and the corporations enter into what are called. "deferred prosecution agreements." These involve doing away with a trial, the corporation accepting a fine, along with a government monitor of its operations, the details of which in many cases are kept secret. That all this is easily subject to corruption became evident when in one case $52 million was paid to serve as monitor to the firm of the former Bush Administration Attorney-General John Ashcroft. Such agreements, once rare, but now becoming commonplace, allow the corporations, while not contesting the charges, to avoid admitting guilt. And the kicker is that that after two or three years the charges are permanently dismissed.

Corporations are fond of pleading *nolo contendere*, or no contest, which, while equivalent to a guilty plea, permits them to issue the self-serving statement that they are now and have always been law-abiding. Pleading *nolo contendere* also has the advantage of putting obstacles in the way of private lawsuits. Of course, *nolo contendere* is not an option for the perpetrator of street crime. In fact, as we shall note, the severity of the street criminal's sentence depends on whether he pleads guilty and, further, whether he expresses remorse, which also affects his chances of obtaining parole. The dual standard of justice, evident in the sharply disparate treatment of corporate and street criminals, has been justified by U.S. District Judge Warren J. Ferguson in Los Angeles, who expressed the opinion of many of his colleagues in these words:

"All people don't need to be sent to prison. For white-collar criminals, the mere fact of prosecution, pleading guilty -- the psychological trauma of that is punishment enough."[39] Of course, right-wingers have no problem with this kind of "bleeding heart" judge.

One of the more interesting aspects of the law as it relates to the elite is how often it has been turned into the *opposite* of its original purpose. Anti-trust laws against corporations were first used to prosecute *unions*; the 14th

Amendment, designed to protect the rights of African-Americans, became a means to grant extraordinary privileges to corporations; the Voting Rights Act, the crowning achievement of the civil rights movement, turned into an instrument for prosecuting *Black* Alabama and Texas election activists trying to get out the vote; anti-discrimination laws are twisted, as in the Bakke case, to make it impossible to remedy the legacy of past discrimination. Deregulation of industry, supposedly designed to stimulate competition and lower prices, has strengthened monopoly and caused prices to soar, as in the case of cable TV and the power industry.

Another device available to the rich and powerful is the tactic of *delay*, and it is true indeed that justice delayed is justice denied. So even if a law is passed for the people's benefit, and even if that law is validated in court, the government or the big corporations can string matters out so as to frustrate the victory. Merck provides a perfect example. Its drug Vioxx, shown to have caused heart attacks, was withdrawn in 2004. By that time, more than 20 million people in the United States had taken it, and an estimated 100,000 were stricken by its deadly effects. But the courts refused to consolidate the tens of thousands of lawsuits that were piling up. So far, fewer than 20 of them have reached juries. At that rate, it will take decades to work through the backlog so that many plaintiffs will die before they get their day in court. But even when they prevail, as it is anticipated that many will, it would take additional years for the plaintiffs to get their just compensation. Merck has appealed every case it has lost. The company's strategy has been to game the legal system. And the strategy has worked beautifully. Finally, Merck and a group of lawyers for some plaintiffs have recently proposed a settlement of $5 billion, representing only nine months of Merck's profit, to cover 27,000 lawsuits. In addition to Merck, the biggest winners will be the victims' lawyers (par for the course), who will take about 40 percent of the settlement amount, or about $2 billion, while the victims will get about $72,000 apiece. No surprise that Merck stock *rose* upon announcement of the agreement.

The Supreme Court has now ruled on the EXXON-VALDEZ suit *20 years* after a jury awarded Alaskan residents $5 billion in punitive damages. That award was subsequently cut in half by an appeals court, and the Supreme Court has cut it once again, down to $500 million, or about 10 cents on the dollar. Meanwhile, tens of thousands of the plaintiffs have passed on to what we hope will be a richer reward.

Other examples: 29 corporations convicted of an electrical equipment price-fixing conspiracy were able to hold off punishment for a quarter of a century. And the Aluminum Company of America delayed punishment until 16 years after its criminal conviction.

It is standard practice for the government to keep workers waiting for years for payment of their legitimate Workman's Compensation claims. The same situation exists regarding those requesting Social Security disability benefits, as 750,000 people are waiting to have their claims processed, some as long as three years, many of whom have been forced into bankruptcy. Some facing terminal illness have died waiting for a decision. Hundreds of thousands of the hungry are forced needlessly and illegally to wait for the food stamps to which they are entitled. The National Labor Relations Board allows union contract grievances to pile up by the tens of thousands as they. deliberately stretch out their decisions for years, in many cases making such decisions too late to be of any use to the worker.

When it comes to enforcing civil rights law, delay is the rule. In 1946, the Supreme Court declared that segregation in interstate travel was unconstitutional, a ruling that took fifteen years to enforce, and that only after the bloody sacrifices of the Freedom Riders. The *Brown v. Board of Education* desegregation decision calling for "all deliberate speed" was met by all deliberate obstruction, the process of integration not beginning until 11 years later. Six years after Hurricane Katrina, many of its homeless victims were still waiting for the promised government "emergency relief." All this is in contrast to the alacrity with which the government has sprung to the rescue of the bankers and Wall Streeters in connection with the sub-prime crisis.

The powers-that-be shrink in horror at crime against property. While preaching the sanctity of private property, the elite themselves commit sacrilege upon sacrilege. They instruct us that private property is synonymous with democracy, as opposed to communism or socialism, which they say is synonymous with tyranny. Defense of private property, interchangeable with defense of the "American Way of Life," was one of the key justifications for waging the Cold War, for overthrowing governments, for invading other countries. But when the property of the *small* property owner stands in the way of the big property owner, of big real estate developers, for instance, then the doctrine of the sanctity of private property gives way to the doctrine of eminent domain. Originally intended to prevent individual property owners from standing in the way of an overriding public benefit, the Supreme Court has now blessed the seizure of homes and small businesses for the greater good of erecting shopping malls and large luxury complexes, even gulf courses. It turns out that the "sanctity of private property" is only a slogan to dupe the middle class. For example, the political spinners proclaim that the estate tax (dubbed the death tax) is bad not because it hits the tiniest fraction of the upper class, but because it supposedly takes away the life savings of the family farmer; that the capital gains tax is terrible not because it reduces the income of the big investor but because it, robs widows and orphans of their pittance. And what a torrent of crocodile tears is shed for the little grocery store owner threatened by laws raising, the minimum wage. Of course, the real fear is of the ripple effect threatening the corporate bottom line.

In recent times, the Supreme Court has intensified its actions on behalf of our oppressed corporations, whose record profits have not been record enough and who were being pestered by shareholders who would prefer not to be swindled. The Court has made class action suits more difficult, has slashed punitive damages in a number of cases, and has taken jurisdiction away from states in favor of the more corporate-friendly federal courts. This is done by Right-wing justices on the court professing to be champions of states' rights.

In sum, we see that laws are usually passed to benefit the elite at the expense of the people, that those laws that do benefit the people are usually so watered down that they do little good, or when not sufficiently watered down, are struck down or twisted beyond recognition by the courts. Finally, we see that laws that benefit the people, when they are not watered down or struck down, nevertheless remain a dead letter, are not implemented or else delayed so as to make such laws meaningless. So what can the conclusion be except that *the fix is in?*

Especially important in considering the law's relationship to the elite are the statutes that *should be* on the books and aren't. For example, if the people really were in charge, if the government were really in their hands, the law would guarantee free quality health care for all. If the people were really in charge, it would not happen that 50,000 tenants each year would be evicted for non-payment of rent in New York City alone, or that millions of people would lose their homes through foreclosures. If the people were in charge there would be laws ensuring construction of sufficient decent and affordable housing. If the people were in charge, the law would ensure a living wage for all, would stop giving corporations a cozy deal on taxes instead of having the main burden fall on those of modest means. If the people were in charge, there would be a law guaranteeing the right of collective bargaining, which exists on paper today but only on paper. If the people were in charge, workers would have the right to strike in the public as well as in the private sectors. And there would be laws against closing down plants here and setting them up or subcontracting abroad where exploitation has no limits and where the standard of living of working people presses against the lowest level of physical existence.

Naturally, there would be a law against the bribing of politicians by corporations and wealthy individuals disguised as campaign contributions. And there would be a law requiring that the salaries of politicians be modest so that political office would truly be a public service and not a career path ensuring a standard of living much higher than that of the great majority of the people they supposedly represent.

ELITE CONTROL OF GOVERNMENT:
A PERSONAL EXPERIENCE

It is common for lawyers representing the corporate interests to work at the legislator's elbow, drafting tax and other legislation, a position earned by making the appropriate campaign contributions. But increasingly, the laws which seem to be the product of legislative initiative, are actually crafted in corporate offices. Politicians, finding the work tedious and complicated, just outsource it to the interested parties, freeing their own time for their principal passion of fund-raising.

I can personally attest to this process in the matter of a most important piece of legislation during the Kennedy Administration. In the 1960's, working as an office temp typist, I was sent to the headquarters of Peter Grace, a branch of the vast conglomerate W.R. Grace. My week's assignment was to type up, along with others, what turned out to be the "Alliance for Progress," an ambitious program of development assistance to Latin America, touted as promoting democracy and social justice. But its real motivation was to counter the growing attraction of the Cuban revolution. Of course the public was never told that the actual father of that program was not President Kennedy but the corporation with the greatest investment in Latin America and the greatest stake in seeing to it that the labor and resources of Latin America would continue to be sucked dry for the benefit of US Big Business.

THE POLITICAL PIGPEN

It is a seamless journey from corporate to political crime, from corrupter to corruptee. Similar to our survey of corporate crime, the discussion below is not focused on the crime of the merely self-serving, so pervasive that a US Attorney in New Jersey remarked about officials selling their offices, lining their pockets and making a mockery of their service to the public. There is nothing unique about New Jersey, as scandals across the country regularly attest, the most dramatic being the one involving Governor Blagojevich of Illinois, the state of a thousand corruption convictions in the last 30 years. Currently, there are underway more than 2,000 federal investigations of political corruption nationwide. Quoting the *New York Times*: "...wrongdoing by public officials at all levels of government is deeply rooted and widespread...In 2004 and 2005, more than 1,060 government employees were convicted of corrupt activities, including 177 federal officials, 158 state officials, 360 local officials, and 365 police officers, according to FBI statistics."[40]

Of course, these are only the ones who got caught or whom the authorities decided to prosecute.

"Power corrupts" is the oft-quoted saying. But what is more important is that *corruption empowers*. And the corruption that mostly concerns us at this point is the corrupt relationship of the politicians to the fat cats. The politician's success is not based on sticking his hands into the till. It hinges, rather, on exchanging the fair market value of his political services for the financial backing necessary to advance his political career. Is such an exchange considered corrupt in the eyes of the elite? Quite the contrary. The willingness of politicians to engage in such exchanges is precisely what makes them "safe," "sound," and "reliable." Those, on the other hand, who enter politics committed to serving the people and who remain steadfast in that commitment are deemed dangerous fanatics. As a presidential candidate once advised his rival, businessmen wanted men in office who will not steal but who will not interfere with those who do.

Really large corporate crimes depend on government complicity. Bribery of government officials is a quite normal part of a company's operations. There is the secret, illegal bribery of politicians and officials, and there is the open and legal bribery known as "campaign contributions." Our politicians spend half of their time raising money for their next election campaign and the other half squaring their political debts. It is this which greases the wheels of government. In the course of time each political campaign becomes more expensive. And each year, the gulf grows between the politicians and the people, separated by an ever more immense river of money. As the political favors to the rich and the corporations keep mounting, so do the salaries of our "public servants," which are far greater than those of the vast majority of their constituents. And so we say that, the system hasn't been corrupted; corruption is the system.

It is the stock-in-trade of candidates at election time to tearfully remind the voters of the privation of their youth. What they don't say is that it is a privation to which they intend never to return by upholding foolish moral principles. And so it is as true today as it was 100 years ago when Mark Twain observed that we have the best Congress that money can buy. Meanwhile, Congress passes one campaign financing reform law after another. Unimpressed, a leading lobbyist from the Mortgage Bankers Association put it this way: "It's a structural problem. You may find a temporary solution, but the water will find a way in. Influence is like water."[41] Now in *Citizens United*, the Supreme Court has slammed the door on even the most meager Congressional restrictions.

Bribery takes all forms, only sometimes involving cash. There is, for example, the offer of a job for members of the politician's family, as well as many other favors and special "business opportunities." Now in the era of "globalization," corruption has increasingly gone international. Over 500 U.S. corporations have admitted to bribing foreign officials.

It is important to understand that it is indispensable to the system of corruption, just as in the case of corporate crime, that there be periodic prosecutions of political bribe-takers. The system requires that some unlucky officials be hauled before the, bar of justice. For corruption must be orderly. The system cannot afford total anarchy. Greed must be controlled, not eliminated. And certainly it must not be allowed to harm the interests of fellow members of the elite.

Old-fashioned bribery, the secret passing of money for legislative or executive favors, so commonplace in the Gilded Age and before, has been largely modernized, given a respectable appearance. Beginning in the last quarter of the 19th century, the bagman gave way to the lobbyist. Paper bags full of cash for the most part gave way to checks signed by corporate treasurers, no longer to be openly distributed as a *quid pro quo*, but depicted simply as a means of "gaining access," access which is denied the vast majority of the American people. It has been calculated that on the statewide level alone, lobbying transactions total over $1 billion annually. There is an average of five lobbyists for every state legislator and a similar ratio around the halls of Congress as well as the inner sanctum of the White House. In addition to campaign contributions, there are junkets paid for by trade groups and corporations and there are large payments to politicians in the guise of speaking engagements. Even Supreme Court Justices are the beneficiaries of this type of "honorarium," which has nothing honorable about it.

Not that the older, more vulgar style of influence-peddling has disappeared. It's merely less important. Thus, the *N.Y. Times* reported that Chicago's "infamous political machine, an apparatus that many had said had faded away, like the stockyards, is actually alive and well, according to federal prosecutors -- and illegal, too."[42]

The Supreme Court has set straight those misguided individuals who believe that the obscene amounts of money in politics have totally corrupted democracy. Placing limits on campaign contributions, it has ruled, is equivalent to attacking free speech. So 99 percent of the First Amendment belongs to the wealthiest 1 percent, while 1 percent of it belongs to the 300 million rest of us.

We call the politicians criminal, even those who adhere most scrupulously to the letter of the law and do not engage in abusive self-serving. These generally are the independently wealthy who do not need to resort to petty graft. But in order to successfully climb the career ladder, politicians *must* be corrupt, must be willing to serve the elite of this country at the expense of the interests of the working people and even of the middle class. Since politicians and officials take an oath to uphold the Constitution which in its preamble proclaims the duty to "promote the general welfare" -- the general welfare, and not the exclusive interests of Big Business -- politicians and officials are in constant violation of their oath of office. This should be a serious criminal offense, but in our system such a notion is considered the height of political absurdity.

The politician's career is aligned with the powerful. At the same time he must throw a few bones to his base of hangers-on, doling out patronage on the basis of cronyism and nepotism, handing out small jobs with outlandish salaries and, of course, taking care of himself, his family and friends. It's a good deal all-around. Nobody gets hurt except the people.

It is more than a little ironic that those who are generally viewed by the public -- and for good reason -- as thoroughly corrupt, sleazy, double-dealing, treacherous, hypocritical -- in short, thoroughly loathsome human beings -- we are speaking here of course of the politicians -- are in the forefront of the moral crusade against street criminals.

THE OLD SHELL GAME

Nearly half of our "public servants" in Congress are millionaires. But again, what is of interest here is not how the politicians feather their own nest, not the personal corruption of the politician, but the *systemic* corruption of which politicians are an integral part. That corruption operates through the half-real, half-mock skirmishes between the Democratic and Republican Parties. On the one hand, there is a genuine battle over the choice morsels accompanying office. "To the victor belongs the spoils." Moreover, the struggle between the parties reflects different interests *within* the elite. Then, too, there are differences in tactical approaches on how the elite can best be served. But the struggle between the parties is also half-mock. For while each party defends the system of elite privilege, the politicians of the two parties need to convince the people that there is a genuine battle going on. Above all, the people must be kept from turning to *independent* politics, must be kept from forming a genuine people's party.

Just one of many recent examples of the sham nature of Democratic Party "opposition" was the authorization by leading figures in the Democratic Party of the use of force against Iraq while at the same time claiming not to have authorized its invasion. And then following the invasion it voted repeatedly and unfailingly to fund the war which, had it not done so, would have been brought to a quick end. The commitment by both parties to the needs of the US oligarchy in foreign affairs is expressed in the well-known adage, "Politics stops at the water's edge." The

Democrats, like the Republicans, fall all over themselves glorifying a military that is knee-deep in atrocities and on a mission of world domination, praising the "heroism" of US troops, and calling their acts on behalf of the U.S. empire defense of our freedom. Since so many of our political institutions -- Congress, the Executive branch, the courts, the political parties – are held in such popular disrepute, it should not come as a shock if one day we awaken to a military dictatorship.

The foreign policy of the Clinton Administration was supported by the Republicans and was indistinguishable from that of the senior Bush Administration, the war on Serbia being a case in point. Republicans and Democrats alike are champions of "free-trade agreements," have supported the economic policies of neoliberalism, which have brought ruin to the peoples of the Third World, and are now bringing ruin to Europe and to our own country.

On some domestic issues, the parties thunder about their differences, but always come together on matters affecting the basic interests of the elite. Thus, the hundreds of billions handed over to the banks to shield them from the consequences of their reckless and criminal activities, as well as the trillions that continue to be made available to them by the Federal Reserve Bank, won and continue to enjoy widespread bipartisan support. It was the Democratic President Clinton who "ended welfare as we know it," with the support of the Republicans. And with the support of his party and the Republicans, Clinton hastened to prove he could be just as "tough on crime" as the Republicans. He was instrumental in getting legislation passed which opened the door to a massive prison construction program (if you build it, the prisoners will come), pushed laws that created dozens of new categories of crime subject to the death penalty, as well as provisions for mandatory life sentences, greatly escalated the "War on Drugs," which has proven to be nothing more than a war on people of color, especially Black men, put through a law providing for eviction of public housing tenants if any member of the household were convicted of a drug infraction, even unbeknownst to other members of the household. At the same time, Clinton presided over the slashing of funds for public housing, which is now in the process of being privatized, again with the blessings of both parties. Obama is continuing that process and is now encouraging the privatization of public schools.

While the Republicans fiercely resist throwing even the driest of bones to working people and the poor, the Democrats are prepared to make concessions to them, but in a way that does not seriously impair corporate profits. Thus, the health care law, which Obama claims is a major step toward guaranteed universal coverage, turns out to be a gift to the health insurance industry. The only thing guaranteed are healthy profits to the HMO's. Similarly, while the Democrats support subsidies to the landlords to provide for the housing of a quite limited number of poor people, they will not support the massive public housing construction that alone will address the housing problem.

In step with their Republican brothers, the Democrats, since the pressure of the social justice movements subsided, have ignored the plight of the poor, the decimation of labor unions, the decline of US living standards. The Democrats, including the Obama Administration, have staunchly supported the neoliberal corporate agenda, which includes deindustrialization of America, which will eventually turn it into a Third World nation and thus will be "competitive" with the other Third World nations. The Democrats have been complicit with the Republicans in the rollback of the gains made by African-Americans during the 1960s and in ignoring the growing crisis in the Black communities. The Democratic Party, which traditionally has received a smaller proportion of Big Business money than the Republicans, has made more noise about curbing some of the worst election campaign abuses. Yet after Bill Clinton vowed to clean up those abuses, he helped the Democratic Party become the biggest recipient of corporate largesse, ignoring pledges of reform once he landed in office. Barack Obama, devotedly following the Clinton model in all things, has gone down the same path.

Democrats accept the fundamental premises of the Republicans about the "war on terror," and under Obama have increased aggression in the Muslim world, expanding Bush's policy and waging war, overt and low-intensity, including economic warfare, on Afghanistan, Pakistan, Iran, Syria, Libya, the Sudan, Somalia, and Yemen. He has also adopted a more belligerent policy toward China, and is continuig to encircle Russia. By essentially merging the CIA and the Pentagon, the Obama Administration has signaled that its wars and aggressive activity will in future increasingly be kept hidden from the American people's scrutiny.

On environmental issues, the Obama policy has been oil-company friendly, while masking that policy with rhetoric about "clean energy" and renewable energy. As previously mentioned, Obama stubbornly refuses to commit the government to a serious reduction of greenhouse gases, while scientists say we are approaching a point of no return with regard to global warming, warning of the ultimate extinction of human life.

In trampling on our civil liberties Obama, with the Democratic Party in tow, has gone far beyond the Bush Administration. He has supported and expanded the "Patriot Act," has deported more immigrants than any other administration in history, has prosecuted more whistle-blowers, has cracked down on peace activists more aggressively than previous Republican Administrations, has expanded the domestic role of the CIA, contrary to law, has opened the door to the detention without due process not alone of foreigners but of US citizens as well, and is the first President in history to openly proclaim a policy of targeted assassinations.

Nevertheless, to say that the parties are merely tweedle-dee and tweedle-dum is to miss the crucial point. When the Republicans move to the right, the Democrats move to the right with them, taking care to allow only the barest sliver of daylight between them, just enough to continue to be seen by their constituency as "the lesser of the two evils." While the evils steadily grow worse, the lesser steadily becomes less lesser. Then when the people become fed up and move to the left in their thinking, the Democrats move left, too, in order to prevent the formation of a genuine People's Party. It is this which constitutes their basic role in the system.

That the two parties are "kissing cousins" is further illustrated by the game in Congress and in the state and local legislatures of logrolling, also known as "You scratch my back and I'll scratch yours." Republicans frequently seek Democratic Party support for projects on behalf of their special interest constituencies (corporations), which the Democrats grant them in return for Republican support for Democratic projects on behalf of their own special interest backers. In addition, although Democrats and Republicans, when controlling a statehouse try to give themselves a partisan advantage, they will connive to carve out – gerrymander – political districts that favor the incumbents of both parties, which is why there are so few genuinely contested elections. The two parties also gang up to prevent independent parties from gaining ballot access. While each party bombards the electorate with warnings of the disaster awaiting the country should the other prevail, corporations remain quite unperturbed, contributing to both political parties simultaneously, thus ensuring they are always on the winning side.

The election campaigns of both parties, which are supposed to be the ultimate exercise in democracy, turn out to be the ultimate exercise in cynicism, with their smear campaigns, mud-slinging, promises the candidates have no intention of keeping, shameless demagogy and pandering to the politically illiterate.

The fact of the matter is that the two-party system is basically a scam, a hustle, a shell game with only two shells. The shell is always empty, whichever one is lifted. Nevertheless, we're told we've got to stick to the game. The

Republicans will give the corporations everything they ask for; the Democrats, in order to be the "lesser of the two evils," will only give the corporations three-quarters. Each party plays its assigned role in preserving the status quo.

Politicians must be good salesmen, in other words successful con artists. One of their most important jobs is to convince us that we have a democratic form of government, that the people have real power, that we can "put the politicians' feet to the fire." Actually, the public is not heeded but handled, managed, manipulated, lied to, deceived, given as little truthful information as possible. The politicians whip up imaginary perils, distracting attention from real problems and the real enemy. And in their noble mission of keeping the public bamboozled and befuddled, they can always count on the mainstream media for assistance. Politics has been called "the art of the possible." And it is indeed the art of testing just how much it is possible for politicians to get away with.

All this, we will be told, is distortion, wild exaggeration. There are plenty of instances, it will be pointed out, where laws are passed for the public good. Indeed there have been such occasions, but they have always been enacted under duress, only when the people have swung into action, when they organize and mobilize outside the framework of the two-party structure, when a movement arises that threatens a popular upheaval. It is then that those who rule come to the conclusion that discretion is the better part of valor. Better to defuse the situation and make some concessions than defy an aroused public opinion. To ignore the people in those circumstances could raise the political ante to a new and unaffordable or at least much more expensive level.

The politicians and government officials are incessantly plotting. They plot in the White House, in Congress, in Governors' mansions and in the state legislatures. They plot in all those specialized agencies and departments to which few people pay any attention. Naturally, this will be dismissed as paranoia, conspiracy theory. But there is nothing remarkable about conspiracies. Since the interests of the powerful few are diametrically opposed to the interests of the overwhelming majority, the elite and their representatives cannot very well pursue their objectives in the full light of day. The elite must act behind the scenes, in concert with their colleagues and their hirelings. How could they promote their aims except through conspiracy? Our government cannot but be a conspiracy, corporations cannot but be a conspiracy, all the institutions serving either or both have no choice but to be conspiracies.

THE DEMOCRATIC PARTY: A SUMMARY

The Democratic Party is the lightning rod of discontent. It adapts itself to radical movements more readily than the Republicans. It bends. It is flexible. And one of its main functions is to prevent the formation of a genuine people's party, a party that would express the interests of the working people, of the oppressed peoples, and of all the sectors of our population interested in peace and fundamental social change.

And so it accepts reform -- as much as necessary but as little as possible -- in order to calm the people's anger, to coopt the people's leaders, and ride out the storm until the crisis has passed. It then gradually curtails those reforms and cuts back programs in the people's interest. In periods of popular apathy the Democratic Party takes on a very conservative hue, and then takes on a pinkish coloration as the masses once more get into motion and begin making radical demands.

The political stance of the Democratic Party is a kind of litmus test of the strength of the people's movements. Of course, there are limits beyond which the Democratic Party will not go in the interest of assuaging popular discontent.

It is just the inability of reformists of the Left to understand the function of the Democratic Party within the system of political control which is the two-party system that leads it into the impasse of accepting the theory of the "lesser of the two evils" or chasing the will-o-the-wisp of capturing the Democratic Party, thinking that it is, for example, merely a matter of gaining a majority of convention delegates, and failing to appreciate all the impregnable tentacles of control which fasten the Democratic Party to the elite.

GOVERNMENT DOMESTIC CRIME (continued)
Federal Agencies

The President, his cabinet and Congress, get the lion's share of the spotlight. Behind the scenes there is little scrutiny of how the various executive departments carry out the bidding of Big Business. As we previously observed, agencies created as public watchdogs to prevent industry abuse have been perverted into means of facilitating such abuse. Many of them are staffed by former executives from the very industries whom the agencies are supposed to oversee. In their hands, naturally, regulations designed to safeguard workers, consumers, and the public at large, are "interpreted" to suit the corporations, are ignored, flouted or weakened.

We have already mentioned the connivance of the **Food and Drug Administration** with the drug industry. We have also mentioned the orgies at the **Department of the Interior,** where a top auditor revealed that his bosses were prohibiting him and his colleagues from recovering hundreds of millions of dollars in royalty payments from oil and gas companies, and in fact were steadily reducing the auditor staff. the **Securities and Exchange Commission** actually fired officials who blew the whistle on the shady activities of hedge funds. Rather than protecting the investing public, which is its primary mission, the SEC works to shield from lawsuits the corporations and their executives it is charged with disciplining. The **Occupational Health and Safety Administration** (OSHA) ignores corporate flouting of worker safety and health regulations. The **Mine Safety and Health Administration** not only fails to make the necessary inspections it is legally required to carry out, but lies to cover up that failure. Naturally, mine accidents are on the rise, in spite of which the number of mine inspectors has been cut almost 20 percent. The **Environmental Protection Agency** was severely admonished by a federal judge for making false and misleading statements about the quality of air at New York City's Ground Zero. A dozen states are suing the EPA for weakening regulations that require corporations to report on the toxic chemicals they use, store and release. Then there is the **Federal Energy Regulatory Commission** which has smoothed the way for price gouging through collusion of the power companies. The **Nuclear Regulatory Agency** ordered one of its inspectors to change his findings exposing an Ohio company's negligence in operating its nuclear reactor. **Internal Revenue Service** agents complain they are being discouraged from collecting the full amount of taxes owed by the big corporations. The IRS is even preparing to turn over regulation of the tax henhouse to the foxes, that is, to lobbyists whose life work has been to minimize tax liability for its business clients.

The entire area inside the Washington Beltway ought to be roped off as a crime scene and everyone inside its perimeter should be hauled before a grand jury.

State and city agencies similarly protect Big Business at the people's expense. Lobbyists ply their trade at the state and municipal levels, ensuring that the special interests are well taken care of. For at stake are lucrative business contracts, franchises, leases, zoning regulations, flotation of state and municipal bonds, utility rates, the making of key government appointments, the apportionment of tax burdens, including the creation of special tax breaks, a host of subsidies, the conferring of eminent domain, and on and on. Often going through the motion of an open-and-above-board process, almost all government decisions are actually made behind the backs of the people.

THE MYTH OF FREE ELECTIONS

American "free elections" are touted as the envy of the world, the most brilliant jewel in the crown of US democracy. Actually, the Constitution, even with its amendments, has for over two hundred years ensured that while we have a *little* democracy, we don't go overboard. The political system is saturated with institutional arrangements designed to thwart the will of the people, or as the Founding Fathers put it, the "passions of the mob," the "popular tumult" that was their great dread. But beyond that, elections, the periodic scramble for power by the various factions of the elite, have generally been saturated with fraud and violence.

We shall skip the fact that the great majority of people for the greater part of our history were not eligible to vote, and even fewer eligible to run for office. We shall not linger over the vaunted "universal" suffrage of "Jacksonian Democracy" for white males only. We haven't time to examine the electoral intrigues and corruption, the vote rigging -- ballot box stuffing, vote buying, and vote suppression -- surrounding corrupt big city machines and equally corrupt rural courthouse gangs. Let us move past the gerrymandering, the carving up of political boundaries for partisan advantage, which has been a favorite method of undermining democracy, a practice engaged in by both political parties for almost 200 years and still for the most part permitted by the courts. Let us move past systems of representation favoring conservative rural areas against the urban working people, which also lasted for almost 200 years before being partially struck down by the Supreme Court under pressure of the ferment of the 1960s (still manifest, for example, in the electoral college and the institution of the Senate). Let us not dwell on the extraordinary legal obstacles put in the way of the formation of any genuine people's party. We simply point to the controlling influence of money, more overwhelming each year, making the claim of free elections in the United States sheer fantasy. And the media is a key agent of the influence of money, always working to keep the masses ignorant, but especially during election time.

Of course, contempt for free elections was nowhere more on display than in the Jim Crow South during and after the violent overthrow of that brief, relatively democratic period of Reconstruction. Here is how the prominent historian C. Van Woodward described elections in post-Reconstruction Mississippi: "Independent candidates were run out of their counties, beaten, or murdered...Ballot boxes were stuffed, fraudulent returns were made, and thousands of opposition votes were thrown out on technicalities. With mock solemnity, newspapers reported that boxes containing anti-Democratic [Party] majorities had been eaten by mules or horses."[43]

During the election in Louisiana in the 1890s, "armed bands of Democratic [Party] "Regulators" roved the northern parishes, beating, killing and intimidating... The *Times-Democrat* admitted that in many precincts the ballots reported were 'two, three, and four times as great as the number of males of voting age."[44]

After an election in Wilmington, North Carolina in 1898, a mob demolished a Black newspaper office, shot up the Black district, killed 11, wounded a large number, and chased hundreds into the woods. Similar events took place in Georgia, where Atlanta mobs looted, plundered, lynched and murdered for four days.

When violence and fraud had largely accomplished its objectives, Jim Crow elections in the South and the disenfranchisement of African-Americans could proceed in a more "orderly" fashion.

But it was not Southern Blacks alone who suffered from this system. Millions of poor Southern whites were also disenfranchised. But rather than make common cause with the African-American, they settled for the consolation prize: At least they weren't "niggers." And so they condemned themselves to a poverty even shocking to European travelers who were familiar enough with the terrible conditions of their own destitute classes. Yes, at least they weren't "niggers." And with that comforting thought they languished for decades in hopeless poverty, illiteracy, sickness and disease, wages lower than those of whites anywhere else in the country, nonexistent social services, paid attention to only when there was need for a lynch mob, and used as cannon fodder abroad. That income differential, incidentally, is now being used to drive down the standard of living of Northern automobile workers, who are being pitted against Southerners working for Japanese auto companies attracted to the South's "right-to-work" laws.

Armed mobs no longer keep African-Americans from the polls. Today's instruments of disenfranchisement are racial gerrymandering, insufficient or broken voting machines in districts of color, and an infinite number of dirty tricks, such as switching poll locations in African-American communities at the last minute, intimidation by police, misinformation about voting procedures, etc. The latest contribution to our free elections, triumph of modern technology, are versatile voting machines which can secretly flip a vote to register the opposite of what was intended. But the most serious curb on Black voting is *felony disenfranchisement*, which we shall address presently.

Such is the democracy which Washington demands of the rest of the world, often at the point of a gun.

THE CONSTITUTION

The Constitution is the foundation of the legal system, supposedly. And indeed, the history of the country is that of constitutional rule. But it is equally the history of the trampling of the Constitution, particularly the Bill of Rights. Obviously, batteries and African-Americans are not included. For 150 years, workers found that freedom of speech and assembly did not apply to them, especially when it came to the right to organize. In periods of hot or cold war, economic crisis, and social ferment generally, civil liberties have been repeatedly tossed out the window. In such times the Bill of Rights is considered by the elite an unaffordable luxury. And those who dare challenge the oligarchy's foreign policy aims or its social control at home have found themselves prosecuted for sedition and subversion, imprisoned or deported, driven from employment, while the media can be counted on to shape the necessary public acquiescence. Nor is there ever a shortage of judges ready to railroad the "trouble-makers." During and immediately after the First World. War, after the frenzy of repression against those deemed unpatriotic, after the wave of persecutions of war protesters and labor radicals, after the Palmer Raids and deportations of immigrants simply because of their political associations, Supreme Court Justice Oliver Wendell Holmes set forth his famous phrase that was to become the guiding principle of the Court to the very present. That principle is now hailed by liberals and civil libertarians as guaranteeing freedom at all times -- at all times except when there was a "clear and present danger." Meaning that you can holler away, demonstrate to your heart's content, carry on your protest activities, as long as your influence extends to only a few. Up to that point opposition will be cheerfully tolerated. But when as a result of the exercise of your rights, large numbers of people begin to seriously challenge elite rule, that's when "clear and present danger" kicks in. So much for the **First Amendment.**

Judicial permission for no-knock entries is granted for ever flimsier reasons. Illegally obtained material is now permitted to be introduced into evidence. Arbitrary stop-and-frisks have reached epidemic proportion. In 2011, there were 700,000 in NYC alone. Thanks to "anti-terrorist" legislation, FBI agents may enter anyone's home and surreptitiously search it, may even look into whatever is in one's computer files. Eavesdropping, phone tapping, "data mining," are on the rise as the government gathers information about every aspect of people's personal lives, including their health and finances. The telephone companies have recently revealed that they have turned over comprehensive information in just one year on over a million cell phones to law-enforcement agencies. All making a mockery of the **Fourth Amendment**, which asserts the right of the people to be secure in their persons, houses, papers and effects against unreasonable searches and seizures.

Much of the First and Fourth Amendments never make it into the public schools, where the principals are a law unto themselves.

The **Fifth Amendment** has been severely eroded.

During the height of McCarthyism, a concept emerged of the "Fifth Amendment Communist." Invoking that amendment before witch-hunting bodies almost invariably meant the loss of one's job, as well as other sanctions. While using a rubber hose in the back room of police stations to exact confessions is a thing of the past, and while one cannot be forced to incriminate oneself, the Fifth Amendment can no longer be invoked to avoid incriminating others. Enter the concept of "use immunity" whereby people are hauled before grand juries and forced to testify about the activities of others on pain of being held in contempt and jailed. This procedure has been repeatedly used against anti-war activists and Irish and Puerto Rican freedom-fighters. The Fifth Amendment bar to double-jeopardy has been ignored. People are frequently prosecuted for essentially the same offense in both state and federal courts. The Fifth Amendment requirement of due process before being deprived of one's life and liberty has been routinely ignored by the Bush and Obama Administrations which deny that the Constitution applies to the alleged terrorists being kept at Guantanamo and other prisons, as well as to hundreds of others kidnapped and taken to secret locations. The provision in the Fifth Amendment that private property cannot be taken for public use without just compensation is being increasingly flouted. In fact, "eminent domain," as we have previously mentioned, has been abusively extended to now apply to property seized for private use.

The **Sixth Amendment** which, among other things, requires that the accused shall have the right to a speedy and public trial by an impartial jury, as well as other rights in the conduct of his defense, has been trumped by "anti-terror" legislation which allows detainees to languish in prison for years, and trials to take place using secret evidence and unidentified witnesses, among other abuses. In fact, it is not uncommon for ordinary prisoners to be kept in jail for six months or more before finally getting their day in court.

Habeas corpus, enshrined in the first article of the Constitution, and certainly implied in the Fifth and Sixth Amendments, has been disposed of at Guantanamo, along with other quaint notions such as the prohibition against torture, enshrined in the Geneva Conventions.

The **Seventh Amendment** providing for trial by jury, while honored in theory, has been scrapped in practice, as more than 90 percent of criminal trials end with plea bargains.

The **Eighth Amendment** concerning excessive bail is widely ignored. While the amount set often appears modest, "modest" is beyond the reach of the majority of defendants, who are indigent. New York Supreme Court Justice Bruce Wright made the mistake of taking the Eighth Amendment too seriously. He was dubbed by the tabloids "Cut 'Em Loose Bruce" because he refused to go along with imposing on poor defendants bail they could not possibly raise. For his conscientious application of the Constitution, Judge Wright was removed from the Criminal Division and transferred to civil cases, demonstrating once again that it is altogether proper to toast the Constitution on ceremonial occasions, but woe to those in authority who apply it in defense of the powerless! As for excessive punishment, the august Supreme Court with all due gravity has sanctioned a 50-year sentence without possibility of parole for a man who stole videotapes from a K-mart store, has let stand a sentence of 50 years for a parolee who smoked one joint of marijuana, and has refused to hear the appeal of a man serving a 15-year-to-life sentence because it was filed three days too late, and that only because of the trial judge's erroneous instructions. The widespread use of the death penalty, "Three-Strikes-and-You're Out" laws and the draconian sentences associated with drug offenses make of the Eighth Amendment pretty much of a dead letter.

The **Fourteenth Amendment**, guaranteeing to African-Americans all the rights of citizenship, has not been enforced to this day, despite the great movements of the 1960s and that decade's torrent of civil rights laws and court rulings. Housing is more segregated and more unequal than ever; the schools are more segregated and unequal than ever; the economic chasm between Black and white is wider than ever; racial disparities in the health care system are growing steadily, as is the resulting gap in health and life expectancy. And racial disparities within the criminal justice system are wider than ever.

The **Fifteenth Amendment**, extending to African-Americans the right to vote was ignored in the South for 100 years. The Voting Rights Act of 1965, which should not have been necessary if the Fifteenth Amendment had been enforced, was itself flagrantly violated in the presidential elections of 2000 and 2004, when Bush stole the elections largely through suppression of the Black vote.

The so-called War on Terror is being used to shred

137

still further the tattered remnants of the Bill of Rights. For example, international treaties such as the United Nations Charter or the Geneva Conventions are treated with utter contempt, even though under the Constitution they have the same force as domestic law. This did not start with the Bush Administration. As a matter of fact, it began with the long and shameful history of the US government's flouting of treaties with the native peoples.

It bears recalling that the elite never desired a Bill of Rights in the first place, as evidenced by the actions of the Founding Fathers, who did not include it in the Constitution they produced at Philadelphia. Only later was it reluctantly accepted by them when it became clear that the people would never ratify the Constitution without a Bill of Rights. In fact, it was violated by the new American government almost immediately. The Alien and Sedition Acts passed at the behest of President John Adams, resulted in the jailing of his political opponents and the closing of opposition newspapers, a repression aimed at the Jeffersonians, who looked favorably upon the French Revolution, which was then (and now) viewed with horror by the commercial and monied elite.

Thus began the long and dreary record of government persecution of those struggling against elite privilege – the imprisonment, harassment and physical assault upon workers trying to form unions or going on strike; the ban on anti-slavery petitions to Congress, or anti-slavery literature sent to the South through the mail; the arrest of those helping fugitive slaves; the century of Fascist-type Southern rule after Reconstruction; the 1897 execution of the anarchists Albert Parsons and August Spies, convicted of killing policemen in a dynamite attack in Chicago's Haymarket Square, their unforgivable crime being agitating for social justice; the imprisonment of citizens and deportation of aliens opposing US entering the First World War; the 1915 frame-up and execution of labor troubadour Joe Hill, who left the inspiring message, "Don't mourn, organize!"; the 1917 frame-up of Tom Mooney, like Parsons and Spies accused of a fatal dynamite attack, his unspeakable crime being his effectiveness as a labor organizer. Mooney, whose innocence was eventually admitted even by the trial judge and jurors, nevertheless languished in prison for over 20 years until eventually released as a result of worldwide pressure; the 1927 railroading of the anarchists Sacco and Vanzetti, executed for murder but really found guilty of raising the consciousness of workingmen. Presiding Judge Webster Thayer was heard to declare his intention to get "those anarchist bastards"; the widespread persecutions in the era of McCarthyism with its loyalty oaths and blacklists; the martyrdom of Ethel and Julius Rosenberg, executed for the technically impossible feat of stealing "the" secret of the atomic bomb. Presiding Judge Irving Kaufman held a flagrantly illegal secret meeting with the prosecutor before issuing his death sentence, a crime for which he was rewarded by appointment to the Court of Appeals; the imprisonment of Communists and those who would not inform on Communists; the vicious "black bag" operations (also known as COINTELPRO) against militant Black activists; the assassination or imprisonment of legions of

African-Americans, from the early victims of Southern lynch law to the martyrdom of such Black freedom-fighters as Mumia Abu-Jamal (whose presiding judge stated that he was going to "fry the nigger"), on death row for over 20 years and still behind bars, Also, Geronimo Pratt, George Jackson, and so many others; Leonard Peltier, still behind bars after 30 years, his crime being the defense of the rights of indigenous people.

Just a small sample of democracy American-style. All this repression and all these frame-ups were orchestrated against the political bogeymen of their day: syndicalists, anarchists, communists, Black militants, now Muslim and Arab "terrorists."

Years after the events, it becomes fashionable for historians and law professors to declare them travesties of justice, some of which were later even reversed by the courts themselves. But such criticism and such reversals never arrive in time to repair the damage. The powers-that-be achieved their political ends when it counted. It is only when it has become safe to do so that regret is expressed at past "excesses." Then college professors congratulate America on the progress which the country has made since that "regrettable" period, assuring their students that such things could never happen again, until they do.

Constitution or no Constitution, the FBI has under every President been given the green light to act in police-state style, has sent provocateurs into political organizations to instigate violent and criminal actions, has spied on political dissidents, broken into offices of political organizations and the homes of individuals, with and without warrants, wiretapped, opened mail illegally, compiled millions of dossiers, and threatened economic reprisal to force people to become informers against those whose only crime was to defend peace and democratic rights.

But the FBI are pikers compared to the CIA, which operates on a grand international scale, organizing coups, carrying out assassinations of foreign leaders, kidnapping foreign nationals, financing opposition organizations and parties, subverting foreign governments, engaging in military commando operations -- all in flagrant disregard of international law. Forbidden by US law from operating domestically, the CIA has nevertheless intercepted domestic mail, carried out wiretapping and other forms of domestic surveillance against anti-war activists and those who oppose the status quo, have secretly subsidized reporters, student organizations and literary groups, engaged within the country in mind-control experiments unbeknownst to their victims, and covertly tested chemical and biological weapons on civilian populations, including our own. Currently, the CIA alone maintains a list of 300,000 individuals and organizations within the United States, illegally coordinating its work with police agencies inside the country. The black-bag activities of military intelligence are still more secret than those of the CIA.

During every repressive period of our history, those who were counted on to stand up for democracy -- the vast majority of liberals, union leadership, most academics, the Democratic Party -- have consistently caved in or even enthusiastically supported the undermining of our liberties.

During tranquil times they pose as democracy's ardent champions. *But when the chips are down and when standing up would make a difference, these cowards and hypocrites are either nowhere to be found or in the trenches of the enemy.*

THE LAW

At this point it will be useful to step back and examine a little more closely what law is, who makes it, how it is enforced -- or not -- and for what purpose.

The elite are forever proclaiming that the foundation of society rests on respect for the law. But for themselves and their class, law is merely a matter of expediency. So when the law favors their interests, they demand that it be followed to the letter. When the law is inconvenient, they ignore it and generally have the clout to escape the consequences, except when it comes to injuring the interests of fellow members of the club. But every now and then their real attitude toward the law slips out in some unguarded utterance, occasionally even in some openly arrogant display. The greatest of the railroad magnates, Cornelius Vanderbilt, whose railroad fortune was made from deals that ranged from shady to shadier, declared: "What do I care about the law? Hain't I got the power?" Expressing the attitude of the Southern ruling class after the federal courts outlawed segregation, Birmingham's notorious chief of police Bull Connor proclaimed: "We don't give a damn about the law. Down here we make our own law." John J. McCloy, at one time one of the country's most powerful attorneys, head of the US occupation regime in Germany, stated quite frankly when he was Assistant Secretary of War "You are putting a Wall Street lawyer in a helluva box, but if it is a question of safety of the country [or] the Constitution of the United States, why, the Constitution is just a scrap of paper to me."[45]

Another telling moment in history: Back in the early days of the republic, in a rare display of intellectual and moral integrity, the Supreme Court, headed by John Marshall, ruled against the State of Georgia's attempt to seize the land of the Creek and Tsalagi (Cherokee) people. President (and slaveholder) Andrew Jackson thereupon famously declared, "John Marshall has made his decision; now let him enforce it." And to this day, the Democratic Party celebrates its hero in its annual Jefferson-Jackson Day dinners. At the same time historians slobber about how the Jackson administration inaugurated a great era of democracy.

It has often been said that the law is what nine Supreme Court Justices say it is, actually, what five justices say it is, decisions often being made by a 5 to 4 vote. Moreover, that "distinguished" body over whose selection the people have no direct say, serves for life, thereby insulating the court from "popular tumult" and "popular passion" -- in other words, the democratic will.

The Supreme Court, tackling the weightiest questions of state, has often been packed with legal nonentities, with men selected for their political loyalty to the President and his party, rather than for any special constitutional expertise, and are often drawn from the ranks of corporate attorneys. Naturally, decisions of such a court reflect the dominant values and prejudices of the class whose interests they had previously made a career in defending.

The judges take great pains to pretend that their rulings are governed by strict legal reasoning and that they are indifferent to political considerations, are "above the fray." How little this is the case was seen in the example of the bizarre decision that installed George W. Bush in the White House, defying both settled law and simple logic, demonstrating not only that the Supreme Court is political, but that it is prepared to flout the Constitution in the interest of the narrowest considerations of partisan, in this case Republican, politics.

Extraordinary are the number of flip-flops made by the Supreme Court, given that it is supposed to be guided by fixed principles enshrined in the Constitution and an almost religious devotion to precedent. With serene assurance it has rendered its opinion one day, and then with equally serene assurance, sometimes soon thereafter, rendered an opposite opinion. The fact is that the courts, including the Supreme Court, are subject to the influence of popular pressure, of popular movements, which cause them to bend to the prevailing political winds. And the reason they do this, despite their absolute insulation from the electoral process in the case of the federal courts, and their relative insulation in the case of the state courts, is that they understand that there can be serious consequences if they fail to adjust to public opinion and the temper of the times. They know that if they go too far in antagonizing the people, matters might be taken completely out of their hands, as well as out of the hands of all those holding on to the levers of power.

Equality before the law is as bedrock a notion as it is mythic. Generally speaking, the law goes to the highest bidder. In criminal court, the chances of a defendant obtaining a favorable outcome increase in proportion to his resources, something that is not denied even by the most ardent defenders of the criminal justice system. As the African-American attorney Johnny Cochran put it: "One is innocent until proven poor."

But precisely because there is little *substance* to equal justice, those in charge, given that we are a "democratic" country, take special pains to create the *appearance* of equal justice. They fill the process with all kinds of formalities that supposedly protect the defendant's rights. This contrasts with the situation in many openly authoritarian countries whose rulers have no need for most of the sham.

As with everything else that is generally true about law and justice under this system, exceptions can always be cited which serve to mask the underlying reality. In fact, such exceptions are vital to the maintenance of the system, helping to nourish illusions which keep the people pacified, or at least not so outraged as to put an end to the farce.

What is the law? For many years piracy against the merchant ships of one's own nation was punishable by death, while it was richly rewarded when aimed at the ships of rival nations. Many an American fortune was made through piracy -- excuse me, privateering -- against English shipping during the Revolution and the War of 1812.

For over 250 years one could be a law-abiding citizen and at the same time a kidnapper, a trader in human beings, could hold people captive and work them under the lash, sometimes to death, be a destroyer of families and a serial rapist. The criminal was the slave who escaped or tried to escape. To assist a runaway was also a crime, North as well as South. Not only were the lords of the lash not considered criminal, but the more victims they possessed and tortured, the higher were they held in esteem and the more influential were they in the halls of government. So, for centuries, respect for the law was consistent with perpetrating the most monstrous crime in history.

The South moved on, with Northern encouragement, from slavery to serfdom and peonage, that is, slavery by another name. The plantation elite not only owned the land but the arithmetic, as well. The sharecropper was in trouble if he couldn't keep track of what was owed him but in even deeper trouble if he could. Having been swindled, as he universally was, should the sharecropper appeal to the law,s the sheriff could be counted on to hold the rope. Clearly, African-Americans are owed restitution for the labor performed by their ancestors under slavery and its accompanying pain and suffering. But so are the descendants of sharecroppers owed reparations for the century of labor performed in conditions of landlord larceny and state terror.

Today, law and barbarism continue to happily coexist. In a number of states there are actually statutes denying additional assistance to women who bear a child while on welfare. To starve a mother and/or her children, then, is not only sanctioned but demanded by the law. In these United States it is lawful for a family unable to pay the rent or mortgage to be tossed into the streets. It is also lawful for a company to fire its workers at any time it sees fit, with all the accompanying family suffering, including, of course, that of their children, in order that corporate executives and fat-cat stock market speculators may line their pockets. The squalor in which the poor are forced to live is absolutely lawful. Nor is any law violated when people die because they are unable to afford medical treatment.

But is it not criminal that each year 15 million children starve to death in a world in which the food supply is plentiful? That each year eight million babies die at birth despite the current state of medical science that in theory should make infant mortality a thing of the past? That by the tens of millions people die from diseases curable with the most modest of resources? That hundreds of millions are homeless despite there being the productive capacity to house everyone? That more than a billion suffer from illiteracy though the means exist to easily eradicate it?

An indignant Martin Luther King charged those in power with being "on the side of the wealthy and the secure, while we create a hell for the poor." But there is no law against creating a hell for the poor, except in the People's statute books where it is a crime of monstrous proportion. In the People's statute books it is an unspeakable crime for masses of people to lack the necessities in a world overflowing with the fruits of today's scientific and technical achievements and productive abundance. And it is a crime, above all, because society's crying inequities are the deliberate product of policies of the world elite.

Here is Milton Friedman, the guru of today's dominant theory of trickle-down economics (an apt name, recalling the ancient water torture), hero of the free-marketeers (or freebooters, as they should be called). Contemptuously sweeping aside the hopeless sentimentality of liberals who plead for a humane capitalism, Friedman declares: "Few trends could so thoroughly undermine the very foundations of the free society...as the acceptance by corporate officials of a social responsibility other than to make as much money for the shareholders as possible."[46]

What is the law? History shows that the law is primarily a device for imposing the will of the rich and powerful on those below them, as well as a means of solving in an orderly manner conflicts among themselves.

Sometimes laws actually benefit the great majority of the people. But such laws always require enormous pressure, some cataclysmic event like the Great Depression. They require masses pouring into the streets, great mobilizations, strikes, and enormous sacrifice. Such laws are passed with the greatest resistance, the elite conceding as little as possible. The wave of reform legislation during the height of the civil rights movement, for example, was recognized by Harry Ashmore, astute editor of the *Arkansas Gazette*, as being passed "not to advance the Negro cause, but to control and contain it." Laws benefiting the elite, on the other hand, are often enacted by stealth, soundlessly, like a thief in the night.

But there is more. Having engaged in a titanic

struggle to get good laws passed, the people find that they often turn out to be null and void because they "accidentally" have loopholes in them. Or the courts will "interpret" the teeth out of those laws, or twist them to become the opposite of what was intended.

But let us say the people manage to get a good law on the books, and there are no loopholes, and the courts don't outlaw it or render it unrecognizable. Then it requires about the same amount of struggle to get it enforced. For violators of such a law are rarely prosecuted. And if they are, the punishment is so light that it is no deterrent. For the elite control not only law-making but law enforcement. Take the laws on the books against monopoly, for example. These were passed back in the 1890s when an enraged public rose up against the great trusts, particularly the railroad trust, which had an absolute stranglehold on the life of the nation. Yet looking around today, over a century later, concentration is greater than ever. One finds market domination by a handful of companies in every industry, nationally and even internationally. And as previously mentioned, the wave of mergers and acquisitions continues to accelerate.

Again, as we have pointed out, if the elite are unable to directly defy laws which are in the people's interest, they can delay compliance.

We have cited *Brown v. Board of Ed.* For ten years the ruling proved toothless. "With all deliberate speed," was the Court's order. Today, schools in the North are more segregated than ever, while those in the South are being resegregated, all with the Supreme Court's sanction.

Everyone has gone through the frustration of dealing with bureaucracy. But it is especially outrageous when to the bureaucracy's normal indifference to the people's needs is added a deliberate stonewalling. Thus, millions of the disabled wait for years to have their legitimate claims processed, the average time now 515 days. Even when one wins a lawsuit against a corporation, it will usually take a decade to gain some compensation. The corporations have all the time in the world; the individual needs immediate relief. So the person with modest means often caves in and agrees to an unjust settlement, one that is far smaller than deserved.

FOREIGN POLICY CRIME

We are taught from elementary through graduate school that US foreign policy, whatever its past "mistakes" -- admitted in hindsight and usually in very safe hindsight -- is driven by the purest of motives, by democratic ideals and a generous spirit. And if the country occasionally resorts to arms it is only because evil forces have left it no other choice.

We cannot here even begin to list, much less describe, the crimes committed by Washington against the peoples of the world down through the years, the trampling of international law, the bloody interventions, incursions, occupations, wars of aggression, the fomenting of coups d'etats, the countless acts of terrorism, assassination, sabotage, subversion, economic strangulation -- failed or successful -- unmatched by any other country in history. While these crimes have been perpetrated by the government, it should be understood that behind government actions are the interests of Big Business. Not content, however, to leave execution to the professionals, corporate executives have increasingly assumed the *direct* management of policy, periodically taking leave of their corporate responsibilities to enter "public service."

The first foreign policy crimes were committed *within* this country, beginning with the many campaigns of extermination against the indigenous peoples, lasting right up to the end of the 19th century. Of course, participation in the kidnapping of millions of Africans was the ultimate foreign policy crime, a crime, by the way, that went on for half a century past its constitutional ban. Meanwhile, the US went to war against the Mexican "bandits." It turned out the U.S. government was the real bandit, robbing the Mexican people of half their territory.

Then, after 30 years of extraordinary economic growth following the Civil War, the US elite began feeling its oats and was ready to step onto the world stage. Embarking on what is known as the Spanish-American War, it was primarily a war against the Cubans, Puerto Ricans, Pacific Islanders, and especially the Filipinos. Heartbroken over the barbaric treatment by Spain of its colonial subjects, Washington proceeded to give Spain and the rest of the world lessons in barbarism's infinite possibilities. There was, for example, the order by an American general, cited by the historian Thomas Schoonover, to kill all Filipino males over 10 years of age if they were considered capable of bearing arms. Public outrage against the Spanish use of concentration camps had been pumped up to support going to war. For openers, on the island of Samar alone, the US army rounded up a quarter of a million Filipinos and put them into concentration camps lacking in food, sanitation, or medical supplies. Schoonover writes that "The U.S. military introduced the Filipinos to modern war -- burning, looting, scorched earth, rape, pillage, and water torture." And he informs us that despite the American public's outrage as the facts of US atrocities became known, "The tarnished reputation of most U.S. commanders recovered miraculously. Each of the three ranking generals from the Luzon-Samar campaign eventually became the ranking general of the U.S. Army."[47]

To carry out its genocidal policies, the enemy was dehumanized, called "niggers" and "gooks." The latter name so pleased US servicemen that it later carried over into the wars against Korea and Vietnam. There are other parallels with later aggressions. For just as President McKinley declared that the US had invaded the Philippines to "uplift, civilize and Christianize," so the Iraq war has been portrayed as part of a "war of civilizations," Christian against Moslem. And just as the war in the Philippines was said to be motivated by a desire to free Filipinos from the harsh rule of their Spanish oppressors, so the war in Iraq has been justified by the need to free Iraqis from the brutal dictatorship of Saddam Hussein. Albert Beveridge, shorty before being elected Senator from Indiana, in a speech delivered on September 16th, 1898 declared, "Would not the people of the Philippines prefer the just, humane, civilizing government of this Republic to the savage, bloody rule of pillage and extortion from which we have rescued them?"[48] -- a "rescue" in which more Filipinos were killed by Americans in three years than by the Spanish in three centuries. Similarly, then Senator Hillary Clinton told her presidential campaign audiences that the US had brought to the Iraqis "the greatest gift one can bring to a people, "the gift of freedom," omitting that we have also showered hundreds of thousands of Iraqis with the gift of death, millions with the gift of exile, and all Iraqis with the gift of a society brought to ruin. Still, we must remember the old saying that you can't make an American omelet without breaking Iraqi eggs.

The fact is that before their "rescue," the Filipinos had managed to rescue themselves, having by their own efforts freed almost their entire country. Thus, when the Americans reached the islands, they landed without opposition. The final surrender of Manila, as Schoonover tells us, was "staged to save face for the defeated Spanish and for the transfer of control to a white western power rather than a brown-skinned indigenous people."[49]

But how did we get involved with the Philippines in the first place, given that the principal mission was supposedly to free *Cuba*? The real motivation was locked away in the diary of Whitelaw Reid, one of the men charged with negotiating peace with Spain: "If to [Hawaii] we now add the Philippines, it would be possible for American energy to...ultimately convert the Pacific Ocean into an American lake...such a possession would... stimulate shipbuilding, industry and commerce, and...add

153

immensely to the national prosperity."[50]

Sounds to me like the "i" word, imperialism, which no one in the mainstream media, no politician from either party, nor any respectable political commentator these days dare utter in describing current US policy. Back then, however, the oligarchy was proud of its imperialist mission. Senator Beveridge: "We are a conquering race, and must occupy new markets and, if necessary, new lands...the trade of the world must and shall be ours."[51] The good Senator called for world rule of the Anglo-Saxons, as did Winston Churchill a half-century later at Fulton, Missouri, in a speech now regarded as the opening salvo of the Cold War. And it is this which up to this day lies at the heart of the Anglo-American "special relationship."

Just as there has been a disastrous toll of Iraqi civilians, so was the toll of Filipino civilians disastrous, a toll which can only be estimated because in neither case did the US military see any need to count such casualties.

Cuba, too, was "liberated" from Spanish rule, although Cuban patriots had also come close to freeing themselves, having engaged in a protracted struggle that had worn down the Spanish army. The Cubans had already cleared the beaches of Santiago when the US military landed. But as soon as Washington felt their help was no longer needed, the Cuban liberation forces were pushed aside and declared unfit to govern. To Washington it was scandalous that the Cuban masses should have chosen as their leaders dark-skinned rebels, as opposed to white middle-class collaborators with the Spanish colonizers.

About the only thing taught today to our school

children on the war of 1898 is that General Leonard Wood eradicated Yellow Fever, casting the American conquest as purely humanitarian. Not mentioned is that the same General Wood described the Cuban freedom-fighters as an "ignorant, unruly rabble," nor his other expressions of racist contempt for those among them of African descent. It was in that spirit that US Presidents, from McKinley through the great "democrat" Woodrow Wilson, would explain that Washington's repeated invasions and occupations of the nations of the Caribbean and Central America were undertaken with great reluctance and were merely intended to teach fiscal responsibility to still immature peoples who, evidently, needed parental guidance in the handling of money. For they had failed to pay back the loans Washington had earlier forced upon them. And so like a stern but just father, US troops came in, seized their national treasuries, sometimes replacing governments who retained misguided feelings of self-respect, and put the new administrations on an allowance.

It was in that same spirit that President Theodore Roosevelt, desiring to put some meat on the bones of the Monroe Doctrine, enunciated what was thenceforth to be known as the Roosevelt Corollary, proclaiming that the US would oversee the internal affairs of all Caribbean and Central American republics and intervene when necessary to keep them stable. In his December 1901 address, Roosevelt had spoken about "America's duty toward the people living in barbarism... to see that they are freed from their chains and we can free them only by destroying barbarism itself...Peace cannot be had until the civilized nations have expanded in some shape over the barbarous nations." [52]

And so Cuba was "civilized" into a wholly-owned US subsidiary, with American corporations taking over the sugar plantations, the sugar mills, telephone service, and everything else. The American Mafia ran the Jim Crow hotels and casinos. And the beaches were kept sparkling white, Jim Crow white, for the benefit of the highly discriminating US tourists. All this came to be superintended by the murderous dictator Fulgencia Battista. No outrage was expressed by Washington then against a Cuban government trampling on human rights and oppressing its people. Nor did the US have a problem with Cuban sugar workers breaking their backs for four months and starving the rest of the year, their children's bellies distended with hunger, no problem that there was not a single school for the children of the rural poor. No US embargo, no blockade, no bile. After all, who at the UN was more loyal than the Battista delegation?

Fast forward some 60 years later: The guerrilla army of Fidel Castro marches into Havana, sending Battista fleeing to the welcoming arms of Miami, followed hot on his heels by thousands of "freedom-lovers" who had managed to live quite contentedly under his brutal dictatorship. These exiles, bemoaning the supposed loss of liberty in Cuba, proceeded with US assistance to establish a decades-long dictatorship over their fellow exiles *within Miami*. For the fanatical right-wing "freedom-fighters," heavily subsidized by Washington, not only carried out a campaign of terror against Cuba, but through bombings, assassinations and economic reprisals, muzzled those in the Miami community who sought any kind of Cuban rapprochement.

The first outrageous act of the Cuban revolution, which has stuck in the craw of the US oligarchy for half a century, was taking back its resources seized by American thugs -- the Mafia hoods and the still more powerful cutthroats of Corporate America. Havana's second major crime was pursuit of a foreign policy that was in harmony with the interests of its people, choosing its own friends and not allowing Washington to dictate with whom it could have economic and political relations. But the coup de grace, the greatest of Cuban crimes, was adopting a social system that put an end to exploitation of its people by the rich and powerful, whether homegrown or from abroad.

For these crimes Cuba has for decades been the victim of US economic strangulation. For these crimes Cuba has suffered invasion, sabotage, biological warfare, and other terrorist acts, including countless efforts to assassinate Fidel. And all the while, with a straight face, it is Washington that accuses Cuba of being a terrorist state.

During the Cold War, Washington justified its hostility by claiming that Cuba was a "forward base" for Russian aggression and therefore a dire threat to US national security. It was located, after all only 90 miles from its shores. It never pointed out, of course, that the "colossus of the North" was only 90 miles from Cuba's shores. That the so-called security threat was a mere pretext was proven after the collapse of the Soviet Union when Washington's hostile acts grew even more intense.

Now Washington justifies its venomous policies on the grounds of Cuba's supposed lack of democracy and human rights. Yet the US has always had good relations with the most brutal dictatorships throughout the hemisphere. There was no blockade, for example, no sabotage, no attempted assassinations against the Guatemalan dictatorship, which exterminated hundreds of thousands of its indigenous; no blockade against the succession of genocidal regimes of El Salvador, which engaged in a similar slaughter of its peasants and others made in the image of God; no action taken against the military dictatorships of Argentina, Brazil, and Chile, whose former rulers are now being put in the dock by their own people for crimes against humanity. There was no blockade against the Venezuelan dictator Marcos Perez Jiminez, the Paraguayan dictator Alfredo Stroessner, the Haitian dictators, "Doc" and "Baby" Duvalier, the seemingly eternal dictatorships of Rafael Trujillo of the Dominican Republic and Anastasio Somoza of Nicaragua. Why has the supposed absence of democracy been intolerable in the case of Cuba, but not only tolerable but worthy of economic and even military assistance in the rest of Latin America?

In fact, Washington has had the most amicable relations with dictators around the world, such as the South Korean dictator Syngman Rhee, Philippines dictator Ferdinand Marcos, the Shah of Iran Mohammed Reza Pahlevi (beneficiary of a CIA coup), Pakistani dictator Pervez Musharraf (recently pushed aside by the people in spite of Washington's best efforts), the dictators known as the Saudi royal family, the royal dictators of Kuwait and Jordan, and that genocidal dictator of the Congo, Mobutu Sese Seko, installed after the Western powers organized the assassination of its elected premier Patrice Lumumba. Nor did Washington make any attempt at "regime change" during the reign of any of the many other dictators on the African continent.

While Washington was constantly tightening its economic sanctions against Cuba, it would not apply such sanctions against the racist regime of South Africa. In fact, the African National Congress, headed at one time by Nelson Mandela, was placed on Washington's list of terrorist organizations. Incidentally, answering the call of the Angolan government for assistance following an invasion of the country by the apartheid South African regime, Cuban troops played a major role in South Africa's crushing defeat at Cuito Cuanavale. And it was that defeat that led to the end of the apartheid regime.

Washington denounces Cuba for trampling on human rights. But is not the highest human right the right to life itself, the right not to starve? In these United States, 11 million people, including almost half a million children, skip meals, sometimes go without food all day. One in ten Americans suffer from food insecurity. By contrast, and though far behind in economic development, according to UN reports "on average Cuba consumes much more then the recommended daily amount of calories." Is not shelter a human right? There are millions of homeless in the wealthiest nation in the world; in Cuba there are none.

All right, but at least the hungry and the homeless

in the United States can vote in free elections, the nature of which we have already described. Actually, not only are US elections not free, but they are the most expensive in the world.

Puerto Rico, still another nation "liberated" from Spain, over a century later continues to be held as a US colony, although Washington insists it is not a colonial but a "special" relationship. That special relationship resulted in the US sterilization of a third of the women of the island without their knowledge, just as for the purpose of ridding the world of an "inferior" population and unbeknownst to them, African-American women were similarly sterilized. Puerto Ricans have been used as guinea pigs for pharmaceutical companies testing birth control pills. The island of Vieques was laid waste for many years, having been used for target practice. And its people will suffer for decades from the testing of such toxic weapons as Agent Orange and shells tipped with depleted uranium. The final result of the "special relationship" is that a good portion of Puerto Rico's population has been forced by their desperate circumstances to move to the "mainland," where many continue to live in poverty, while many who remain on the island live not only in poverty but in humiliating dependence. The latest World Bank figures show that. Puerto Rico ranks 211th out of 215 countries in its rate of economic growth.

We have spent so much time on the Spanish-American War because it was then that the United States set the pattern of US aggressions throughout the next century,

We go on.

"Uncle Sam," having now tasted blood, proceeded to attack Nicaragua, Panama, Honduras, the Dominican Republic, Korea, Cuba again, Nicaragua again, Honduras again, Panama again, Nicaragua still again, Honduras still again, China, Panama, Honduras, Nicaragua once more, the Dominican Republic, Mexico, Haiti, the Dominican Republic, Cuba, Russia (whom the US invaded with 13 other nations to "strangle Bolshevism (socialism) in its cradle"), Panama, Honduras, Guatemala, Honduras, Panama, China, El Salvador.

In this connection, upon his retirement, Major-General Smedley Butler, Marine Commandant, made a remarkable admission. Said Butler:

"I spent 33 years...in active military service...And during that period I spent most of my time being a high-class muscle man for Big Business, for Wall Street, and for the bankers. In short, I was a racketeer, a gangster for capitalism...I helped make Mexico...safe for American oil interests in 1914. I helped make Haiti and Cuba a decent place for the National City Bank boys to collect revenue in. I helped in the raping of half a dozen Central American republics for the benefit of Wall Street...I helped purify Nicaragua for the international bankers house of Brown Brothers in 1909-1012...I brought light to the Dominican Republic for American sugar interests in 1916. In China I helped to see to it that Standard Oil went its way unmolested...."[53]

The history of US-Haitian relations is particularly shameful. For over half a century, the United States refused to recognize the independence of the Black republic,

161

which was born out of the first successful slave uprising in history. For the US government was terrified at the example it set for its own slave population. With the outbreak of the Civil War, Lincoln finally established diplomatic relations, but it was not long thereafter that Washington set to work to sabotage Haiti's development, a course pursued to the present day. Having for decades supported the corrupt and brutal Duvalier dictatorships, it proceeded to topple the popularly elected Aristides government that was charting a course of reform. When that coup and the return of the old terror spawned a flood of Haitian refugees trying to reach our shores, they were intercepted by the US Navy and interned at Guantanamo. As their numbers mounted, Clinton was faced with growing political embarrassment. So he sent Aristides back to Haiti, along with the Marines, but as a virtual political prisoner. Later re-elected, Aristides fell victim to still another US coup. Today, compounding the devastating effects of the earthquake are the devastating effects of Haiti's political disaster. For Haiti is strangling under the imposition of a Western protectorate masked by the UN flag. While the Haitian people live in utter misery, it being the poorest country in the hemisphere, the situation is quite satisfactory to those who have so much at stake in the notion of Black incompetence and inferiority.

Retracing our steps again: Woodrow Wilson, who introduced Jim Crow to official Washington, who ordered a number of those Caribbean and Latin American invasions, has gone down in the history books as noble promoter of the self-determination of nations. After campaigning for the presidency on a platform of keeping

America out of war, Wilson sent hundreds of thousands of young men to their death in World War I "to make the world safe for democracy." And when the. smoke cleared, the world indeed remained safe...for imperialism, as the victors simply took over the colonies of the defeated. While Wilson was moralizing about self-determination, his British partner Winston Churchill declared that he "had not been made Chancellor of the. Exchequer to preside over the dismemberment of the British Empire." Again to make the world safe for democracy, Wilson dispatched troops to help put down the revolution in Russia. Sadly, his gift of democracy was rejected by ungrateful Soviet workers and peasants, who drove the American and 13 other interventionist armies out of their homeland, some of which were soon put to work putting down revolution in their own countries.

The Second World War was unique in that our cause was just, a war in which over 60 million people lost their lives and for which the Nazis bore the main responsibility. Rather than putting those beasts out of circulation after the war, Washington saw them as being quite useful in its anti-Soviet crusade. So many of the old Nazis were reinstalled in the "new" Germany, under US tutelage, filling up two-thirds of the governmental apparatus. At the same time the German corporations that financed the Nazi war machine were allowed to keep their factories and their wealth. And the German war machine, with US assistance, was built up once again.

Some of Washington's interventions led to prolonged occupations: five years in Cuba (1898-1903); eight years in the Dominican Republic, (1916-1924); 10 years in

Nicaragua (1912-1923); 19 years in Haiti (1916-1934); half a century in the Philippines; a 110-year occupation of Puerto Rico and still counting. And so far, ten years in Afghanistan and nine in Iraq.

The United States was forced into World War II, but it was not forced to commit war crimes, not forced, for example, to drop atomic bombs on Hiroshima and Nagasaki, which claimed hundreds of thousands of civilian lives, including those of tens of thousands of children, while many of those who survived wished they hadn't. Not being instantly cremated, they suffered for decades the slow and agonizing death of radiation poisoning. Those weapons of mass destruction were not used to shorten the war, as claimed, for the Japanese were on the point of surrender. Their real purpose was to serve notice on the Russians that the United States intended to be top dog in the postwar world.

In Korea, the forces of South Korean dictator Syngman Rhee, who had promised to conquer the North, were themselves routed, only to be saved by the US in a war that was less about Korea and more about Washington trying to undo the Chinese revolution. Conducted with unbridled barbarism, the "police action" foreshadowed the savage conduct of the US war on the Vietnamese. Millions of Koreans perished under the pounding of indiscriminate US firepower. After saturation bombings of civilian areas, south as well as north, US Air Force Major General Emmett O'Donnell reported to the Senate in 1951, "Everything is destroyed. There is nothing standing worthy of the name."[54] Syngman Rhee, that great symbol of the democracy the US was supposedly defending, was eventually overthrown by his own people.

The Vietnam War, one unending atrocity: Villages torched, mass assassinations of civilian leaders, hundreds of thousands herded into concentration camps, (resurrecting the old US strategy in the Philippines), widespread torture of prisoners, massive use of Agent Orange rendering large areas uninhabitable and dooming future generations to appalling birth defects, and routine use of napalm. More bombs were dropped on that impoverished peasant country than on all of Europe during World War II. Victims in the millions. Throw in for good measure the methodical carpet-bombing of Cambodia with its untold casualties. (Washington would later insist that even after it had been overthrown, the UN should continue to recognize as Cambodia's legitimate government the Khmer Rouge genocidal clique, a gang which had exterminated a third of its own people.)

Meanwhile, the people of the Dominican Republic were carrying out a popular insurrection against the 30-year dictatorship of Rafael Trujillo — this coming on top of the Cuban revolution, from which Washington was still smarting. So here come the Marines again.

And then Panama, again. The American sheriff came riding in to arrest the "notorious drug dealer" President Manuel Noriega (who had at one time been on the CIA payroll, as had Saddam Hussein. Both men got in trouble when they began charting an independent policy). The "law-enforcement" operation that brought Noriega back to a US prison involved a bit of "collateral damage," as 7,000 of Panama's poorest died fiercely defending their country's sovereignty. The US Supreme Court has since determined that sovereignty, other nations' sovereignty, that is, is an obsolete principle, ruling it was perfectly legitimate to kidnap Noriega or any other foreign national. And so the legal precedent was set for the Bush Administration's "extraordinary renditions,"as such kidnappings are now called, Washington proceeded to install the next Panamanian president who, as it turned out, was a well known and even bigger drug dealer than Noriega.

The invasion of Grenada deserves special mention in the annals of US valor. Declaring that island a threat to US security, whose population could barely fill a football stadium, Washington put an end to its people's dreams of social justice previously embodied in their beloved leader, Maurice Bishop.

And then Iraq, and Iraq again, the first time using hundreds of thousands of fleeing Iraqi soldiers as aerial target practice. Between the first and second invasions, economic sanctions were responsible for the deaths of a million Iraqi children, who perished from lack of medicines, clean water and electricity, dying silently except for the wail of mothers. Nothing there for the US peace movement to demonstrate about.

The second US invasion was motivated by George W. Bush's core values, namely, three trillion barrels of oil times their market price. Now that the country has been brought to its knees, the Iraqi government is signing "arms-length" contracts with the oil companies. The balance sheet: A hell for the Iraqis, a disaster for the American people, but a bonanza for US contractors and the oil barons, truly bearing out the old saying that "It's an ill wind that blows no one some good."

Then there is the mystery of Afghanistan, which is how the US Air Force, equipped with the most sophisticated tracking systems, the most accurate "smart bombs," the most precise laser-guided missiles, can repeatedly manage to "mistakenly" rain death on peaceful villagers.

We have not exhausted the list of victims of American military prowess. But let us move on, for military incursions have only been a part of Washington's lawlessness. Many of its aggressions were carried out through proxies, such as the Contras in Nicaragua, a terrorist army that blew up schools, assassinated schoolteachers and civic leaders. The invasion of Somalia by Ethiopia, which has now resulted according to UN officials in the world's worst humanitarian disaster, was coordinated with US forces. Then there is the "strategic alliance" with Apartheid Israel, the "democratic oasis" in the Middle East, an oasis which turns out to be a mirage. Showering it for decades with unprecedented amounts of money and weaponry, Washington has enabled Israel to seize Palestinian land and impose the cruelest occupation in modern history. For Israel has been the US oligarchy's trump card, the key policeman in the region, performing invaluable service in fighting the tide of Arab nationalism that threatened and continues to threaten US corporate interests, especially oil interests. Unwavering, also, has been Washington's support of Arab despots, most of whom sit on enormous oil reserves which are used exclusively to enrich their families and the cliques around them. Strangling the social and national

167

aspirations of their peoples, they collaborate with both Israel and the US, and but for American protection they would have been overthrown long ago.

Washington claims its aim is to set up and/or support democratic governments around the world -- at the point of a gun where necessary. However, if existing democratic governments do not follow the line of our oligarchy, then it sees to it that they are overthrown. Such was the fate of democratically-elected Jacobo Arbenz in Guatemala, at the behest of United Fruit Company; Salvador Allende in Chile, at the behest of International Telephone & Telegraph; Mossadegh in Iran, for the benefit of U.S. oil companies; Juan Bosch in the Dominican Republic who, like the other victims of US-instigated regime change, had attempted to carry out desperately needed social reforms. Particularly tragic was the coup against the democratically-elected Patrice Lumumba, premier of the mineral-rich Congo, leading to the bloody 40-year rule of the Mobutu kleptocracy and the slaughter of five million Congolese, the most bloody conflict since the Second World War, but being African lives, hardly worthy of US media attention.

Then there are the ongoing covert operations of the CIA with its trail of sabotage and assassinations, only a tiny portion of which have ever been officially admitted. And finally, US economic warfare against nations that did not do Washington's bidding, bringing down Michael Manley in Jamaica, Kwame Nkrumah in Ghana, Cheddi Jagan in Guyana, but failing to eliminate Fidel Castro, despite a half-century of trying.

Not to be overlooked was the ubiquitous man in the three-piece suit, stepping out of a commercial airliner landing in a Third-World country, carrying with him the Structural Adjustment Program of the Washington-dominated International Monetary Fund, wreaking more havoc than a Marine division. That program is now even being imposed on Europe, with terrible consequences, and increasingly on the people of this country, as well.

The brainwashing of the people has still left it confused about who was responsible for the heinous crime known as the Cold War, launched by the United States immediately upon the end of World War II. In fact, it began on the day the US dropped the atomic bomb on the cities of Hiroshima and Nagasaki which, as we have pointed out, was not intended to shorten the war and save lives. For the Japanese were ready to surrender unconditionally, except for the detail that they wished to keep the Emperor as a figurehead. The two atomic bombs, while dropped on Japan, were really aimed at the Soviet Union. Thus commenced a half-century of attempted regime change by Washington, actually, of *system* change. For the elite in this country would never accept the existence of socialism anywhere on the planet. This class hatred of socialism was masked as patriotism. To further its aims, the oligarchy proceeded to stoke national hysteria: "The Russians are coming!" Domestic Communists were painted as nothing but spies and saboteurs undermining our defenses. So Washington launched an arms race, including the manufacture of massive numbers of nuclear weapons of ever more terrifying destructiveness, resisted

Soviet disarmament proposals, and pressured the nations of the Third World to join in the anti-socialist crusade. The Cold War was portrayed as a titanic struggle between freedom and tyranny, freedom and slavery, between democracy and dictatorship, although, strangely enough, those who joined us included the world's most naked and bloody dictatorships.

In a sense, the Cold War actually began after the failure of military intervention in Soviet Russia in 1918. For 15 years after being forced to pull out, Washington refused to recognize the legitimacy of Soviet government, just as later Washington would for 30 years similarly refuse to recognize the legitimacy of China's socialist government.

"Freedom" and "democracy" turned out to be the freedom to make profits from the exploitation of the workers, and freedom to plunder the natural resources of underdeveloped nations. How many trillions upon trillions of dollars which could have been spent on social needs ended up as useless military hardware? How many nations abroad suffered invasion, coup d'etats and destabilization in the name of pursuing Washington's Cold War aims? What was the psychological damage done to the people of the world living under the constant threat of nuclear annihilation? How many lives were ruined in the hysteria known as McCarthyism? And how does one calculate the damage done to this country as progressive movements for social justice were destroyed under the pretext of their being part of the "Red menace"?

With the political awakening of the 1960s, the nature of US foreign policy came to be increasingly understood, especially by the young generations that fiercely opposed the war in Vietnam as well as Washington's subsequent never-ending aggressions. But the minds even of progressives in this country have not yet been cleansed of Cold War propaganda which remains a barrier to a true understanding of the wellsprings of US foreign policy, an anti-human policy which is not simply the product of this or that misguided Washington Administration, but the natural expression of an anti-human economic system.

"THE WAR ON TERROR"

Foreign Policy/Government Domestic Crime: Two for the Price of One

Today, it is the so-called war on terror which is used to justify Washington's bloody deeds, a war whose targets are everywhere, whose duration is infinite, whose means of combat is restricted by neither national nor international law. (Incidentally, we are told that terrorists are motivated not by political grievances but purely by their hatred of the American Way of Life, by envy of its prosperity and its freedom, a way of life that now has 40 million Americans gulping down pills for anxiety disorders.)

The truth is that when it comes to terror, the US government far and away sets the gold standard, raining down death and destruction on Iraqis and now Afghanis, threatening the annihilation of Iran, carrying out torture at Abu Ghareib and Guantanamo or transferring that torture to countries willing to carry out the CIA's dirty work, pounding the people of Libya with missiles, carrying out murderous drone attacks upon -- is it four countries now?

It should be remembered that the rationale for the invasion of Afghanistan was the Taliban's harboring of Al-Quaeda terrorists. The Bush Administration threatened dire consequences for any country that gave terrorists refuge. But it turns out terrorists can be good as well as bad. Emil Constant, head of the Haitian terrorist gang FRAPH, responsible for the killing of 7,000 when he was part of a Haitian coup regime, boasted of being on the CIA payroll. Fleeing to New York City when the dictatorship was overthrown, for years he lived openly and in tranquility while Washington refused a democratically elected Haitian government request to extradite him. Now the murderous thug has been convicted in the United States of business fraud, but as to answering for his mass murders, the US government continues to protect him. Similar is the case of Luis Posada Carriles, also in the employ of US intelligence, whose career has consisted of an endless string of acts of sabotage and murder against Cuba and Nicaragua, including shooting down a Cuban civilian airliner with 73 passengers on board. Extradition requests by both Venezuela and Cuba have likewise been rejected.

Under cover of the "War on Terror" the government is taking away what little there is left of our precious rights -- carrying out indefinite detentions, detentions without charges, putting people on trial using secret documents, secret witnesses, confessions extorted by torture, refusing detainees the right to counsel, engaging in massive warrantless wiretaps, targeting Muslims and people of Arab descent within our borders and deporting many without justification or due process, as well as persecuting legitimate Muslim philanthropies.

There is a huge watch list of American "terrorist suspects," now numbering more than a million. And this list has been disseminated, no one knows how, to companies who are using it to refuse credit or employment. Clearly, this is nothing but ethnic profiling as well as Mc Carthyite targeting of people suspected of opposing US foreign policy. Anti-terrorism laws are now used against ordinary street criminals and gang members, resulting in a significant increase in their sentence upon conviction. These laws are also being used against environmental activists, whom the government labels environmental terrorists. The machinery for allegedly fighting terrorism will no doubt eventually be used against political dissenters generally, unless the people muster the strength to put an end to the ever more brazen acts typical of a police state.

THE GROWING POLICE STATE

Today, between our intelligence and police agencies, there are 50 million names in US dossiers. We have the world's highest number and highest percentage of people behind bars. There is a growing wave of arbitrary stop-and-frisks, especially targeting people of color. Ever more ubiquitous surveillance cameras sprout on city streets and in private offices. Police departments are being militarized. Tasers are now standard issue for police and prison guards, despite being denounced as barbaric by human rights organizations. Our communications -- telephonic and via internet -- are being routinely monitored. And government secrecy increases in tandem with our ever-shrinking personal privacy.

A "lawless administration," the *Times* called the Bush regime.[55] In no way has the Obama administration proven to be less lawless. In fact, he has in many ways gone further than Bush in shredding the Constitution.

The corporations, the banks, the elite, have always been the driving force in every repressive era in our history, and the threat of a police state, military dictatorship, or some form of Fascism will never be eliminated until we destroy the power of the source of virtually everything anti-human in our society.

THE MEDIA

When we speak of the media, we always have in mind the mainstream media -- the corporate media as well as so-called public broadcasting which, while not taking commercial advertising, accepts corporate underwriting and whose political line is virtually indistinguishable from that of the corporate media. We have spoken about the role of the corporate media in abetting the crimes of the elite. Gone are the days when the media routinely accepted subsidies, hidden and open, given by political parties, the government, or corporations. This type of corruption has, for the most part, been replaced by more modern and "cleaner" bribery in the form of commercials and advertising, from which it derives the lion's share of its income.

The media can be counted upon to convince us that in foreign policy matters our leaders in Washington never lie, just as Washington's opponents abroad never tell the truth. The media happily obliges the government in dutifully transmitting official handouts as gospel, happy to be the conduit of official "leaks," a convenient way for the government to get its message across without taking official responsibility. But should it happen that particular reporters or media outlets challenge the government's line and refuse to play the game, they are frozen out of the information pipeline, a fatal handicap when having to compete with one's commercial rivals. Happily, such situations hardly ever arise, for the media bosses are content to "get with the program" and are rarely

175

consumed with any dangerous urge for truth-telling. Besides which, the elite, including the media elite, are all one big happy family. For the mainstream media are themselves mighty corporations, in fact, oligopolies, a half-dozen of which dominate each sector of the industry. Mainstream media shares the Big Business point of view on those grounds alone, and therefore they share the point of view of the political establishment which serves Big Business. Moreover, there are important connections between the media and the rest of the corporate world, expressed in interlocking directorates. Such is the case of the *New York Times*, for example, where its representatives have sat on the board of Merck, Morgan Guaranty Trust (now J.P. Morgan-Chase), Bristol Myers, American Express, Scott Paper, Sun Oil, etc. And representatives of various major, corporations sit on the *New York Times* board. When the media tells the truth, it is only to sell a lie, to preserve its credibility while throwing dust in the people's eyes, to shield the elite against the danger of an informed public opinion. In lockstep, the media manufactures the news; in lockstep it suppresses it. Its job is not to alert but to anesthetize.

The media has had centuries of experience in perfecting the tricks of its trade, honing the art of deceiving and misleading, of slanting facts when not making them up out of the whole cloth, demonizing foreign leaders as the US foreign policy of the day requires. The media is expert at pumping up moral outrage in the service of the grossly immoral, at manipulating emotions so as to becloud reason, at using loaded words and phrases undetected by many of the public who are unable to think critically.

In suppressing the truth about the crimes of the oligarchy committed at home and abroad, in hiding the real relationship between the corporations and its government hirelings, in presenting politicians through the prism of their personalities rather than by revealing the corporate interests they serve, in other words in promoting public naivete about the political system, encouraging uncritical deference to authority figures, civil and military, and in exploiting popular weaknesses, pandering to narrow-mindedness, racism, xenophobia, scientific illiteracy, and the voyeurism of large segments of the public, the media strives to keep the people befuddled and submissive in the interest of maintaining the criminal status quo.

Media collaboration with the government is closest in the area of foreign policy, always supporting Washington's wars (cold and hot) and military interventions. When Washington's relations with this or that country are antagonistic, the media's coverage of that country is invariably hostile as well, and in both its news coverage and editorials it will make sure no positive feature of the life of that country sees the light of day. Invariably, tears will be shed about that country's long-suffering citizens, their alleged lack of democracy and their government's trampling on human rights, their people's economic privations, reaching supposedly, to the level of mass starvation. Finally, the media makes it clear that as long as that regime is in power the American people will not be able to sleep safely in their beds.

Dissidents abroad who oppose the government of a country we have labeled as our enemy are sure to receive the most generous publicity, however insignificant their numbers, while our own country's dissidents are ignored or given the most, perfunctory coverage. One recent example is the sustained campaign against China, especially during the period of the Olympics, focusing on protests concerning Tibet, with TV network cameras following the Olympic torch as it was being carried around the world in order to be sure to catch a glimpse of any incident that would highlight the anti-Chinese message. Now the spotlight has been put on a dissident Chinese "human rights activist" while the media ignores the hundreds of human rights activists who are assassinated or buried in dungeons of countries who play ball with Washington. When demonstrations take place in this country against the policies of the oligarchy, if they are covered at all, the numbers participating are always minimized, and the lion's share of the coverage will be on some isolated incident of violence, usually instigated by the police, which the media highlights to discredit the demonstrators.

If a nation on Washington's enemies list eventually comes to terms with Washington, then all its internal problems, real or fabricated, suddenly and quite magically disappear, never referred to by the media again, unless there is another falling out with the US government. On the other hand, if military intervention is in the works, then the media can be counted upon to provide a steady drumbeat of vituperation, growing ever louder, so that the public reaches a point where it is absolutely intolerable that the government sit idly by in the face of enemy "provocations."

If sections of the media move into opposition regarding some particular aspect of foreign policy, it is only because a portion of the oligarchy has likewise gone into opposition, something which usually happens only when that policy has clearly failed, has backfired, is seen as harming the interests of the elite or sections of the elite themselves. But even in opposition, the media strives to prevent the people from understanding Washington's real motives, its heartless amorality, its bottomless cynicism, its indifference to human life everywhere, not excluding the lives of its people at home. Instead, the media will take the government to task for "flawed" policies, "errors" in judgment, good intentions badly executed. Even when in opposition, the media suppresses the voices of those who dare question the sincerity, integrity and good will of the governing group. The media keeps the people in ignorance and so the war crimes of today are followed by the war crimes of tomorrow.

The media rejects the charge that it functions as an organ of the government. It is simply a coincidence, you see, that it always follows the government's foreign policy line.

If, despite everything, there arises some little "misunderstanding," say, an honest story by an over-eager reporter or editor, the Pentagon or White House steps in to quash the offending piece. A threat to banish the reporter or news channel from the information loop is usually sufficiently persuasive to prevent its recurrence. There was the case involving Phil Donahue, at the time WNBC's most popular television talk show host. Because he had invited guests who expressed opposition to the Iraq war, his show was abruptly cancelled, just as every liberal radio commentator after World War II was dropped from the networks, victim of the Cold War.

Corporations, as well, have little to complain about. The threat of pulling their advertising is generally enough to keep the media in line. Most business pages consist of corporate press releases, often printed verbatim. A *Houston Chronicle* executive was blunt: "We do nothing controversial. We're not in the investigative business. The only concern is giving editorial support to the ad projects."[56]

Back in the Progressive Era, at the beginning of the 20th century, muckraking magazines unmasked the machinations of the Robber Barons, exposed the sleazy operations of the trusts (monopolies), such as Standard Oil, the railroads or meatpackers. Fed up with these disclosures, J. P. Morgan and the Rockefeller interests simply bought those magazines out, fired their managers, and put an end to an important journalistic era.

Books that step on corporate toes are refused publication by the major publishing houses. A by no means unique example was the fate of a manuscript submitted by the distinguished progressive professor Noam Chomsky to Simon & Schuster, then owned by the Gulf & Western conglomerate. Despite it having been at first enthusiastically received by a senior editor, the manuscript was returned, for political reasons, on orders from the publisher.

Ben Bagdikian, former dean of the Graduate School of Journalism at the University of California at Berkeley, has laid out how corporate censorship operates. Corporate advertisers, he has written in his book, *The Media Monopoly*, demand that messages supporting the status quo be reflected in news, editorial and entertainment content. "The readers, listeners, and viewers do not know that these messages are planted by advertisers. They are not supposed to know. They are supposed to think that these ideas are the independent work of professional journalists detached from anything commercial." There is journalistic latitude, continues Bakdigian, but there are limits to that latitude. "The most obvious limit is criticism of the idea of free enterprise or of other basic business systems. In other words, while some reporters may criticize specific corporate acts and offend certain corporate leaders, there is a taboo against criticism of the corporate system."[55] Environmental pollution by corporations is another taboo topic. Until recently, CBS was owned by Westinghouse, a huge corporate polluter, while NBC is owned by the world's biggest corporate polluter, General Electric.

The Federal Communications Commission, charged with ensuring that the airwaves are run in the public interest, for by statute they belong to the people, has been actively assisting ever-accelerating media consolidation. It also strives to prevent those with an anti-corporate viewpoint from gaining access to a significant audience.

That the public's steady diet of media lies and distortions is spooned out without direct government orders, that the media is not government-controlled, is supposed to prove that America has freedom of speech and the press. What it really shows is the effectiveness of our *informal* system of thought control. It is true that there is little direct government control over the media (although more than most people realize). But there is no need for such control since the media takes responsibility for its own censorship, an arrangement that has rarely given the government reason to complain. (We leave aside such practices as the secret planting of stories by the CIA, a practice in which the media has often cooperated, secret CIA subsidies of media personalities, the use of overseas reporters as government spies, or even the most recent revelation that supposedly independent retired military media pundits were secretly coordinating their "punditry" with the Pentagon.)

The vaunted American freedom of speech that is trumpeted around the world turns out to be the exclusive freedom of billionaires to shape public opinion, while those without resources are permitted to squawk away out of public earshot. But even when these squawks occasionally get through, the people have been so safely inoculated, so solidly conditioned, that the clear truth of a "squawker" is rejected as incredible because it is so much at variance with what the people have been told the other 99 percent of the time. Political "opponents" routinely invited by the media to debate issues in the name of fairness and balance have far more in common than that which separates them. The people not only do not hear genuine opposition views but are given the impression that such views do not even exist. Thus, the media works to create and sustain a deadly conformity.

The media not only supports the oligarchy with regard to its criminal foreign policy, but likewise supports its criminal domestic policies, takes the side of Big Business against labor, the corporations against the consumer, the elite against the people generally. We have touched on the environmental havoc the corporations have been wreaking, the illness and disease they have caused, their primary responsibility for the earth's unprecedented climate devastation, about all of which the media is silent. They are silent about the conspiracy of the oil companies to hijack the people at the gas pump. They are silent, as well, about the crooked activities of Wall Street and their stooges which have now brought the country into the throes of an unprecedented economic crisis. As Gary Weiss, a long-time writer on Wall Street scandals, has pointed out: "The media did expose some of the major Wall Street calamities of recent years. However, the media was a conduit for the relentless hype that made those calamities possible...and are making future calamities possible...by failing to expose regulatory fakery."[57]

While the media suppresses information about elite crime, or grossly understates it, it exaggerates and sensationalizes the scope and impact of street crime. For example, in 1992 through 1993, television coverage of street crime more than doubled, while murder coverage tripled, although such crime itself had actually decreased. No surprise, therefore, that despite a steady decades-old decline in crime, the great majority of the public still believes it to be on the increase and out of control.

In addition to the steady drumbeat of street crime stories conveying a sense of a raging epidemic of rape, murder and mayhem, the media focuses on Black crime perpetrators, from "welfare queens" and drug pushers at the bottom of the social ladder through crooked Black politicians, up to Black celebrities who run afoul of the law, material which the police and prosecutors are all too happy to furnish on the basis of their selective targeting, and always accompanied by the obligatory TV "perp walk." A mug shot of an alleged Black perpetrator is four times more likely to appear in a local television news report than that of a white one. Further, an accused African-American man is twice as likely as a white man in a local TV news report to be shown physically restrained. Even former president of CBS News Lawrence Grossman admits that TV newscasts "disproportionately show African-Americans under arrest." No surprise, therefore, that in the public mind, Blacks overwhelmingly make up the "criminal element."

Tapping into its audience's racism, the media howls for ever-harsher punishment, incites the public about an imaginary coddling of street criminals, and calls for "zero tolerance." But when has the media ever denounced the real coddling of corporate or political criminals, or demanded "zero tolerance" regarding their crimes? And why are white politicians and corporate executives who have been convicted of crime never referred to as perpetrators or "perps," never referred to as co-conspirators or accessories before and after the fact? And why is the entire bunch not called career criminals?

One of the jobs of the media is to prepare public opinion, when necessary, for some government assault. Thus, after a heavy media campaign about "welfare cheats," already meager state welfare benefits were slashed, while the civil liberties of those receiving such assistance came under sharper attack. (Even if a segment of the poor is guilty of "getting over" to survive, why is it that such petty chiseling receives much greater attention and enrages the media more than the massive swindles of the rich?) On the heels of another media campaign, with appropriate horror stories about crack cocaine users, came the racist laws penalizing crack offenses 100 times more severely than powdered cocaine.

Black youth are especially beloved media targets. One survey showed that half of the stories on youth involved violence, while more than two-thirds of the stories on violence involved the youth. Yet juveniles comprise less than 20 percent of those arrested for violent crime. Again, the media and the politicians work hand in hand. After a lurid media barrage about Black teenage assaults on white grandmothers, there followed laws providing for juveniles to be sent to adult prisons, where they frequently graduate hardened, embittered, and more expert in the techniques of the criminal trade.

The media pretends its function is to inform. Its real function is to misinform, and increasingly to distract, to entertain. Nor is this optional. For the central truth from which all else follows is that the interests of the elite are diametrically opposed to the interests of the great majority. And it is the media's job, its most important job, to obscure this fundamental reality. Thus, the corporate media bigwigs must rightfully take their place in the dock with the other arch-criminals with whom the people must one day settle accounts.

INEQUALITIES

The wages of sin is death, but evidently for the upper class, the profits of sin is not death but a lion's share of the wealth. In 2005, the country's top 10 percent received almost *half* the national income, up from roughly one-third in the 1970s, their largest share since 1928. The working people, while producing ever greater wealth, have seen their real wages sliding downward as corporate executives play leapfrog in getting ever more lavish salaries and bonuses. The CEO of Home Depot, for example, walked away from company failure with a $210 million severance package. Despite the Ford Motor Company's record losses, its chief executive earned $28 million in his first four months with the company. 36 corporate executives who were *ousted* last year because of their companies' poor performance took with them a total of over $1 billion. The top 25 hedge fund managers last year made more than $14 *billion* - taxed at the same rate as that of ordinary workers. The combined rise in earnings of 93 *million* non-farm workers in the seven years from 2000 to 2006 equalled only one-half of the amount given in the latter year alone by *five* Wall Street firms for *bonuses*. And next Christmastime, Wall Street executives paid themselves billions in such bonuses even as their firms were drowning in a sea of red ink, brazenly announcing their intention to do so again the following Christmas, with US taxpayer bailout money, supposedly given to save the economy from total collapse. This is the bling of the real thug life.

While constituting only 5 percent of the world's population,

186

Americans have amassed a third of the world's wealth. And of that third, 40 percent belongs to the top 1 percent, equal to that of the entire bottom half of the population. Moreover, it is the top tenth of that 1 percent that has the lion's share owned by the 1 percent. Thus, five major banks dominate the economic and political life of the country.

While the share of wealth gobbled up by the elite is rapidly *escalating*, their tax burden is equally rapidly *shrinking*. The tax code is corporate welfare incarnate. Leaving aside the numerous loopholes specifically created for individual companies or corporate sectors, the percentage of taxes paid by corporations has been steadily declining over decades, shifting the tax burden onto the working people, so that the super-rich are actually taxed proportionately far less than the average worker, and in some cases like General Electric, one of the largest corporations in the world, avoid paying taxes altogether. Such is the big payoff for elite crime. Rank hath its privileges, and the privileges are indeed rank.

CONCLUSION

It should be clear from what we have laid out that the mega-corporations (and the politicians who serve them) are nothing but a gang of arch-criminals who should be put in the dock for crimes against humanity. Moreover, they are even ultimately responsible for the vast majority of crimes committed by lowly street criminals. For it is the elite who constitute the real power of the state, control society, and are therefore responsible for society's limitless inequities, including the obscene maldistribution of wealth and the degrading conditions of poverty and racism. It is the elite who control the educational system, which is for many nothing but organized child abuse. It is the elite who make a mockery of notions of law as an instrument for the public good. The crimes committed by our very best citizens, our pillars of society, are supposedly washed clean by their distributing a small portion of their loot to educational, cultural and charitable institutions, funding scholarships, contributing to humanitarian research, supporting public-spirited efforts often down to the smallest not-for-profit community organization. In reality, they are simply making sure that while easing to some small degree, at best, certain social ills (of their making), society is kept under tight control, free from the virus of revolution.

The extraordinarily prosperous bunch enjoying their yachts, jewelry, country clubs, mansions, servants and mistresses (or pool boys) – in short all the rewards that can be bestowed by a system rooted in injustice – are infinitely more loathsome and immoral than the despised stratum at the bottom of the social ladder whose fate is to be stuffed in cages, those gated communities of the poor.

Perfectly reflecting the morality of the elite is Ayn Rand's *Atlas Shrugged*, hailed as one of the most influential works of modern American literature, which unashamedly extols the virtue of *selfishness*. 400,000 copies of this vulgar message are handed out to high school students each year so that they may properly sharpen their claws for the dog-eat-dog world they will soon be entering. This callous anti-social tract has been called his bible by, among other movers and shakers, Alan Greenspan, who for decades served as the chairman of the Federal Reserve, the most powerful financial institution in the world. Greenspan played a key role in smoothing the way for the looting which finally led to the economic debacle that has brought so much suffering to our people and people around the world.

We should just note in passing certain norms of the business world that are not part of our economic textbooks: the ever-greater compromises of one's integrity made in order to rise up the career ladder; the petty backbiting and intrigues of office politics; the shabby tricks perpetrated on consumers that fall under the commercial heading, "Buyer Beware!" caveat emptor, or less classically phrased, "Never give a sucker an even break"; the culture of valuing people only to the extent they can be used and exploited, a culture in which it is not only acceptable but desirable to capitalize on the people's basest impulses and even twist for commercial ends the people's most humane and generous sentiments.

Such is the moral climate of our "free enterprise" system – free, that is, of scruples, ethics, and concern for the masses of the people. Look carefully at the flags flying over the White House and the Capitol Building, over the

Governors' mansions and City Halls, over Wall Street, over every corporate headquarters, flying over factories and office buildings, by day the Stars and Stripes, by night the Skull and Crossbones. Without wishing to be alarmist, the people should be alerted to the fact that tens of thousands of social predators are at large among us.

Compared to the despicable acts of the elite, whose consequences few in society manage to escape, the deeds of street criminals are petty indeed. And street criminals are much more honest in owning up to their transgressions, possess far more humanity, and have an infinitely greater sense of justice. Their crimes are often a natural response to oppression, deprivation, discrimination, humiliation, and hopelessness. They are a protest, conscious or unconscious, against conditions that ought not to be the lot of human beings. It was the renowned psychiatrist Karl Menninger who remarked: "I suspect that all the crimes committed by all the jailed criminals do not equal in total social damage that of the crimes committed against them."[58] In a similar vein, the illustrious historian C.L.R. James observed: "The cruelties of property and privilege are always more ferocious than the revenge of poverty and oppression."[59]

While the elite find street crime distasteful, they also find it useful. For with the help of the media, street crime provides a wonderful distraction. Promoting fear and insecurity, overladen with racism, is invaluable in maintaining the status quo. The "war on crime" as well as the "war on terror" conditions the public to give up its liberties, to accept a police state whose full fury will one day come down on all who do not sign on to the corporate program.

190

THE CRIME OF PUNISHMENT

STREET CRIME

INTRODUCTION

Having established that the criminality of the elite as a class is universal and not a matter of a "few rotten apples," let us climb out of their moral sewer and enter the cleaner air of the street criminals, those who are at the bottom of the social pyramid, blows raining down on them from all directions, about whom the public is goaded into a frenzy and upon whom falls the full force of society's vengeance.

Any discussion of street crime – how it is perceived, how it is dealt with – is inseparable from a discussion of the history and present condition of African-Americans. This is *not* because street crime is overwhelmingly perpetrated by them but because in the minds of the general public, crime is equated with street crime, and street crime is just another name for Blacks. We must delve into the history and present condition of African-Americans because (1) they constitute half the prison population, which is explained by their alleged inherent criminality, and (2) that inherent criminality is supposedly the product of some combination of bad family, bad culture, and bad genes.

We will examine the validity of those ideas. For if it turns out that they are false, if it turns out that the huge racial disparities at every level of the criminal justice system can be accounted for simply by the racist nature of the criminal justice system, then the question must be raised as to why these ideas are being promoted.

The charge that the criminal justice system is racist is not of recent date. It did not originate with the Civil Rights or Black Power movement. Over a century ago at Harper's Ferry, scene of John Brown's heroic anti-slavery raid, the leading Black figures of their day declared:

"We want the laws enforced against rich as well as poor, against capitalists as well as laborers; against white as well as Black. We are not more lawless than the white race, we are more often arrested, convicted and mobbed."[1]

IS STREET CRIME BLACK?

We have already shown that elite crimes constitutes the vast majority of all crimes. Needless to say, it is committed overwhelmingly by those of European descent – "whites." But what about street crime?

That street crime is primarily a nonwhite phenomenon seems to be confirmed by statistics derived from the FBI Uniform Crime Report, which in turn are compiled from various law-enforcement agencies. The FBI report is considered authoritative, but it can be highly misleading. For one thing, more than half of all crimes go unreported. While FBI statistics show that African-Americans commit aggravated assaults at three times the rate of whites, one needs to consult crime figures from another source. The National Crime Survey based on interviews is far more comprehensive and freer of bias. And it reveals, for example, that the proportion of Blacks and whites committing violent offenses is virtually identical. Of course, it is considered sacrilege or treason to doubt the FBI, the embodiment of rectitude. The FBI was led for almost all of its existence by J. Edgar Hoover, a man who associated with mobsters and told us there was no Mafia, but saw Communists under every bed, who called Martin Luther King "the most notorious liar in America." It was Hoover who set in motion the Counter-Intelligence Program (COINTELPRO) using the most violent, unscrupulous and illegal methods in an effort (largely successful) to destroy the Black and native peoples' freedom movements.

During the late 1960s and '70s there was a dramatic upsurge of street crime. Accompanying it was a campaign of racist incitement by the politicians and the media. More than two-thirds of the public saw Blacks as responsible for what they perceived as an out-of-control crime wave and believed it ti be linked to the "insolent" demands and behavior of a civil rights movement now manifesting itself in urban riots, The demand went up for an end to the supposedly scandalously light sentences handed down to Black criminals by "bleeding heart" judges and an end to "revolving door" justice, meaning humane parole policies which supposedly were responsible for a high rate of recidivism. Legislators fell all over themselves to mandate ever stiffer sentences. The conditions of incarceration became ever harsher. The rights of the accused as well as the rights of the incarcerated, expanded through the struggles of the 1960s, were again being stripped away.

It was an era when California passed more than 1,000 new criminal statutes, an era of "Three Strikes and You're Out," with draconian punishment for second and third nonviolent offenses. Seventeen times more Blacks than whites were charged in that state under the "Three Strikes" legislation.

It was an era, also, of "Truth-in-Sentencing" laws which put "truth" in the hands of prosecutors and took it out of the hands of judges, an era when the federal government subsidized prison construction to encourage states to stretch out the time that inmates had to serve, from the customary one-third to 85 percent.

It was an era of "One Strike and You're Out," whereby if any member of a family living in public housing was found guilty of engaging in a criminal drug transaction, even outside the home, and even without the knowledge of other family members, the entire family faced eviction.

As has already been pointed out, the media played a vital role in fabricating a sense of crisis, providing the public with a daily diet of rape and murder, splashing in print or on TV the Black face that invariably accompanied accounts of the latest criminal outrage. The word of the day was "incarcerate." And incarcerate they did, facilitated by a crash program of state prison construction. Federal parole boards were eliminated.

And sure enough, as incarcerations soared, the crime rate dropped, confirming what "everybody" knew. But hidden from the public was the data showing that there actually was no correlation between the rate of incarceration and the rate of crime. For example, while in some states crime went down as the incarceration rate went up, in other states the crime rate went up even though the rate of incarceration also rose. Of 10 states with the highest increases in their incarceration rates, none had a crime decline above the national average.

We are told that there is nothing racist about the fact that there is a disproportionate number of African-Americans in our prisons. This is only to be expected, it is claimed, given that Blacks commit the crimes disproportionately. (We set aside the fact that white collar criminals, who are disproportionately of European descent, in fact overwhelmingly of European descent, hardly ever go to prison.) We shall see, on the contrary, that the grossly disproportionate Black presence in the prison system can be mostly accounted for by the cumulative impact of racial targeting and discriminatory treatment by police, prosecutors and judges. That is a truth rarely told, and when it is, it usually only reaches the tiny audience who follow the alternative media and the little publicized work of social justice organizations.

STREET CRIME AND FEAR

The public is conditioned to associate street crime with violence. Actually, the vast majority of street crimes are committed with no weapons and involve no violence. On the other hand, we have laid out the bloody and violent record of the elite, the wars waged abroad on its behalf and the casualties sustained at home as a result of corporate greed. The victims of elite crimes are far more numerous than those of violent street crime. Yet the public is kept on edge with daily accounts of street crime, while the injuries and deaths caused by corporate greed are passed over in silence.

As the power structure understands all too well, nothing works better in maintaining social control than promoting insecurity, frightening people with imaginary demons and then stepping forward as the people's protector, requiring only that the people relinquish their hard-won liberties. Throughout the history of this country, the elite have found it useful to fan hysteria against one group or another, demonizing, for example, sympathizers of the French Revolution in the early days of our Republic, later calling Catholics agents of a diabolical Vatican, and still later portraying immigrants as bomb-throwing anarchists. After World War I, the public was kept in a state of alarm by a supposed Bolshevik threat, atheists who had nationalized Russia's women and would do the same thing here, if given the chance. Then there was the great panic during the Cold War: the Russians were coming! And American Communists and Communist sympathizers were painted as spies and saboteurs trying to pave the way for the imminent invasion. As McCarthyite hysteria receded, the African-American bogeyman came to the fore, with raised fist shouting "Black Power!" while his brother, the "crackhead," leapt over the white picket fences of tranquil white suburbs, grabbing the white man's property and terrorizing his women.

Now, after the events of 9/11, we are supposedly locked in a great "clash of civilizations" with Islam, the outcome of which will determine our very survival.

STREET CRIME: CAUSES OF AND RESPONSES TO

So how does one account for the huge numbers of people of color, especially African-Americans, who are caught in the clutches of the criminal justice system? Both Right-wingers and liberals have a good deal in common in their explanations. To the Right-winger, the commission of crime (by which, as usual, they mean street crime) is simply a question of making bad choices and therefore a matter of bad character. "We don't need a lot of sociological mumbo-jumbo...the guilty criminal...is a free moral agent who, confronted with a choice between right and wrong, chooses to do wrong...."[2] says Morgan Reynolds. He and others like him scoff at explanations that trace crime to social deprivation and inequities. They call that "victimology" and sneer at those who raise the issue of social injustice, which they claim promotes a "victim mentality." To them, racism, poverty, and inequality are so many pitiful alibis. (In this they have been joined by elements of the Black middle class, including such figures as Professors Shelby Steele and John McWhorter, comedian turned social commentator Bill Cosby, and his partner Harvard psychiatrist and historian Alvin Poussaint, as well as radio journalist Juan Williams, among a host of others. They swear loyalty to the old civil rights movement and exalt Martin Luther King while twisting his message beyond recognition. For unlike these smug stereotype-mongers who have achieved enormous popularity within Right-wing circles as they insult the Black poor and admonish them about their lack of morality, absence of ambition, and all their other supposed personal inadequacies, at the close of his life King was not about rebuking the poor but mobilizing them, not about blaming the victim, and not about denying or belittling the damaging effects of institutional racism.

Liberals hasten to distance themselves from "victimology," as well. While they agree that social factors are part of the crime equation and therefore urge social reforms, they insist that individuals can overcome social handicaps and make the "right choice." They agree with the Right-wingers that criminals have simply made the wrong one.

The issue is not whether a few outstanding or lucky individuals can break out of their harsh environment. The question is what is the likely *group* outcome? The opportunities, and therefore the choices, available to the poor fall within a quite narrow range. Success of an individual is offset by the lack of success of many others, and this can be calculated with great statistical reliability.

This, of course, raises the question of free will. The liberals, like the Right-wingers, strongly oppose any "deterministic" argument and agree that everyone can rise above their circumstances. To believe otherwise, they say, is fatalistic and encourages passivity. What is needed is for people to "apply themselves," study and work hard, keep their nose clean, stay away from the wrong crowd. The recipes offered are for individual escape from the problems of the community.

But the fate of individuals is bound up with the fate of their communities. The aim is not for *a few individuals to beat the odds*. The solution lies not in rising *above* their community but *with* their community, not in *escaping from* ghetto conditions but in changing those conditions. And this requires *collective* struggle. What is not addressed is precisely how the community can escape. Actually, the real determinists are those who believe that "poverty will always be with us," that the social conditions which breed street crime will always be with us.

The great majority of those who wind up on the wrong side of the law – and, as we have shown, for the most part they represent the more petty types of criminals – are themselves victims of enormous social injustice. Now, while liberals will concede that many street criminals have been dealt lousy hands, what is not acknowledged is that those lousy hands have been dealt by card sharks from the bottom of the deck.

To recognize that one is being victimized is not to resign oneself to such victimization, to bob along rushing waters over which one has no control. On the contrary, acknowledging one's victimization and, even more, correctly identifying the forces behind that victimization, is the beginning of self-empowerment. Understanding that it is not God's will, fate, bad luck, or personal failure, but that there are *social forces sabotaging the chances of one's success* and similarly sabotaging the chances of the success of one's community, moreover that these forces can be fought and defeated, is not only self-empowering but, more important, *community empowering.*

It is obvious that street crime is linked to poverty, deprivation, and/or a consciousness of the system's unfairness. Alcohol and drug abuse, which usually accompany street crime, are part of self-medicating the pain of hopelessness and anger which can seemingly find no other outlet. While alcohol and drug abuse are for other reasons equally present among the more affluent, the negative behavior caused by such abuse in middle class or elite circles is generally shielded, covered up, and is much less likely to result in its members becoming enmeshed in the criminal justice system. And on the occasions when they are, the consequences are much less dire.

Nevertheless, it must be stressed that poverty, deprivation and inequality are what contribute toward street crime and not crime generally, not the crime of the elite, which is the major kind of crime, the crime of the greedy, rather than of the needy.

CRIME AND BLACK BIOLOGY

Quite in vogue today are explanations of crime as rooted in biology, particularly the crimes ascribed to African-Americans. Without embarrassment, many of the same people who say that crime is a matter of free choice and that pointing to social conditions is deterministic, champion the most deterministic explanation of all. James Q. Wilson, considered by some to be the most influential writer on crime in the United States, claims that "biology is destiny." Biological explanations for crime are generally tied to racist stereotypes. Since it is assumed that Blacks commit the great majority of all crime, the question of why people commit crimes has morphed into why Black people commit crimes.

In the good old days, pseudo-scientists attributed the crimes of the Black man to his "jungle blood," which was supposedly responsible for his periodically savage behavior. That such savage behavior was only periodic was believed to be due to his being under the control of whites. While such sentiments are no longer expressed openly, they continue to be conveyed subtly and through innuendo. Thus, in the midst of hurricane-ravaged New Orleans, after almost all whites had fled the city and many Black people were left on their own, the media portrayed New Orleans as being in a frenzy of looting, murder and rape. And such will be the lasting impression despite subsequent revelations of media distortion and outright falsifications. It was no ignorant "redneck" nor even a Right-wing intellectual, but Fred Goodwin, the director of the Alcohol, Drug Abuse and Mental Health Administration under President Bill Clinton, who declared: "...maybe it isn't just a careless use of the word when people call certain areas of certain cities 'jungles.' For the inner cities have lost some of the civilizing evolutionary things that we have built up...."[3]

One can track the creation of the image of the Black savage to the political needs of the elite of both South and North. In the South, promoting that image helped the plantation owners swing poor whites over to their side and overthrow Reconstruction. Thus was destroyed the tenuous alliance of Blacks and poor whites which for a brief moment offered prospects for a life of dignity for both. In the end, the poor white, though without a pot to piss in, though an object of contempt of his white "betters," was comforted knowing he was no "nigger" and that, protected by his biology, as low as he might be in the world he at least would never descend to the "nigger's" level.

To re-establish a regime of white supremacy, an iron fist was needed to deal with the freedman: night riders, KKK, rule by terror. No longer useful was the image of the happy-go-lucky, banjo-strumming Sambo, who loyally guarded his mistress while the white plantation menfolk went off to fight the Yankees. Sambo was created to show that the "darkies" were happy with their enslavement. When slavery ended, Sambo was transformed into the hulking Black brute.

Meanwhile, in the North, the ruling industrialists, facing growing unrest among their own workers, became increasingly sympathetic to problems of labor control (Black) below the Mason-Dixon line. Further, they desired a stable environment for their growing southern investments after the Civil War. And so they threw their support to the old Confederacy. Moreover, stepping onto the world stage, they joined the other great powers in assuming the "White Man's Burden," enthusiastically embracing the racist ideology that justified imperialist expansion.

Biological explanations for Black behavior have a long tradition. There was the discovery of the disease known as "drapetomania" which ,when infecting slaves, caused them to try to escape. Later, learned phrenologists explained Black inferiority by charting the bumps on their head. "Science" has come a long way since then. "Jungle blood" has been replaced by genetics. Now we are told that there are genes for violence and crime, or that at least there is a genetic basis for a predisposition to violence and crime. And since it is a given that African-Americans account for a hugely disproportionate amount of crime, the conclusion is inescapable that African-Americans must be the primary carrier of such genes. What such scientists have yet to explain is how genes, the formation and alteration of which ordinarily require thousands of years, can account for increases or decreases, sometimes quite sharp, in the crime rate over 10 or 20 years. Further, it is yet to be explained how biology is related to criminal acts, given that acts that were once defined as crimes have become legal, that acts once legal are now considered crimes, that some acts are legal in one locality and illegal in another – in other words, how biology can explain what are actually social constructs.

California, leading the way in the number of incarcarated and in the harshness of its prison regime, also leads in the promotion of biological theories of criminality. Influential figures in that state have called for mandatory medical treatment of criminals, recommending that they should be housed in clinics, rather than prisons. Naturally, if no effective treatments have yet been discovered, then they suggest that criminals be held indefinitely. There have even been investigations into the use of neurosurgery to heal damaged centers in the brain which it is believed are associated with aggressive behavior.

Biological explanations are, of course, never offered for white collar or corporate crime. No attempt is made to locate the gene for corporate fraud, nor the gene for wanton destruction of the environment. No attempt is made to locate the gene for mass murder in those manufacturing and marketing cigarettes. Nor has there been any effort to isolate the gene for police brutality. No one has studied President Harry Truman's DNA (which can now be done posthumously), given that his order to drop atomic bombs caused the deaths of more than a quarter of a million people. Of course, no one is curious about exploring the genes of all those responsible for the ceaseless wars that have caused the loss of life of hundreds of millions.

Our "objective" scientists assure us that there is no racist element in their biological theories. They deny they are picking up again from the American eugenics movement of the 1920s, subsequently embraced by the Nazis to justify extermination of "inferior beings." (It should be recalled that by 1931, 27 of our states had passed laws allowing compulsory sterilization of the "feeble-minded," the "insane," and the habitually criminal.) Rather, those good scientists insist they are guided by the most humane of motives: simply to discover the source of the "cancer" that is growing from birth in the African-American male and to forestall his otherwise inevitable anti-social activity. In that way, they say, not only will society as a whole benefit, but African-Americans will be protected from their own nature. Similar thinking has led to race-based explanations of disease, drawing this comment from Dr. Troy Duster, past president of the American Sociological Association, and grandson of the great Black leader Ida B. Wells:

"African-American males have twice the prostate cancer rate that whites do. Right now, the National Cancer Institute is searching for cancer genes among Black men. They're not asking, 'How come Black men in the Caribbean and in sub-Saharan Africa have much lower cancer rates than all American men?' A lot of money is currently being spent to find a drug for Black hypertension. That's a lot cheaper than a war on poverty, which might alleviate the root cause of a lot of hypertension."[4]

CRIME AND BLACK CULTURE

If biology doesn't work to explain Black criminality, let's try culture. Thanks to the Black freedom movement, the ugly stereotypes that characterized white supremacist thought for a century after the Civil War were replaced in some quarters by libel of a more "sympathetic" nature. This has taken the form of a good deal of sighing and tongue-clucking about the Black man's desertion of his family, about female-headed households, "children having children," the alleged promiscuity of Black women on welfare, all pronounced with missionary tender-heartedness. Under the leadership of former Democratic Senator Patrick Moynahan, the notion of Black family pathology became the incontestable truth of both liberal academia and Right-wing think tanks. According to Moynahan, such pathology is rooted in slavery. And although African-Americans, he said kindly, are not responsible for their enslaved past, that long history has left an unavoidable stain on their nature. It is perfectly understandable, therefore, that criminals should come from a people that has never known true family life, should come from parents who are typically neglectful or abusive, perfectly understandable that Black parents should be less responsible than white parents and should not inculcate proper moral values in their children.

Study of "ghetto pathology" or a post-slave syndrome of one kind or another, has produced a veritable cottage industry for learned sociologists. Of course, it does not take a Ph.D. to understand that people do not respond well to oppressive treatment. This is certainly part of the picture. But what remains a closed book to those social thinkers and to an increasing section of the Black middle class is how, tempered in the furnace of the Black experience, a culture has emerged of astonishing beauty, power, and moral grandeur, a culture described by historian Paula Giddings in connection with Black women seeing "not only the degredation but the triumph of transcending what the system would make of them."[5]

If we accept that the high rate of crime committed

by Blacks is the result of a historically dysfunctional family life going hundreds of years back into slavery days, how then (as in the case of the biological explanation) can it account for the *doubling* of the Black prison population in just 20 years? And again, where are the investigations of the family life of corporate and political criminals? Where are the attempts to identify the source of family dysfunction in our elite predators?

It will be instructive at this point to examine the real history of the Black family. Here I extensively cite *The Black Family in Slavery and Freedom*, 1750-1925, by the outstanding historian Herbert G. Gutman.

THE BLACK FAMILY IN HISTORY

A common myth, according to Gutman, is the supposed lack among slaves of feelings of parental and marital attachment. This was certainly a convenient belief when family members were routinely sold and ripped away from their loved ones. This myth was so widespread that even many white Abolitionists denied that slaves had a family consciousness.

A leading reference authority in the world, the *Encyclopedia Britannica*, declared in its 1884 edition that Negroes were "nonmoral." A decade earlier, the leading Southern newspaper, the "moderate" *Atlanta Constitution*, would state: "Now, what does the negro know about the obligation of the marriage relation? No more, sir, than the parish bull or village heifer."[6]

Most of the adult slaves were married. As a matter of fact, a larger percentage of slaves were or had been married at the time of death than Southern whites. And marriages under slavery were long-lasting. In contrast to the picture of the Black male slave routinely abandoning his family, it was his family ties that served to discourage his escape. Some runaways often stole away from their plantation to visit their immediate family members and other kin living at some distance, and then returned, prepared to take the lash.

Slavery, of course, did disrupt many Black marriages. That disruption, however, was caused by forcible separation. One study, for example, showed that in Mississippi, among men and women age 30 and older, nearly one in four men and one in five women had suffered such a separation.

Many freedmen, veterans of the Union army, returned to their former home to fetch their wife and children but were often driven off, beaten and threatened with death should they come back again to claim their families. That African-Americans cherished the marriage institution was also shown after Emancipation when large numbers of former slaves rushed to legalize their relationships, something done despite what was for them the considerable fees involved.

Despite the extraordinary pressures of slavery upon family ties, and the "excessive attention given to what has been called 'pathological' in the Afro-American historical experience, as Gutman has written, kinship bonds were extraordinarily strong, as revealed in the adaptive capacities of the extended kinship networks that developed first among the slaves and then among their free children and grandchildren.[7]

Frederick Douglass marveled that despite so many hardships, there was not to be found among any people a more rigid enforcement of the law of respect for elders. As the freedmen faced a grim new reality with no resources, bonds of feeling and empathy remained high. A Lumberton, North Carolina, a white clergyman was astonished that following Emancipation, "All indigent or helpless people are being supported by relations, parents, or friends." Another Northern missionary declared: "It is surprising to see how ready they are to help out one another to the last dollar."[8] After the Civil War, impoverished freedmen took into their homes thousands of Black children orphaned or separated from parents who could not be located. That this was typical of the ex-slave throughout the entire South is one important reason, Guzman concluded, that over its full lifetime, the number of ex-slaves requiring material assistance by the Freedmen's Bureau amounted to less than one percent.

Upon Emancipation, the formerly enslaved determined that the women were no longer going to work in the fields. They would, like the white women, devote themselves to their homes and children, something which was highly irritating to the landowners and the political ancestors of our present moralizers about "family values." This commitment to properly raise their children was viewed as "female loaferism." (Today, too, single mothers on public assistance are depicted as loafers and are forced to enter the labor market, often at the expense of their children's proper care. Once again, the double-standard: In the decade following the Second World War, women were urged to be "homemakers," were given the title "domestic engineers," their housekeeping chores glorified. But, of course, all this pertained only to white women of the middle class.

Just who it was that possessed family values was clearly revealed immediately after the Civil War when Southern white legislatures enacted the Black Codes. These provided for African-American children to be torn from their families through forced "apprenticeships" so as to at least partially make up for the loss of slave labor. Gutman describes boys of 12 to 14 being taken from their parents under the pretense that their families were incapable of supporting them, while the younger children were left to be maintained by the parents. Children were indentured by judges who declared their parents vagrants before they had enjoyed their freedom for a single week. Every able-bodied African-American boy would be taken from his parents just at the time when they were becoming able to help in supporting their families.

The importance of family bonds to African-Americans is reflected to this day in the widespread custom of gathering together in annual reunions the often widely dispersed family, including extended, often very extended, family members.

As for the single-mother household and all the rest of the "pathology" of the Black family, Gutman informs us: "...at all times – and in all settings – the typical Black household (always a lower-class household) had in it two parents."[9] That is, until the cataclysm of the 1960s. Gutman cites studies showing that in the 1880s, both rural and urban Black households in the South (where 90 percent of African-Americans resided), were overwhelmingly composed of two parents. The situation was similar in the North. In 1905, five out of six New York City Black households contained either a husband or a father. Again Gutman: "Through the early part of the 20th century, the. two-parent household, North and. South, was not limited to better-advantaged African-Americans but was just as common among unskilled workers and day laborers."[10] His conclusion: "As measured by the types of households inhabited by most poor southern rural and urban Blacks and by poor migrant northern Blacks between 1855 and 1925, enslavement had not created among them a 'tangle of pathology.'"[11] As late as 1940, only a little more than 10 percent of the overwhelmingly rural Black families in the South were headed by females.

Surveying the data, Gutman concludes that right up to the 1960s, the disintegration of the Black family was a *myth*. Since then, however, the Black family has indeed been facing severe strains, the reasons for which lie not *within* the Black family but elsewhere.

THE CAUSE OF BLACK FAMILY "PATHOLOGY"

Between 1940 and 1975, four million African-Americans poured out of the Southern countryside into the cities, especially Northern cities. First, thanks to the labor shortage caused by the Second World War, the gates of industrial plants swung open to Blacks, previously barred. With the war's end, however, they were, as usual, the first to be fired. While some managed to hang on to their jobs, many faced the new experience of prolonged unemployment, without land or kinfolk to fall back on. Meanwhile, whites were pouring into the suburbs, assisted by the government which, through the Federal Housing Administration, refused to underwrite anything but white-only mortgages for white-only neighborhoods.

Then, the freedom movement of the 1950s and '60s challenged the Southern reign of terror and the super-exploitation such terror enforced. At a time when the employment of Black field labor was cheaper than using machines, sharecropping made sense. But now the political basis of the sharecropping economy was being undermined. So the plantation owners mechanized their farms and drove tens of thousands of Black families off the land (this on top of the tens of thousands who had already been driven off in the 1930s by the agricultural policy of the New Deal). Between 1950 and 1970, most of the displaced families migrated to major Northern cities. Resourceful and self-sufficient Black farmers, masters of the art of "make-do," who had performed wonders of adaptation to an extraordinarily difficult environment, were now seen in the urban setting as without skills and unemployable. Unlike previous Black migrations, this one took place not during wartime labor shortages or an expanding Northern economy, but when automation was eliminating a million-and-a-half unskilled and semi-skilled factory jobs.

Moreover, as African-Americans filled center cities and their public schools, the original move of whites toward suburban bliss was transformed into a tidal wave, away from the nightmare of the Black presence. Again the government could be counted on to strengthen apartheid, now through "urban renewal." Suburban white commuters had been forced to drive through nasty Black neighborhoods. So whole blocks were bulldozed in the middle of Black communities, and highways were cut through to permit passage at a safe 40 miles an hour. Urban renewal meant people removal (Black and Latino), abandonment of retail trade, and withdrawal of vital social services, causing further community desolation. Factory work gave way to office jobs, from which Black men were barred because they would be in unnerving proximity to white females. Corporations found it convenient to set up branches in the suburbs, inaccessible to those in the inner cities.

Under all those circumstances, African-American men could not provide for their families. Under those circumstances there was no choice but to apply for state assistance. There is an African-American saying, "First you shit on me and then you tell me I smell bad." As large numbers of African-Americans were being forced to seek state assistance, rules were set up barring aid to families where there was an able-bodied man in the house, which effectively forced the unemployed husband to desert his family for the sake of the survival of his wife and children. No surprise, therefore, that the rate of family break-up increased between 1950 and 1970.

In slavery days, the Black father was ripped away from his wife and children with a bill of sale. A century after Emancipation he was ripped away with the bill of goods that was the "welfare state." The Black woman got her cheese and powdered milk; the sociologists and criminologists got grants to study female-headed households; and the politicians got their election plank.

Strangely enough, Black genes and family pathology are apparently catching, for similar symptoms of disintegration are being increasingly exhibited by the white family.

The reality is that no people have fought so tenaciously to maintain or repair their families than African-Americans, during and after slavery. *The real destroyers of Black family life have always come from outside, from the institutions and policies of the white elite.* So it is not the pathology of the Black family that is at the root of ghetto misery but the controlling political and social system that has deliberately undermined what had previously been the Black community's pillar of strength.

Sociologist and pioneer in the field of community studies Hylan Lewis hit the nail on the head when he wrote: "The answer to the problem of family disorganization is not one of inculcating marriage and family values in young couples; there is ample evidence that they exist. The critical test is to find ways and means for the young adult male to meet the economic maintenance demands of marriage and family life."

In a nutshell, just provide good jobs. The family will then take care of itself. The tangle of pathology turns out to be nothing but a slipknot.

CRIME AND BLACK EDUCATION

We are told that African-Americans engage in crime because they have rotten genes and/or rotten families. Also, a rotten education. It is true that a good number of those in prison are functionally illiterate. Many can't read beyond the fourth grade level. The reason for this, supposedly, apart from their innate stupidity, is that ghetto students and their parents are indifferent to education, even hostile. And this is proven by the fact that poor Black parents have no books in the house, don't help with homework, and don't come to parent-teacher conferences.

The reality is, as Hylan Lewis documented in his study of poor Black parents in Washington, D.C., they have the same ambitions for their children as those of the middle class, but those ambitions are tempered by street wisdom, also known as realism.

Further, we are told that the children don't try to do well in school because to them getting good grades or speaking "proper" English means "acting white." Long articulated by Right-wing white racists, this line has now been taken up by middle-class Blacks. There is a clear parallel between these middle-class attitudes with those of 19th century middle-class German Jewish immigrants. Harshly critical of the impoverished Jews from Eastern Europe who came after them and who settled in the teeming ghettos of the Lower East Side of New York, they, too, were ashamed of and condemned their brethren's criminality, uncouthness, and culture, a culture alien to their own middle-class values. For the more affluent German Jews feared that despite their own respectability, at which they had worked for so long, the Jews of Eastern Europe would bring down on them added troubles in a country already rife with anti-Semitism. Similarly, middle-class Blacks, having found a comfortable, if tenuous, niche in White Supremacist America, fear that the behavior of those in the "hood" is fanning racism and jeopardizing their own still precarious future.

Now let's get real.

The function of the public school system for a good period of our post-slavery history was to prepare the mass of African-Americans for their predetermined role as field workers and menial labor. Obviously, this did not require much in the way of education. In fact, too much education was considered a detriment, for it would only create misfits and malcontents. In addition, the job of the school was to train African-Americans to accept their role at the bottom of society as both proper and inevitable, conforming to their generally accepted limited abilities. So the schools not only had to under-educate them but undermine their confidence in their ability to learn, had to convince them not only of their own inferiority but that of their forebears, including their African ancestors, in other words, to pump into them that their inferiority was *congenital*.

It was also the job of the schools to see to the children's moral training, to condition them to suppress their natural sense of what was just, and to punish them when they didn't exhibit sufficient deference.

From the time public education was first provided to the great majority of African-Americans – and it took a civil war to accomplish this – Blacks have received inadequate and inequitable educational resources, have been forced to accept a curriculum which distorts U.S. history and ignores or demeans the African-American's place in it, a curriculum meant to inculcate in Black youth a sense of worthlessness. Academic tracking has been a constant device to support society's race and class hierarchy. Only the forms of such tracking have changed over the years, in response to political pressure and to the elite's economic needs. Today, it is expressed in middle-class white students mostly attending four-year colleges, while the two-year community colleges are organized for the majority of students of color, that is, for the half who actually make it through high school. The two-year college is a preparation for the better kind of dead end jobs – for example, technicians assisting white professionals.

Yes, but we have made progress, as we are always being told. IQ tests replaced phrenology, and SAT and similar standardized tests have replaced IQ tests. But whatever the means used, the results always just happen to confirm presumed Black inferiority. Then there are the "special education" classes, created for the mentally retarded and emotionally disturbed. Naturally, such classes are overwhelmingly filled with Black boys. At the other end of the spectrum there are the classes for the "intellectually gifted," the track for the college-bound, overwhelmingly not filled with African-Americans.

School discipline is imposed in a racially discriminatory way. Corporal punishment, legal or not, is more likely to be laid out on Black than on white schoolchildren. In 2000, the *Washington Post* reported the "long-standing pattern of Black students being suspended and expelled from school more frequently than white students. That disparity has persisted for at least 25 years."[12] While Black children constitute only 17 percent of public school students, they make up twice that percentage of those suspended, often for "defiant" or "disruptive" behavior.

Schools are becoming increasingly militarized, especially those whose students are predominantly of color. Metal detectors are commonplace, police and "peace officers" swagger through the hallways. As high school student Ryan Kierstedt stated in a New York Civil Liberties Union newsletter, "This is not a school anymore – it's a future prison. They're preparing us for prison."[13]

Educational disparities have in the last few decades only worsened. With the radical changes in the country's economic structure, with the growth of a knowledge-based economy, it was found to be cheaper and more desirable to bring in skilled immigrants than to train African-Americans from scratch. As agribusiness has replaced family farming, as manufacturing has been outsourced, and as we have become increasingly a service economy, even the traditional place for Black labor has sharply contracted. The educational system, therefore, is no longer preparing the majority of Black students even for the evaporating dead-end jobs. So many are either dropping out of school or being pushed out, finding in prison the only institution whose practice of affirmative action we are confident the Supreme Court will never declare unconstitutional.

AFRICAN-AMERICANS AND EDUCATION: A HISTORICAL SKETCH

Indifference to education? History says otherwise. *No other people have sacrificed so much for schooling.* During slavery times, many secretly strove to become literate despite the threat of the lash. As Civil War battles raged, Black soldiers poured over primers in their knapsacks in every lull in the fighting. Following Emancipation, there was a huge thirst for education among the freed men and women, who worked full time during the day and attended school at night. Charlotte Forten, a Black New Englander who came down to teach in the Carolina Sea Islands, attested to that passion. Writing for *The Atlantic* in May, 1864, she observed that for Black children, "coming to school is a constant delight and recreation to them. They come here as other children go to play." White Presbyterian missionary Thomas Calahan, teaching Blacks in Louisiana after the Civil War, reported, "...everyone pleading to be taught, willing to do anything for learning...Their cry is for Books! Books! Books! When will school begin?"[14]

While receiving assistance from Northern

philanthropy, the great majority of schools of the ex-slaves were built with their own efforts, out of their nickels, dimes, and carpentry skills. Which raises the question: If today there is a lack of educational motivation among some Black children, who or what unmotivated them? What is it that has stripped them of their joy in learning, a joy which nevertheless persists today in the early grades?

The problem is not Black indifference to education but the stubborn resistance of the white power structure, which continues to do everything in its power to prevent, stunt, and distort the education of African-Americans. It was African-Americans who were the driving force behind public education during Reconstruction, and it was the Southern white elite who fought public education, not only for Blacks but for poor whites, as well, gutting public schools as soon as they returned to power. For almost a century after the Civil War the white oligarchy, North as well as South, spent (and for the most part continue to spend) only a fraction on Black education compared to that on whites, maintaining a separate and unequal school system (despite the *Brown* ruling), North as well as South.

Equal, quality education was one of the priorities of the Black freedom movement. Have those scenes already been forgotten of heroic Southern Black parents and children braving insults, abuse and physical assaults, and defying inevitable economic retribution, as they challenged school segregation? Have their efforts been forgotten in setting up their own freedom schools when the public schools were closed down by the white power structure rather than submit to the courts' integration orders? Have the massive school boycotts of Northern Black parents been forgotten, protesting against inferior education, their later bitter struggles for community control of their schools, for a relevant curriculum, for appointment of Black teachers and administrators theretofore scarce as hen's teeth, and for college open enrollment? Was it the African-American community which shut down affirmative action programs in higher education, that modest attempt to rectify historic injustices? Or, rather, was it the courts of the white oligarchy which declared affirmative action unconstitutional, waxing indignant at the "victimhood" of the white man?

Would it not be more fruitful to attribute the inadequate preparation of Black students to a political system organized around the principle of White Supremacy? Since *Brown v. Board of Ed.*, has anything changed except the level of hypocrisy?

Today, there is much fanfare about a law, passed with bipartisan enthusiasm, designed, supposedly, to raise scholastic achievement, especially that of the "minorities." But it has turned out that the No Child Left Behind Act is *predicated on leaving millions of children behind*, most of whom are precisely children of color and who are being driven out of the educational system at an accelerating rate.

Lack of motivation? Is it Black parents who have demanded that the teachers of their children be largely inexperienced, incompetent, and uninterested? Did Black parents insist on the shortage of books in their schools, on the cutbacks in art, music, and other enrichment opportunities taken for granted in the more well-to-do suburban schools? Was it Black students and their parents who clamored for an end to open enrollment? Was it they who closed down affirmative action in higher education? Was it they who requested that tuition be raised to unaffordable levels for those below middle class status? Was it Black prisoners who were responsible for the termination of the Pell grants in 1994, so that higher education is no longer available to them?

And if poor Black youth view as pointless what passes for the education that is inflicted on them, could it be, given the job market, that it is for many of them, in fact, pointless? If some Black youth have come to believe that studiousness is a white trait, who is it who created that stereotype and for generations pounded it into them until it became internalized? And is it surprising that, given the way schools function, Black children see themselves in an adversarial relation with teachers and administrators, see school as a demeaning experience that is part and parcel of the daily humiliation they experience in society generally? It should be clear to those whose eyes are not clouded with bigotry that resistance to the organized child abuse that goes by the name of the educational system should not be interpreted as glorification of ignorance, as it is depicted to be.

Meanwhile, there is a growing educational crisis involving *white* boys, who increasingly view reading and academic achievement as "girly."

RAPE AND THE BLACK MAN

While the Black man is associated in the public mind with crime generally, it is rape which is considered his special domain. David Horowitz, infamous for his McCarthyite assaults on universities in the name of academic freedom and his re-writing of Black history, informs us that in one given year Blacks committed 20,000 rapes against white women while white men committed only 200 against Black women.[15] We shall examine the actual statistics shortly. But let us step back and look at rape and the historical record.

The promotion of the myth of the Black brute lusting for pure white maidenhood was key in launching the terror that overthrew Reconstruction and brought on Jim Crow and Black disenfranchisement. It also helped swing Northern public opinion in support of turning the South back to the rule of the old plantation elite. And it was also used effectively in breaking up the tenuous alliance between Blacks and poor white farmers against the plutocracy during the Populist movement of the 1890s. It has remained a potent staple in justifying racist oppression down to the very present.

The image of the Black rapist received its classic expression in Hollywood's wildly popular *Birth of a Nation*, a film glorifying the Ku Klux Klan. Boasted Thomas Dixon, author of the novel upon which the film was based, "The real purpose of my film was to revolutionize northern sentiment by [our] presentation of history...Every man who comes out of our theaters is a Southern partisan for life." And they came in droves, an unprecedented 27 million viewers. Requested by Woodrow Wilson, it was the first film ever to be shown in the White House. And after the screening, a deeply moved Wilson remarked, "It is like writing history with lightning. My only regret is that it is all so terribly true."[16]

The Big Lie, spread endlessly in newspapers, political speeches, novels, and history books, was part of a more general theme. Concerning the African-American, wrote Ulrich B. Phillips, the most authoritative Southern historian of his time, whose national influence lingers to this day, "Those who were brought to America, and their descendants, have acquired a certain amount of civilization, the result of their association with civilized white people. Several keen-sighted students have already detected a tendency of the negroes, where segregated in the black belt, to lapse back toward barbarism."[17] This theme was also reflected in the popular literature of the day, with such titles as The Negro: A Beast, by Charles Carrol, and Robert M. Shufeldt's The Negro: a Menace to American Civilization.

Rape was the cry that set off howling lynch mobs. Lynching was then the preferred tool of social control, rather than the mass incarceration of recent years, for Blacks were still needed in the fields. Mississippi's Governor Vardaman in 1903 thundered, "We would be justified in slaughtering every Ethiop on the earth to preserve unsullied the honor of the Caucasian home."[18] And 35 years later, Theodore Bilbo of Mississippi, filibustering an anti-lynching bill on the floor of the Senate, denounced "the lust and lasciviousness of the rape fiend in his diabolical effort to despoil the womanhood of the Caucasian race."[19] While the accusation of rape served as the pretext for most white mob violence, it was Black political resistance that was the real cause, such as insisting on going to the polls, being part of a Black militia, demanding payment due for work performed. Even becoming too successful economically invited the noose.

During World War I, the U.S. Army, under President Wilson, sent a dire warning to the French authorities about the uncontrollable lust of African-American troops then stationed in that country. The French were urged to avoid all social contact with them. Two generations later, President Dwight Eisenhower was quite reluctant to enforce Supreme Court integration orders, expressing sympathy for white parents who objected to having, as he put it, a "big black buck" sit next to their daughter.

Just as the leading white women's pacifist group joined in warning against fraternization with Black troops in France during World War I, eighty years later, feminists decided to seize upon the most notorious rape case of a generation to launch an "educational" campaign about violence against women. We are speaking here of the so-called Central Park Jogger case, involving the supposed gang rape of a white female stockbroker by a group of predominantly Black youth. Despite the case's weakness, including clear evidence of prosecutorial misconduct, the feminists attacked anyone who suggested there were some striking similarities to the Scottsboro Boys frame-up of the 1930s. Convicted by the media and a tainted jury, it was only after most of the boys had served long sentences that the real perpetrator of the assault confessed and the boys were finally exonerated -- reluctantly, to be sure.

RAPE AND THE BLACK WOMAN

The solicitude for white maidenhood is indeed touching, hearkening back to the golden age of Southern chivalry, when wives of plantation owners lived in constant humiliation as their husbands routinely raped slave women and often forced them to become their concubines. Gallant Southern gentlemen capable of rape? Ridiculous. One doesn't rape a "whore."

Deborah Gray White in her *Ar'n't I a Woman?*:

"One of the most prevalent images of Black women in ante-bellum America was of a person governed almost entirely by her libido...By the 19th century, coarse jokes about 'negro wenches' were commonplace...It was conventional wisdom that Black women were actually happy to be sexually taken by white men. White men never had to use authority or violence to obtain compliance from slave women because of their loose morals."[20]

In the 1890s, a *New York Sun* reporter called the Black women of South Carolina's St. Helena Island prostitutes almost without exception.[22] And over a century later, national radio host Don Imus would call the Black women basketball players of Rutgers "nappy-headed ho's." Losing his job for a hot minute, he has picked up another multi-million-dollar gig.

Back to Deborah White: "It was only natural that in

the South there was no such thing as the crime of rape of a Black woman...The rape of African women was widely practiced even in the Middle Passage where, unlike the males, the women and girls were not shackled, in order to be more easily accessible to the criminal whims and sexual desires of seamen, and few attempts were made to keep the crew members of slave ships from molesting African women."[22]

While the rape of Black women by white men was commonplace under slavery, it did not cease after the Civil War. Gutman quotes a letter from a Mississippi Black man to the Kansas Governer asking for advice about migration "The white men here take our wives and daughters and do with them as they please, and we are shot if we say anything about it..."[23]

In Richmond, Virginia, Elsa Barkley Brown relates how after the Civil War "the most likely-looking negro women" were regularly rounded up, "thrown into cells, robbed and ravished at the will of the guard." The people in the vicinity of the jail testified "to hearing women scream frightfully almost every night."[24] (We have come a long way since then: the rape of Black female prisoners, while widespread around the country, is now done a great deal more discreetly.)

In the South, until relatively recently, the number of white men convicted of raping a Black woman ranged from zero to none. Either prosecutors refused to charge them or juries refused to convict them or judges lessened the charges, or if found guilty, were simply given a small fine. Nor could Black women expect any justice from the federal government. As J. Edgar Hoover was reported to have remarked, he was "not going to send the FBI in every time some nigger woman says she's been raped."

SO WHO ARE THE RAPISTS?

Let's move from myth to reality. The National Victim Center estimates that almost 700,000 rapes are committed annually. Only 2 percent of the perpetrators of those rapes are convicted and imprisoned. Therefore, the hundreds of thousands of men each year who commit rape are freely walking the streets. Over the course of a decade that number rises into the millions.

Eighty percent of rapes against women are committed by people of the same racial background. Further, the same percentage of Black and white women are rape victims. In fact, more than three-quarters of rapes are committed by people known to the victim, often family or household members. Over half of the rape victims report that their rape occurred in their home or in the home of a friend or relative. Often, the assaults take the form of "date rapes."

As for general assaults on women, more women seek medical treatment in hospitals for injuries from domestic violence than from all muggings, car accidents, and rapes combined. Since the domestic violence that victimizes women overwhelmingly involves partners of the same "race" – the percentage of interracial relationships being quite low – and since studies have shown no significant difference in the rates of domestic violence by men of different racial groups, then given that whites are a large majority of the population, domestic violence is perpetrated overwhelmingly by *white* men.

Putting all these figures together, it is clear that physical assaults on women generally, and rape in particular, is *not* a predominantly Black-perpetrated crime, much less typically a Black-perpetrated crime against white women. What these figures prove is that the great majority of rapists are *white* men, numbering, as we have said, in the millions. But one certainly wouldn't learn this from the mainstream media, which bombards its audience with lurid accounts precisely of the rape of white women by Black men.

Though women are nine times more likely to be a victim of violent crime at home than in the streets, the media never finds such assaults and rapes newsworthy. The hysteria about the Black rapist contains a great irony. For one has only to look at the wide range of complexions among African-Americans today, complexions not found in West Africa from which they were kidnapped, to observe the results of the truly massive scale of the rape of Black women by white men, during slavery times and after.

Just as fear of Black men was stoked to overthrow Reconstruction in the South and restore the regime of white supremacy, so that fear has since been promoted throughout the country to justify every outrage against the Black community generally, and Black men in particular, especially police outrages, as well as to roll back the gains of the Black freedom movement of the 1950s and '60s.

THE DUKE LACROSSE CASE

Some years ago, the media treated the public to a huge man-bites-dog story. A Black woman came forward claiming to have been performing with another Black woman for a number of white jocks from Duke, an elite Southern university, after which she was raped What made it a man-bites-dog story was that the Black woman's claim of rape by white men seemed to have been taken seriously by the local white District Attorney, who began a vigorous prosecution. But here is where the tale reverts back to its familiar formula: Unlike the cases where a Black man is charged with raping a white women, the accused rapists were able to call upon the services of some of the most high-powered attorneys in the country (who would eventually run up a bill into the millions of dollars). Unlike the cases of Black defendants, which are shrouded in silence after the prosecutor's version of events has been dutifully spread by the media and accepted as gospel, and conviction a foregone conclusion, in this case the media's love fest was with *defense* counsel, whose "proofs" of innocence were given round-the-clock coverage, while media pundits consistently ridiculed the prosecutor's case and questioned his motives. Unlike the cases of Black defendants where their alleged white victims were treated with deference and sympathy, here the alleged Black victim was continually referred to as a "stripper" with all the immoral connotations associated with that term, rather than as the college student and mother she was, for whom stripping was but a rarely employed means to pay for her tuition. In the end, the case

231

was taken out of the prosecutor's hands and then dismissed, whereupon, hauled before the local bar association, he was disbarred for perpetrating a miscarriage of justice -- all absolutely unprecedented.

What we find outrageous in the entire affair is that assuming this was a miscarriage of justice, there have been throughout our history and continuing to this day thousands of miscarriages of justice where prosecutors have framed Black men for rape. And rather than being disbarred, the prosecutors have even advanced their careers, thanks to such frame-ups. For such miscarriages of justice no prosecutor has ever been punished, no huge compensation awarded to the falsely accused, as in the Duke case, no huge public indignation, no happy endings. Rather than seeing .in this case confirmation of the racist double-standard by the criminal-justice system and the media, the Right-wingers have turned it into a cause celebre for the proposition that there is indeed a double-standard of justice, but one that discriminates against whites! We are told that members of the Duke lacrosse team were victims of "political correctness," victims of a liberal ideology which supposedly asserts that it is Blacks in every situation who are the innocent parties.

So let us join in offering our sympathy to the golden boys of Duke, coming from the "best families," and just having had a little innocent drunken fun enjoying the degradation of two Black working women.

MURDER AND THE BLACK MAN

Along with rape, the media keeps a drumbeat going on African-American homicide, especially when the victim is white. In fact, as with rape, it is the media which is most responsible for the general impression that Black-on-white homicide is both commonplace and typical. Actually, as in the case of rape, only a small percentage of murders are committed by strangers. A third of female murder victims are killed by their husbands or boy-friends. The vast majority of murders are the result of "white-on-white" violence. (When is that phrase ever used?) "The low number of killings by strangers," observes the *New York Times*, "belies the common imagery that New Yorkers are vulnerable to arbitrary attacks on the streets, or die in robberies that turn fatal."[25] The *Times* does not go on to explain who is responsible for that "common imagery." Invited to be on hand by the local police, the media are Johnny-on-the-spot, capturing the Black man's "perp walk" for local TV's evening news. They are also always obliging in televising the police department's artist sketches of rape and murder suspects on the loose, invariably Blacks or Latinos of dark complexion.

Contrary to the claims of David Horowitz and his band of neo-cons (an apt description, for they are not only neo-conservatives but neo-confidence men), whites are not the victims of Black violence gone wild. In the 30 years from 1976 to 2005, for example, 86 percent of whites were killed by other whites.

While one will look in vain in the media for coverage

233

of the positive achievements of African-Americans (except in sports and entertainment (they've got "natural rhythm"), it is never stingy about publicizing Black crime. And the more grizzly, the more generous the coverage. Such coverage has another motive, in addition to the commercial one of pandering to the public's taste for lurid sensationalism. Its usefulness as a partisan weapon was demonstrated in the George H. W. Bush presidential campaign, successfully tapping into the eternal white nightmare. Here was the Black rapist Willie Horton, paroled by Democratic Party Governor and Presidential candidate Michael Dukakis, immediately committing murder upon his release. So the choice was made clear in the incessant Republican political ads: Either vote Republican or cower before masses of Blacks running beserk. But as we have already pointed out, beyond specific election campaigns, stoking fear of Black crime is indispensable in garnering public support for the Right-wing agenda.

One of the difficulties for those trying to link murder to race is the fact that the *white American* murder rate is much greater than that of *white Europeans*. Jamil Al-Amin, formerly known as the civil rights activist H. Rap Brown (now languishing in prison in revenge for his previous role in the movement, although the official and trumped-up charge is murder), once famously noted, "Violence is as American as cherry pie." And so it is. No other country in the world has been shaped by so much violence, even leaving out of account the genocide against the native peoples, the routine violence surrounding the institution of slavery, and the innumerable wars waged by Washington. The history of the South is particularly murderous. With a much smaller population, South Carolina in 1890 reported three times the number of homicides as New England. While the wild frontier states of Kansas and Nebraska together counted less than 50 murders in that year, Texas had 184. Wisconsin had 20 murders but Mississippi recorded 106. Michigan 31, but Alabama 108

As C. Vann Woodword describes, "The South seems to have been one of the most violent communities of comparable size in all Christendom. The record of violence should not be hastily attributed to the Negro for at least in South Carolina,. Kentucky, and Texas, white men killed much more often in proportion to their numbers, than did Negroes...Nor could lower-class whites bear disproportionate blame, for the newspapers of the day were crowded with homicidal frays between lawyers, planters, railroad presidents, doctors, even preachers, and particularly editors. Guns blazed in banks, courtrooms, and schoolhouses, as well as in bars and ginhouses."[26]

The special violence of the white South can be attributed to a culture in which the plantation owner was his own law, or simply appointed the law in his district, a law sanctioning the brutalization of Black men and women. This could not but have a brutalizing effect on Southern white society as a whole.

As for the struggles of labor, no other country has had such a bloody history, to which we have already alluded.

THE REALITY OF GHETTO VIOLENCE
AND WHAT'S BEHIND IT

It would be absurd to deny that there is a level of violence in the ghetto greater than that of other communities. Drive-by shootings, the killing of gang members and innocent bystanders are real, as well as the complaints of community residents about their insecurity. The percentage of homicides of Black youth does far exceed that of white youth. Surely, it will be argued, this demonstrates the greater proclivity of Blacks for violence and crime.

But the great majority of the violence and criminal activity in the ghetto is connected to the drug trade, to drug turf wars. This kind of violence hearkens back to the 1920s, Chicago being the class example, where rival mobsters – Italian, Jewish, Irish, and German – routinely gunned down one another. Such violence was intimately connected to corrupt cops and corrupt politicians on mob payrolls. Mob turf wars were often tied to the battles of rival political machines. That chaotic situation lasted until a sufficient number of innocent whites were caught in the crossfire, causing a popular uproar that could not be ignored. It was then that crime became "organized" and rival gangs entered into a negotiated arrangement sanctioned by the highest political authorities.

But unlike that situation in Chicago where the killing of innocent whites created irresistible political pressures for reform – a pattern followed throughout the country – the loss of innocent Black life has evoked only a shrug from most of the white public and the powers-that-be. Further, the image of a ghetto out of control is highly useful politically, reinforcing the stereotypes that are so vital for repression of the Black community.

Who is it that organizes crime? Is it the mobs themselves, the Mafia and other criminal gangs that have sprung up more recently? Yes, the various crime families do come to agreements on the distribution of territories, etc., along the lines of modern corporate cartels. But if gang agreements are to be effective, then the cooperation of the police is essential in enforcing those agreements, and they do this in part by putting away the independents, the free-lancers. Thus, everyone gets a piece of the action. Naturally, the police sergeants and captains, and the brass above them, are not going to tolerate the enrichment of the cop on the beat while they themselves are shut out. So there is a distribution up the line. But again, the politicians are not going to stand by and allow all that money to be monopolized by the police. The politicians have to get their cut of the take. Recall the plane which crashed with a Mafia bag man carrying several million dollars to the Nixon campaign. So it is the power structure that organizes crime. The pervasive links of organized crime with politicians are amply documented in the Kefauver Senate investigation into organized crime of the early 1950s.

Incredible? Well, what are Organized Crime's chief sources of illegal income? Drug dealing, loan-sharking, prostitution, illegal gambling, and other rackets. None of these can exist if the public doesn't know where to patronize them. If the public knows, the police know.

To protect their credibility, law enforcement agencies stay active, enough to satisfy the public as well as keep criminal activity from getting out of control. So periodically some lambs are thrown to the wolves, sometimes by agreement with the gangs themselves, and law enforcement is seen doing its job. Yet somehow or other, with all the arrests and convictions, the drugs flow on, the loan sharks shark on. If it was really desired to eliminate organized crime, it could be done, as the power of this relatively small number of armed gangsters is no match for the might of the state. The point is that violence in the ghettos will be sharply reduced when the Establishment decides to *organize* the drug trade there, as well.

And yet are we not contradicting ourselves? On the one hand we dispute that African-Americans commit a disproportionate amount of street crime, and now we admit that they do. No, we do not dispute that African-Americans, like every ethnic group in this country's history during the period they have been at or near the bottom of the economic ladder, have committed a disproportionate amount of street crime. What is challenged here is the actual extent of that disproportion and the wildly disproportionate scale of arrest and punishment, and, again, not only as applied to street crime, but especially to *all* crime.

RACISM OF THE CRIMINAL JUSTICE SYSTEM

We hope we have begun to puncture some of the myths concerning Black criminality. Now we shall put forward an alternative explanation for the vastly disproportionate involvement of African-Americans in the criminal justice system. One can easily drown in a torrent of statistics. At the least it can be mind-numbing. But it is necessary to slosh through some of the figures. For behind them lie anguish, broken lives, the ripping apart of family and community life.

Let us take the example of California, the state with the country's largest prison system. In fact, it holds one out of every five of the prison population nationwide. On any given day, almost half of African-American men in their 20s are under the control of California's criminal justice system. That compares to 10 percent of Latino and 5 percent of white men. For the nation as a whole, one-third of African-American men in their 20s are under criminal justice supervision. Right-wing ideologists will say that all this simply confirms that Blacks commit more crime, no mystery there. And yet –

In 1995, a commission appointed by New York State's law-and-order Republican Governor Pataki found that people of color were treated more harshly than whites for comparable offenses. Another study led by the former president of the American Society of Criminology found little difference in the rate of violent crime by race, and little difference in the crime rate generally by race. What was found were substantial differences between Black and white *arrest* rates. These differences are accounted for by the police *targeting* people of color, especially African-Americans, a word which more adequately describes what is happening than the more benign-sounding racial *profiling*. The police are frank to admit they concentrate on communities of color. But they justify it on the grounds that "that is where the crime is." However, as Tim Wise has pointed out – a writer who has done much to expose many of the dynamics of our white supremacist society – if the police were consistent, they would, for example, be setting up roadblocks in white suburbs to catch drunk drivers. For whites make up the overwhelming majority of DWI's who, by the way, are responsible for the deaths of more than 10,000 people each year, far more deaths than are caused by illicit drugs. Such roadblocks rarely happen. But, like checkpoints in Iraq, they are set up routinely in the occupied Black communities.

This past year, almost three-quarters of a million people were stopped and frisked in New York City (the number has been rising steadily over the years), more than half of whom were African-Americans, in a city where they constitute only 22 percent of the population. Less than 20 percent of those stopped were white, although they constitute 44 percent of the population. Of those stopped, the police found grounds for arresting only a tiny fraction, while a similarly tiny fraction were merely given summonses. So how do the police justify continuing to carry out a policy that produces such meager results. Aside from the fact that their rationale has no legal validity, it has been proven to be utterly dishonest with the recent disclosure of figures regarding stop-and-frisks in the New York City subway system. These have grown ten-fold in the last several years. Blacks and Latinos comprise half of subway ridership but make up 90 percent of those stopped by the police. Whites constitute 35 percent of the riders but they make up only 8 percent of those stopped. Obviously, there is no issue here of crime-prone neighborhoods.

In the nation's capital, 85 percent of Black men will have been arrested at some point in their lives. That African-Americans and Latinos are indeed racially targeted is shown by the disproportionate percentage of their arrests compared to whites that later proved to be unfounded. So, for example, in California there were four times the number of unfounded arrests of Blacks as of whites. In Oakland, the rate of such arrests was 12 times that of whites; in San Diego, six times. In California, as well as in the rest of the country, communities of color also experience a higher rate of searches and seizures that are later ruled to be illegal. Some of the most egregious practices of racial targeting concern Black motorists. Statistics gathered by the police departments themselves reveal that, for example, on the notorious Interstate 95 running through Maryland, 70 percent of the stops made by police were of African-Americans, and only 17 percent were of whites. Yet drugs were not found disproportionately among the Blacks stopped. A Department of Justice study found that nationwide, Black drivers were stopped at about the same rate as whites. But those who were stopped were three times more likely to be searched. And yet searches of white drivers were four times more likely to produce evidence of criminal activity than of Blacks. Similarly, while almost half of those searched by the US Customs Service were African-Americans and Latinos, the percentage of these caught with drugs was less than their percentage in the general population. Black women were x-rayed at Customs more often than white women and yet they were less than half as likely to be found with contraband.

A particularly insidious strategy in targeting African-Americans and Latinos is the crackdown on what are called quality-of-life crimes. This flows from the so-called broken window theory of policing, which Giuliani boasts was responsible for his "extraordinary" success in reducing crime while he was Mayor of New York. The idea is that the commission of serious crimes can be headed off by arresting and imprisoning perpetrators of minor crimes, since such crimes supposedly eventually lead to major ones. Just as hard drug use is supposedly preceded by smoking marijuana, so fare beating, if not dealt with by an iron fist, will surely, lead to homicide.

There is nothing new under the sun, and the recollection by Frederick Douglass of one of his own slave experiences is quite relevant: "Mr. Hopkins always managed to have one or more of his slaves to whip every Monday morning...His plan was to whip for the smallest offenses to prevent the commission of large ones."[27]

All of which suggests that this policy has nothing to do with quality of life and everything to do with quality of control.

(Incidentally, nowhere is the hypocrisy of the "law-and-order" crowd more sickening than as expressed in their adulation of Giuliani, a darling of the Republican Party who, while he was in office, ran one of the most lawless administrations in. New York City history, a lawlessness for which he was repeatedly berated even by a judiciary which has had a high threshold of forbearance in that regard.)

Mass quality-of-life arrests began with Giuliani's Police Commissioner Bratton, who then went on to head up the continuing scandal-ridden Los Angeles Police Department. Under Bratton, those who committed infractions which had previously been ignored or had only drawn a desk ticket, were hauled through the system, including such menaces to society as the wielders of squeegees, graffiti artists, people walking down the street with a bag containing an open can of beer, and homeless men sleeping on park benches, the majority of the latter being war veterans. So pleased with this strategy were authorities across the country that the policy was soon copied everywhere. Arrests skyrocketed, especially for drug use, and among drug arrests, especially those for marijuana. Needless to say, the targets of this crackdown were African-American and Latino youth, whose quality of life and that of their communities profoundly *deteriorated*.

Racist targeting by the police is just the beginning of disparate treatment. It continues in the hands of prosecutors. In California, analysis of 700,000 criminal cases between 1987 and 1990 revealed that every aspect of pretrial bargaining was marked by inequities: whites had their charges dropped, their cases dismissed, their punishment mitigated, and their criminal record wiped clean in far higher proportion than people of color. These disparities continue on into the sentencing phase. Blacks nationwide are 4 1/2 times more likely as whites to be put behind bars for the same offense. Given the same criminal history, they receive longer sentences. African-Americans who have never been imprisoned are six times more likely to be sentenced to prison than similarly-situated whites. In the case of Black teenagers, the ratio is 9 to 1.

In the United States, only about a quarter of inmates are white, but they constitute two-thirds of those on probation.

There is also discrimination in the setting of bail, so that people of color are more likely to be incarcerated while awaiting trial, something which negatively impacts their ability to assist in their own defense, as well as prejudicing jurors.

YOUTH OF COLOR AS SPECIAL TARGETS.

While Black juveniles are treated with ferocity by the criminal justice system, when it comes to white juvenile crime, the attitude is "Boys will be boys." When Black and white teenagers commit the same offense, police are seven times more likely to charge Black youth with a felony. Black youth are jailed at a rate almost ten times greater than even their supposed crime rate would warrant.

While both white and Black youth carry weapons at roughly the same rate, Black youth are arrested on weapons charges at twice the rate of whites. Similarly, while Black and white youth engage in fights at about the same rate, Black youth are arrested for aggravated assault in connection with those fights at three times that of whites.

In 1995, while a majority of juveniles arrested were white, three-quarters of the juveniles sent to adult prisons were youth of color. As a consequence, they were twice as likely to be beaten in prison and five times more likely to be raped. Their rate of suicide in adult prisons was eight times greater than that in juvenile facilities.

The image of the young Black thug is a media staple. But on occasion, challenges to that image have managed to slip in. There was the July 18, 1990 *New York Times* op-ed column by Evan Stark, Rutgers University Professor of Public Administration, which pointed out that while FBI figures showed half of the juvenile *arrests* for the most violent crimes were of Black teenagers, the rate of *incarceration* of Black youth was 44 times higher than that of white youth, that when white and Black teenagers committed the same offense, police were *seven times* more likely to charge Black teenagers with a felony, and courts far more likely to imprison them.[28] Of course, that single blow of truth could not dent prevailing stereotypes.

Years after the Stark piece, a study found that rates of violence for white and Black youth were similar in adolescence but that on arriving at young adulthood, that rate had increased more for African-Americans. This was attributed to their lack of stable employment. Just as the "pathology" of the poor Black family boils down to one thing –lack of jobs – so does the greater rate of street crime among young Black adults. The most reliable correlation in tracking the rise and fall of street crime is not the rate of incarceration or the harshness of punishment but the rate of *unemployment*. For as they become teenagers and acquire social awareness, Black youth come to realize that building a normal family is permanently beyond their reach and that they have been given a life sentence of pauperdom, all before any crime has ever been committed (Like so many other government statistics, such as the cost of living or the US budget, unemployment figures are absolutely fraudulent, grossly understated, particularly when measuring Black joblessness.)

While on the subject of the harsh and discriminatory treatment of Black youth, mention should be made of the foster care system. In New York City, for example, 90 percent of the children taken from their biological parents into foster care are Black.

The repression of youth of color takes a particularly vicious form in the guise of fighting youth gangs. California law, enacted in the late 1980s, permits a member of a gang labeled as criminal to be convicted for crimes committed by fellow gang members, even if that person had nothing to do with the crime. Simply by virtue of gang membership, if convicted of a crime, two or three years might be added to the sentence. In California, as well as in some other states, three or more members of a gang hanging out together in public could be arrested for loitering. The opportunity for harassing youth and denying them the right of peaceful assembly was not long in being acted upon. Beginning in Los Angeles in 1987, authorities used anti-gang laws to get injunctions against alleged gang members for engaging in a long list of *legal* activities. For example, in San Jose, gang members were enjoined in 1993 in a four-block neighborhood from standing, sitting, walking, driving, or appearing anywhere in public view with each other. They were also barred from carrying pens, nails or razor blades, climbing trees or fences, and wearing gang colors in the neighborhood. To grasp the impact of this on the Black community, in Los Angeles County about 70 percent of Black men are listed as gang members. Nearly half of those so categorized have no arrest record. In Denver, while Blacks constituted only 5 percent of the population, they accounted for over 90 percent of listed gang members.

At the 2007 Puerto Rican Day parade in New York City, 207 young people suspected of being gang members were arrested "to prevent violent or threatening behavior." Their crime, in many instances, was simply that of wearing clothing or beads containing "gang colors". This followed on the heels of the arrest of 30 Black youth on the same pretext who were headed to a funeral to pay respects to a murdered classmate. All were jailed, although the charges against them, even if true, warranted only desk appearance tickets.

Typically, liberals who expressed indignation at these sweeps pointed to the fact that many of those arrested were "innocent," that is, were really not gang members. The liberals did not oppose the arrest of *real* gang members, even though those "guilty" of such membership had not committed any crime. The liberals saw the problem in terms of mistaken identity rather than that members of street organizations possess the same civil liberties as everyone else, and that these kinds of sweeps and round-ups are tactics typical of a police state.

247

The fact is that street organizations have long been a feature of urban social life of youth of all ethnic groups. They perform the vital function of giving young people a sense of belonging that is often lacking, extend friendship, affection and protection in an atmosphere of increasing social hostility and police harassment, and provide a support system in an economy that has cast them aside.

Of course, there are street gangs which are organized specifically to engage in crime. Some of these are linked to the Mafia, although they are never called street gangs. But the great majority of street organizations are formed for social reasons. While attention is directed toward street organizations as crime perpetrators, it is the police swarming the ghetto which is the largest and most dangerous criminal gang. Aside from corruptly protecting when not promoting street crime and lining their own pockets, the police department's day-to-day abuse of people of color, intimidation, brutality, false arrests, illegal searches, and their routine displays of disrespect, constitute criminal activity that dwarfs the street crime they are purportedly there to prevent. For the principal purpose of "law and order" in poverty-ridden neighborhoods, and especially the ghettos, is not to protect the community but to keep the community "in line," especially the youth. The role of the police is primarily psychological: to enforce meekness, passivity, obedience to the system of white supremacy, and therefore to the cops charged with enforcing it.

"THE WAR ON DRUGS"

Blacks have always been disproportionately represented in the jails and prisons of the United States. But that disparity sharply increased as a result of the so-called War on Drugs, ushered in by a wave of draconian laws, the most notorious example being the New York Rockefeller drug law which, among other things, called for 15-years-to-life for possession or sale of four ounces of cocaine. The "War on Drugs" caused a sharp upsurge both in the total number of inmates and the proportion of people of color, especially African-Americans.

While first officially proclaimed under the Nixon Administration, the drug war really took off under Ronald Reagan. No accident that he began his presidential run in Philadelphia, Mississippi, a Klan hotbed and scene of the lynching of three civil rights activists, Cheney, Goodman and Schwerner. Reagan's campaign message, though left implicit, was clear: The days of concessions to African-Americans were over.

The "War on Drugs" was part of a strategy of racist repression. While in 1980 African-Americans constituted 23 percent of the drug arrests, ten years later they represented 40 percent, and 60 percent of the drug convictions. Between 1985 and 1995, Blacks sentenced to state prison for drug offenses rose more than 700 percent, while the number of Latinos quadrupled. Today, while half of the whites arrested for drugs are not charged, the same is true for only a quarter of African-Americans. At the same time, while in 1980 there were 600,000 arrested on drug charges, that number had tripled by 2006.

Obviously, the drug war isn't about protecting the public from violent crime. For example, the first two years of operation of the California "Three Strikes and You're Out" law resulted in more life sentences being imposed on marijuana users than on all the murderers, rapists and kidnappers combined. Those imprisoned for drug offenses increased by over 1000 percent. A study analyzing the quarter-million drug law offenders in state prison as of 1997 found that nearly a quarter of them had *no history of violence, no gun involvement, no high-level drug dealing, and no prior convictions for non-drug offenses.*

In New York State, while in 1980 roughly the same number of African-Americans, Latinos and whites were sent to prison for drug offenses, *in the next two decades there was a seismic shift in those proportions.* Thus, within a few years the number of white youth arrested for selling drugs had gone down from 18 to 12, while the number of Black youth arrested shot up from 80 to 21,304. In Baltimore, in 1991, 11,000 of 13,000 arrested for drugs were Black. In Columbus, Ohio, while constituting only 8 percent of the population, Blacks made up 90 percent of the drug arrests. Georgia passed a "Two Strikes and You're Out" law permitting the imposition of a life sentence for a second drug offense and, as of 1995, while life sentences had been handed down to 16 percent of the eligible African-Americans, only 1 percent of eligible whites were similarly sentenced.

Nationwide, by 1996, *90 percent of those incarcerated for drug offenses were either African-American or Latino. 91 percent of those sentenced in federal court for crack cocaine offenses were African-American, while only 2 percent were white,* thus seeming to bear out the impression that crack was the particular drug of choice of communities of color, especially African-Americans. Yet the *National Institute of Drug Abuse reported- .that crack cocaine was smoked by more whites than Blacks.* Thus in 2003, while Blacks constituted only a third of the crack users, they made up four-fifths of those charged. As a matter of fact, the *Los Angeles Times* found that from 1988 to 1994, not a single white was convicted of a crack offense in federal court.

If there were still any doubt about the anti-Black aims behind the War on Drugs, they were surely put to rest with the law making the penalty for crack offenses 100 times greater than powdered cocaine. This has now been admitted to be a miscarriage of justice even by members of the Establishment, including a growing number of judges calling for a narrowing of this disparity. Congress has finally reduced the disparity, but the disparity still remains.

Disparate sentencing was originally justified on the grounds that crack was supposedly much more dangerous than powdered cocaine, that it produces a crazed state more liable to lead to violent crime. It has since been proven that there is little appreciable difference in their effects. Actually, the violence associated with crack stems from turf battles among crack dealers and between corrupt police and crack dealers battling for control of lucrative markets.

Turf battles involving the police? Consult the notorious case of Adam Abdul Hakeem a/k/a Larry Davis, who made the mistake of trying to *stop* selling drugs for the cops. So several dozen of New York's Finest came calling to do him in. (They later claimed they were simply trying to serve a warrant on him, a nonexistent warrant, as it turned out.) Engaging in a shootout to save his life, he wounded six policemen, was tried for attempted murder, acquitted, then tried for murdering some drug dealers, acquitted again, tried once more on still another charge, and acquitted once again. Finally, he was put away on weapons charges. Years later, he was stabbed to death by a fellow inmate while in the process of cooperating in a media project to expose police corruption.

Then there are the string of official commission reports on police brutality and corruption, including complicity in the drug trade, issued with boring regularity. Such reports get 15 minutes of attention and force a periodic dismantling of "elite" anti-narcotics units, which are then reconstituted, only to be dismantled once again. That the police are neck-deep in the drug trade may still be a secret to the white suburbanite but is hardly news to the ghetto dweller.

Government at all levels has rarely gone after the real drug kingpins, concentrating instead on low-level drug pushers and users, targeting African-Americans and Latinos, and generally ignoring white drug criminals. Today, the overwhelming majority of drug arrests are for possession, rather than for their sale or manufacture, and almost half of these arrests are for marijuana possession. While white men are arrested on drug charges at twice the rate of Black men, black men are 12 times more likely to be imprisoned.

The explanation offered for the racial disparities in drug crime prosecution is the same as that offered for the disparities in prosecution of crimes generally: Blacks, we are told, are the most numerous drug users and dealers, and therefore it is only natural that the prison population should reflect this. But here is the dirty little secret: *The Department of Health and Human Services found that between 1991 and 1993, five times as many whites used cocaine as African-Americans. Moreover, five times more whites than Blacks were drug dealers, and dealers generally sell to members of their own ethnic group.* Updates of these studies continue to confirm those findings. A 2007 survey by the Center for Disease Control and Prevention revealed that white high school males are four times more likely than their Black peers to be regular cocaine users, three times more likely to have used heroin, three times more likely to have smoked marijuana, eight times more likely to have used LSD. There are five times more whites than Blacks brought to the hospital for overdosing. As for crystal meth and Ecstasy, among the latest drugs of choice, their use is far more prevalent in white suburbs and rural areas than in urban ghettos.

Despite the fact that whites use hard drugs in greater proportion than Blacks, and bearing in mind that Blacks make up only 12 percent of the population, according to the National Institute of Drug Abuse they comprise
- 35% of those *arrested* for drug possession;
- 55% of those *convicted* for drug possession;
- 74% of those *sentenced* for drug possession.

While whites make up the vast majority of those who use drugs, they make up only 5% of those imprisoned on drug charges.

As in other types of crime, so in the case of drug crimes, whites are more likely to be recipients of official leniency. In California, Latinos are twice and African-Americans three times as likely as whites to be sent to the harsher state prison, rather than county jail or probation. Whites were placed in community-based rehab programs for first-time drug offenses at twice the rate of Blacks or Latinos. And the same holds true regarding drug programs inside prison.

Just how serious the government is in reducing drug use is shown by a fact that while three-quarters of those in prison have a history of substance abuse, prison drug programs are actually being slashed. While in 1991, one-quarter of the inmates were placed in drug programs, six years later the number dropped to one-tenth. Yet the conservative research group, the Rand Corporation, estimated in 1997 that *money spent on drug treatment would reduce serious crime 15 times more effectively than mandatory prison terms*, hardly a revelation to anyone with common sense. The fact that such drug treatment has not been widely implemented only demonstrates that the "War on Drugs" has always been merely a pretext to wage the real war on people of color, especially African-Americans.

Another indicator of the bogus nature of the War on Drugs was the passage, with bipartisan support, after just two minutes of Congressional debate, of the so-called Personal Responsibility Act. That law bars those convicted of the sale or possession of drugs, as well as their families, from ever receiving federally-funded public assistance, including food stamps. Not so penalized are murderers and armed robbers. Instead of discouraging drug use, such measures serve only to reinforce the hopelessness that leads to drug dependence.

The "War on Drugs" has hit Black youth particularly hard as the same disparities apply as in the adult population. Again, contrary to popular opinion (a manufactured public opinion), white youth use and sell drugs as much or more than Black youth, yet Black youth are disproportionately arrested and imprisoned.

Again it must be asked: What really lies behind the so-called War on Drugs?

THE UNITED STATES: WORLD'S ARCH DRUG TRAFFICKER

The supreme irony in the government's war on drugs is that for over half a century *the government itself has been the world's biggest narco-trafficker*. As far back as the 1940s, when the Chinese Red Army drove the US-supported forces of Chang kai-chek off the mainland into Taiwan, remnants of some of Chang's units established themselves in Northern Burma, from which they carried out raids against the new revolutionary government. To finance their operations, they became the major heroin suppliers to the world, a trade which Washington facilitated, because in harassing the Communists they were doing both God's work and that of American imperialism.

Similarly, in Southeast Asia during the Vietnam War era, in the region known as the Golden Triangle because it had become the world's chief exporter of heroin, the CIA used the drug trade to finance the ethnic minorities which had been recruited to fight against the Vietnamese liberation movement. Testimony before Congress exposed the key drug-running role of Air America, a CIA front. Participants in the operation described how CIA and US Agency for International Development (USAID) funds were used to construct more than 150 short landing strips to mountains near opium fields, thus opening these remote areas to the export trade. Said Ron Rickenbach, head of USAID in that region at the time, "1 was on the airstrips. My people were in charge of supplying the aircraft. I was in the area where the opium was grown. I personally witnessed it being placed on Air America planes. We didn't create the opium product. But our presence accelerated it dramatically."[29]

The US-backed drug trade in Southeast Asia ultimately ensnared our own troops, a quarter of whom became addicted. Hailed as heroes as long as they served as cannon fodder, many returning veterans ended up as social debris, homeless, living corpses, to be honored on July 4th and chased off park benches by the police the rest of the year.

A decade later, Washington was confronted with another challenge. The Somoza dictatorship, loyal to the US oligarchy, was overthrown by a popular revolution. The new Sandinista government began a program of reforms to benefit the masses. That was a no-no. And so the CIA was charged with creating the Contras, a small terrorist army made up mostly of former Somoza officers. When, under popular pressure, Congress was forced to prohibit continued Contra funding, a secret operation was set up in the White House basement, which financed the war with cocaine shipped largely from neighboring Honduras.

When the Iran-Contragate scandal was uncovered, Congressional hearings were careful to keep hidden the Government's drug-trafficking role. This would be too shocking to a public raised on the notion of Uncle Sam's rectitude. In the 1980s, a committee headed by Senator and future presidential candidate, John Kerry, nevertheless managed to uncover the fact that the proceeds of drug trafficking operations were used to provide the Contra terrorists with their weapons, planes, pilots, and other supplies. This was confirmed by the CIA's own Inspector General, whose report was, again, buried by the media.

Meanwhile, Washington was giving all-out support to the Islamic mujadaheen of Afghanistan, directly and through its Pakistan ally. Those we denounce today as terrorists were then hailed as freedom-fighters. The CIA organized the flow of heroin from Afghanistan to help finance the predecessors of today's A1-Quaeda in their battle against the Afghan government and Soviet troops. As Alexander Cockburn and Jeffrey St. Clair described in Whiteout: "The Drug Enforcement Agency was well aware that the mujadaheen rebels were deeply involved in the opium trade...Afghan opium production tripled between 1979 and 1982. There was evidence that by 1981 the Afghan heroin producers had captured 60 percent of the heroin market in Western Europe and the United States. These are DEA figures."[30] (See also Alfred McCoy's *The Politics of Heroin*.)

Still later, the US began pouring money into Colombia, which is now the third largest recipient of US foreign aid behind Israel and Egypt. This aid has ostensibly been given to fight drug trafficking, but it is being mainly used to fight a rebel army that proclaims itself on the side of the poor. Actually, it was the Colombian government itself that has for years had been heavily implicated in narcotrafficking, working through paramilitary death squads which it publicly disavowed but which was a creation of the Colombian army. So we have the charade of drug traffickers being extradited and imprisoned in the United States, of US-assisted well-photographed destruction of Colombian coca fields, while cocaine flows across the US border as freely as ever.

Is it surprising, after so many billions have been spent on the war on drugs, after the incarceration of hundreds of thousands, that drugs on the US market are more plentiful, purer and cheaper than ever?

REAL PURPOSE OF THE WAR ON DRUGS

This does not mean that the war on drugs has been a failure. Quite the contrary. For it has scored an important success in snuffing out the African-American resistance movement. First came the government's massive introduction of drugs into Black communities, a huge and complex undertaking obviously beyond the resources of members of the Black community itself. See newsman Gary Webb's detailed account in *Dark Alliance*, based on his series of articles in the *San Jose Mercury News*. It revealed how the White House, the CIA, the FBI, local police, local prosecutors, and judges, among others, were all part of a government drug trafficking conspiracy. For his expose he received not the Pulitzer Prize he so richly deserved but a pink slip, no doubt due to government pressure. His work was ridiculed by the mainstream media, his journalistic integrity impugned. Finally, having been blacklisted and prevented from doing the work that provided meaning to his life, he committed suicide. But even Gary Webb could not believe that the government would introduce drugs into the Black community as part of a deliberate policy to rip it apart and undermine it politically. To conceive that the US government would be capable of that degree of evil is something difficult for even knowledgeable whites to accept, even those aware of the history of so many of Washington's crimes, including its genocidal crimes against the native peoples and those of African descent. But for many African-Americans it is not too much of a stretch. They understand that the introduction of drugs into the ghetto was a form of chemical warfare, that a decision was taken to defuse the "social dynamite" which the Black community represented in the 1960s and 1970s at the height of its militancy. Having made drugs widely available in the ghetto, the powers-that-be then targeted African-Americans for drug prosecutions. Large numbers of Black male youth were put out of action, addicted, incarcerated, or both. Already struggling, the ghettos became scenes of economic devastation. Most important, community solidarity was destroyed as the older generations turned against the youth, while the police set up a network of snitches.

The war on Drugs was not the only strategy used against the Black community. We have already spoken about COINTELPRO. Add police intimidation, especially of ghetto youth, and a policy of non-stop brutality and harassment. These were some of the sticks used to force the community into line. But there were also carrots, among them the "War on Poverty," which slightly improved the circumstances of the masses at a cost of their increased dependency. The "War on Poverty" also winnowed out and co-opted thousands of the most militant and ambitious activists, some of whom became "poverty pimps," supposedly serving as conduits for government programs but in most cases merely siphoning off funds for themselves. Adam Clayton Powell, the Congressman most responsible for originating those programs, complained that at least 70 percent of the monies earmarked for poor communities were going into salaries and administrative expenses, with very little actually reaching the people.

When the government saw that the freedom movement had run out of steam and that the government-funded "grassroots activists" had outlived their usefulness, the anti-poverty programs were shut down. In addition to the poverty pimps, large numbers of former or potential activists, seeing the new opportunities that had been opened up by soul power, turned their back on the movement and entered into an ever-expanding soul-less government bureaucracy, some even achieving the majesty of elective office.

CRIMINAL JUSTICE SYSTEM COMPONENTS

The Police

Let us now break down some of the criminal justice system's various components, beginning with the police, society's "first line of defense."

The perception of the police varies with one's ethnic group and class. The white middle class sees the police as profoundly protective and comforting, a senior version of the Boy Scouts. To many in oppressed communities, however, they are just the opposite: an army of occupation.

At one time, the police were an object of ridicule. In the days of the Charlie Chaplin and Keystone Cops movies, the police were portrayed as bumbling and stupid clowns. It was those whom the cops chased that the audience rooted for. During the 1930s, years of the Great Depression, a time when poverty was general, as was sympathy for the poor and contempt for the fat-bellied socialites, working class whites viewed the police with open hostility, seeing them as protectors of the rich, harassing people who were simply down on their luck. It was a time when the biggest Hollywood stars were Humphrey Bogart, Edward G. Robinson and James Cagney, popular for their gangster roles.

The prosperity brought about by the slaughter of the Second World War, and then the atmosphere of fear during the Cold War, ushered in a growing conservatism and a major shift in attitude toward authority. The supreme virtue was now loyalty, and those who questioned authority were deemed subversive, to be persecuted during the days of Senator McCarthy, and to be treated as objects of contempt during the 1960s, the time of the Hippies and the counter-culture. Conformity was the watchword. The police, and especially the FBI, became the golden boys of US society. Cops were now the defenders of a citizenry under dire threat. There was no end to the number of radio and television shows glorifying the heroes of law and order. It was a time when Blacks replaced Italians in the popular mind as the main perpetrators of crime. And as urban rebellions flared, they were also viewed as the greatest threat to social order. Handcuffed by "bleeding-heart" judges who many believed were literally letting criminals get away with murder, the audience cheered as law-enforcement heroes of the big and little screens burst into homes without a warrant, roughed up prisoners, and cut through other "red tape" (also known as the Bill of Rights).

Portrayed as engaging in dangerous work, risking their lives to protect the public, the real-life situation is quite different. Thus, there are 12 deaths in the line of duty per 100,000 police officers, compared to fishermen who die on the job at a rate almost 10 times greater, loggers 7 times, miners 3 times. Farmers and agricultural workers die at twice the rate of law enforcement officers. Even the job of groundskeeper is more risky. As for the FBI, a grand total of about 50 have been killed in the past 100 years.

The labor movement has become so weak and passive in the past few decades that it is forgotten that the role of the police has been not only to keep Blacks in their place but to make sure that workers of all ethnic backgrounds remain under tight control, especially during strikes. Up through the first third of the 20th century, and even beyond, it was part of the cop's job description to beat up strikers and protect scabs. Today, they are instructed to act with more prudence. But their role in protecting company interests has not changed. When workers are unjustly fired, when there are mass layoffs, when factories close and then re-open half a world away, one surely does not call the police for help.

The police do get summoned in times of political tension to act against "agitators," dissidents, radicals, those who demonstrate in the streets, however legal and peaceful their activities. To this day, police departments around the country have their "Black Desk" and their "Red Desk." Of course they now have their "Muslim Desk," with pervasive and widespread spying on Islamic communities, mosques and campus organizations by the NYC Police Department, even going beyond the borders of the city. It wouldn't be surprising to learn that police departments have now added an "Ecology Desk" to deal with "environmental terrorism."

The police brass are carefully screened to ensure that their oath to the Constitution does not constrain them from trampling upon the liberties of those who oppose the status quo. They, in turn, see to it that the proper attitude filters down through police ranks and becomes part of the "police culture." For the police must be "reliable," ready to carry out whatever lawless deeds are required of them. Where there are doubts about such reliability — for sometimes the rank-and-file do have scruples about carrying out certain actions -- then "elite" units are formed. It is precisely these "elite" units, carefully screened and receiving special training, that turn out to be the most vicious and lawless (just as the School of the Americas, as it was called until recently, trained "elite" Latin-American officers who then became leaders of death squads and supporters of coups when they returned to their home countries). No surprise that the "elite" units are almost all lily-white, at least much whiter than ordinary police units. One of the most notorious of these elite groups was New York Mayor Giuliani's Street Crimes Unit, whose chilling motto was "We Own the Night." That group committed so many atrocities that it was finally forced to disband. But others, "riot police" and SWAT teams, constitute a growing part of the ever more militarized police landscape. The use of SWAT teams has increased tenfold in the past decade.

The history is long and unbroken of the wanton

killing of unarmed Black men and youth by white cops, killings that are almost never punished. (Hundreds of such killings are identified in *Stolen Lives*, published by the October 22 Coalition.) Once in a great while, a killer-cop may receive some mild departmental discipline. On the rarest of occasions, due to public pressure, a policeman may actually be put on trial. But things are so arranged that he is almost always acquitted, whether by a judge or a jury. Most shocking in recent times was the acquittal of the police assassins of the African immigrant Amadou Dialo, shot 43 times in his hallway as he was about to enter his apartment. Not trusting a Bronx jury, which is the one New York county where people of color predominate, the trial was moved to a conservative, overwhelmingly white venue upstate where the jury agreed that Dialo's body was riddled in accordance with proper police procedure.

It should be understood, however, that police misbehavior is not primarily a product of the viciousness or racism of individual cops, is not a matter requiring "sensitivity training." *For the chief function of the police is to be the pit bull of those who rule society, the ones who are holding the leash.*

POLICE VIOLENCE AGAINST BLACKS HISTORY OF

Blacks have always been the special target of police violence, whether by slave patrollers or southern sheriffs. Their job was to preside over a permanent regime of "shock and awe," ensuring due deference both to the institutions of white supremacy and to white people personally. But this has not been limited to southern law-enforcement. In the era of white race riots, North as well as South, when African-Americans were victims of mob beatings, arson and murder, "law and order" invariably joined the mob in the attacks, and then arrested the Black victims rather than the white aggressors. The notorious sheriff Bull Connor in Birmingham had his counterparts in Police Chief Frank Rizzo of Philadelphia and Chief Parker of Los Angeles. A year following Sheriff Jim Clark's savagery at the famous march in Selma, Alabama, the National Association of Sheriffs in a gesture of solidarity elected Clark as their president.

One of the "reforms" won in the 1960s freedom struggles has been that the cop swinging his stick on Black heads may himself be Black. After undercover cops pumped 50 bullets into a car killing African-American Sean Bell and wounding two other Black passengers, all unarmed, New York City Police Commissioner Raymond Kelly professed to be perplexed at how anyone could conceive that the shooting might have had racist overtones. After all, among the undercover shooters were several nonwhites. With that logic there could be nothing racist about law enforcement

266

under the South African apartheid regime. For most of those charged with maintaining order were also Black. Nor could slave whippings be related to white supremacy since they were often carried out by Black slave drivers.

Police brutality is routine and never-ending, even descending to the level of torture. 192 people stepped forward a few years ago to accuse police officers in just two Chicago precincts of beating them, shocking them with electrical devices, and using methods of near-suffocation during a period from the 1970s to the early 1990s. In this connection, the UN Committee Against Torture noted that these allegations received little investigation.

From 1994 through 1997, New York City paid out more than $100 million in damages for police brutality. This shows just how vital such brutality is to the system, that city authorities would rather agree to huge settlements than eliminate the evil, just as corporations consider fines for their criminal behavior a necessary cost of doing business.

Liberals, recognizing that there is a police brutality problem, suggest a need to reform the "police culture." It is indeed a brutal and racist culture, frankly expressed by police benevolent associations and sheriff fraternal orders, who invariably spring to the defense of their members after every incident of unjustified use of force, including murder. A particularly eloquent example of this police culture was the response of New York City's 13 Precinct, located in a Dominican neighborhood in Washington Heights after one of its officers murdered 16-year-old Kevin Cedeno, shooting him in the back after he followed

267

orders to lie prone on an apartment floor. This heroic deed was duly recognized by the cop's colleagues who named him Officer of the Month.

But the police department is not an independent body. It is accountable to the political authorities and it receives the scrutiny of the media, all of whom can be counted on to energetically defend almost every police outrage. Police brutality is the norm, whether the mayor is Democrat or Republican, liberal or conservative. Not only are politicians complicit in it, but the courts, as well, routinely ignoring evidence of the vicious beatings of those in police custody who come before them.

The most barbarous and indefensible actions of the police often receive white popular support. For it is their perception that the cops constitute a thin blue line between them and the jungle, as stated by a juror who exonerated the cops in the notorious Rodney King beating. What he was saying was the Blacks are animals. But the truth is that *the cops are not protecting us from the jungle; they are protecting the jungle. The jungle is the savage system where the nation's wealth and power is monopolized by a ruthless few.*

The violent, kneejerk response of the police in the ghettos at even the mildest verbal expression of "disrespect" not only reflects the arrogant and racist attitudes of individual officers but is encouraged by their superiors as necessary in enforcing the social order. God help those in the hood who dare utter the word "rights." It may well be their last.

Police departments have historically been knee-deep in corruption. Originally set up to *suppress* vice, they proceeded to methodically *license* it. In the 19th century, as Kristian Williams wrote in Our *Enemies in Blue*: "Discipline was lax, corruption was sanctified, and bribery was a major source of income at every level of the hierarchy. In this context, it was the job of the police to protect illicit businesses."[31]

We have made reference to the numerous commissions set up to investigate police corruption and misconduct. As far back as 1895, the New York Lexow Committee detailed police payoffs and extortion. Then there was the Wickersham Commission (1931); the Knapp Commission of 1971; the Mollen Commission (1993); and the Ramparts investigating committee (2000), among others. In Detroit, Los Angeles, Miami, Philadelphia, Oakland, and elsewhere, official commissions have repeatedly uncovered evidence of police misconduct, of cops routinely framing defendants, shooting unarmed suspects and planting weapons beside their bodies, of cops routinely giving false statements and perjuring themselves in court (a practice that has entered the popular lexicon as "testilying." Frank Serpico, the star whistle-blower at the Knapp Commission hearings (and about whom a motion picture was made), had to flee the country to escape the threats of fellow officers.

Yet little has changed, despite the reams of commission recommendations. Some minor reforms are adopted whose results are generally short-lived. As public anger dies down, the old abuses return. It must be admitted that police graft has decreased over the years. The routine preying upon shopkeepers has been greatly reduced,

269

replaced by generous pay, particularly when overtime is added, along with pension plans that are the envy of the vast majority of workers. Nevertheless, history shows that there is a kind of gravitational field which pulls police conduct back down to a corrupt norm – and brutality is the highest form of corruption.

The rising epidemic of police brutality, or rather the rising intolerance of police brutality in some communities, has led various cities to institute some form of permanent civilian complaint review board. Invariably, however, such boards are not elected by the people, their members being appointed by the police brass themselves and/or the very officials under whose watch police brutality went unchecked. So the boards are toothless, designed not to curb abuses but to appease public opinion. As the former leader of the New York Civil Liberties Union Norman Siegel admitted in the case of the Civilian Complaint Review Board he helped create "with big hoopla," fewer officers are disciplined now than under the old system. This sobering experience did not prevent Siegel, however, from once again participating in a charade, a commission set up by Mayor Giuliani, then running for re-election. Giuliani needed to placate voters of color who were aroused by a torrent of police murders of young African-Americans and Latinos. The commission was charged with recommending measures to improve "police-community relations." But, of course, as everyone but Siegel understood, it was only a Giuliani campaign ploy. Sure enough, once Giuliani was re-elected, the commission's recommendations were thrown in the waste basket. Liberal illusions die hard or, rather, they are immortal. With them it is not "Once bitten, twice shy," but "Once bitten, twice bitten, and for the nth time bitten.

Police Brutality - What Lies Behind It?

It would be a mistake to point the finger at the police as the ultimate source of brutality and other "excesses." As we said, while the police are the pitbulls and have to be curbed, one has to see who is holding their leash. The police are only there for the sake of protecting certain interests – and that is not the masses of the poor, nor even middle class America. The police will occasionally come to the aid of ordinary people, for it would be politically untenable for them to be used exclusively to serve the rich. But their primary function is to guarantee the safety and property of the elite, and in so doing, brutal police methods are *indispensable*. The only way, therefore, to solve the problem of brutality by the police is to take the power away from the elite whom they serve.

Prosecutors

Let us move on from the police to the prosecutors – the US Attorneys and the state and city District Attorneys. According to law school theory, dispensing justice in the United States is based on the adversarial system where the truth emerges through legal combat on a level playing field. And while the duty of the defense counsel is to serve his client, the prosecutor's job, as a representative of the democratic state, is to serve justice. Thus, even when there is an acquittal, if justice has prevailed, then the prosecutor wins. So much for law school theory.

The reality is that, first of all, for prosecutors, an acquittal is a blow to their careers. So in order to gain a conviction, many will not shrink from employing whatever means are necessary, however unscrupulous and even illegal. The more high-profile the case, the more important the case politically, the more will the prosecutors be tempted to abandon ethics and even the law. In this they are amply encouraged by their superiors, including the political authorities. But even beyond the issue of his (and increasingly her) political career, the prosecutor is an agent of the state, and the state is an instrument of the white elite, as we hope we have demonstrated in the first part of this book.

In February, 2006, the attorney for William Brunson, whose conviction for attempted murder was overturned after his having served a dozen years in prison, filed a lawsuit charging the prosecutor with withholding evidence and misleading juries in a broad pattern of misconduct leading to dozens of wrongful convictions. A state court judge found that Brunson's prosecutor had indeed withheld exculpatory evidence. Was this an isolated example, one "rotten apple" in an otherwise beautiful prosecutorial orchard? Brunson's lawyer went on to cite 84 instances in which criminal convictions in Queens County alone were reversed by higher courts for prosecutorial wrongdoing, adding, "These cases are just the tip of the iceberg."[32] The only difference between the malfeasance of Queens County prosecutors and prosecutors elsewhere in the country was the zeal of one defense lawyer in exposing it.

We have cited examples where prosecutorial wrongdoing has been corrected by conscientious judges. Soon we shall see just how typical such judicial conscientiousness is. But in anticipation we might point to a study by the Northern California Innocence Project which found that where established, misconduct by prosecutors is punished only 1 percent of the time.

Prosecutors depend on the police to make their cases, and so they must generally ignore, when they do not actively encourage, the police perjury that is not an uncommon feature of criminal trials. Their touching devotion to the police is most evident when they are called upon to prosecute cops involving brutality against victims of color. Public pressure may sometimes force them to actually bring an indictment. But then quite experienced and able prosecutors suddenly forget how to try a case. A typical example was the "inept" and "amateur" prosecution of the detectives charged in the Sean Bell case, with the predictable unjust outcome for the victim of racist violence. Similarly, a judge recently threw out a murder charge against seven New Orleans policemen on the grounds of prosecutorial "errors" and misconduct. In that case, they had during Hurricane Katrina shot in the back two African-Americans who were scrambling to keep from drowning. That exoneration, however, caused such a storm of protest that they were tried anew, found guilty, and sentenced to prison time.

When police perjury is not sufficient, prosecutors will use the perjured testimony of jailhouse snitches, who are notoriously unreliable and who will lie in return for prison privileges or a reduction in prison time.

In many cases, through their peremptory challenges, prosecutors do their best to minimize the presence of Black jurors. In that regard, a Philadelphia District Attorney was caught on tape instructing his colleagues on the techniques of how to get away with this racist and illegal practice.

Another miscarriage of justice is the selective prosecution of African-Americans of prominence. For example, there was the prosecution of baseball star Barry Bonds, the only player to be convicted for taking steroids, although the Commissioner of Baseball's own investigation revealed the practice was widespread; the conviction of Michael Vick, sentenced to lengthy prison time for promoting dog fighting, a cruel sport but widely engaged in around the country and almost never prosecuted; the extraordinarily harsh sentence of film star Wesley Snipes for tax evasion which, as we have already noted, is routinely engaged in to the tune of tens of billions of dollars by corporations and business executives, often without penalty; the jailing of track star Marian Jones, to my knowledge the only runner sent to jail for using performance-enhancing drugs -- again, widely used in all sports; the indictment of disproportionately large numbers of Black office holders on corruption charges, for which one could convict the entire political class. A sworn affidavit from a former FBI agent, Hirsch Frieddman, read into the Congressional Record by Representative Mervyn Dymally, then Chair of the Congressional Black Caucus, revealed that the FBI routinely investigated without probable cause prominent elected and appointed Black officials in major metropolitan areas on the assumption that they were intellectually and socially incapable of assuming major governmental responsibilities. Then there was the unprecedented FBI raid on the offices of Black Congressman William Jefferson, later ruled unconstitutional. Of course, when it comes to the criminal prosecutions of Black entertainers and athletes, the media can be counted on to give it maximum publicity.

Behind all this is the implicit message that *even the most successful African-Americans cannot escape their innately criminal nature.*

In today's so-called War on Terror, government prosecutors are going after Muslims and Arabs, fabricating cases using entrapment and *agents provocateurs.* They inflame the public with lurid pre-trial declarations, working hard to create jury prejudice. And the media, again, is always willing to lend a helping hand. One case, involving prosecutor Richard Convertino, began smelling so bad that the Justice Department itself had to feign outrage, concluding after an "investigation" that the jury had received false, misleading and prejudicial information, that exculpatory evidence had been suppressed, along with a string of other unethical and illegal practices, but omitting from their findings that the Justice Department had itself collaborated with the prosecutor's office in every phase of the trial.

Prosecutors often use their position as a springboard for political office or a judicial career. The bench is filled with far more former prosecutors than former defense counsel, another factor tilting the balance against defendants. Again, it is not a matter of individual prosecutors being evil. They are for the most part only carrying out the bidding of their political higher-ups. Rather, we must look at the system in which it is expected that prosecutors will play their role in upholding the status quo.

Originally justified on the grounds that it limited arbitrariness, prejudice, and uncertainty, and that it corrected widely disparate sentences in different jurisdictions, mandatory sentences were introduced. This was supposed to result in greater justice both for criminal defendants and for society. Actually, such laws simply took sentencing out of the hands of judges and gave it to prosecutors. Since it is the prosecutors who decide which charges to bring, it is they who control the sentence. Under the "Three Strikes and You're Out" laws, for example, the prosecutor decides whether to charge a crime as a "strike," with all its draconian consequences, or a lesser offense. The prosecutor also determines whether to steer a case to state or federal court, a decision which also influences the degree of punishment. Quite naturally, prosecutors, anxious to retain their enormous and often abused power, have unanimously opposed efforts to return sentencing discretion to the judges. We shall touch upon the impact of this power on defendants a little later.

Mandatory sentencing laws have been used as another potent weapon against African-Americans. At the same time, the indeterminate sentence has also been gravely abused by prison authorities, especially against African-American inmates. *All this demonstrates that however well-meaning reforms may be, virtually every seemingly progressive measure can be twisted to serve the opposite purpose for which it was intended. For the power to interpret and execute it is in the hands of the oppressor.* While the Supreme Court has recently declared federal mandatory sentencing guidelines illegal, it has refused to review the sentences of hundreds of thousands of those whom those guidelines have already victimized, not wishing to open a Pandora's Box and peer into the criminal justice system's racist heart.

Public Defenders

Confronting the enormous resources of the state are the criminal defense attorneys, The vast majority of them do not defend men of wealth but rather work as public defenders for state-subsidized agencies or are court-appointed, receiving shamefully low fees and almost no investigative resources. In 1985, the Bar Association of New York City found that those representing the poor were overworked and underpaid. The average sentence for clients of public defenders is almost three years longer than that for clients of private lawyers.

Public defenders in a growing number of states have refused to take on new cases because of rising workloads and state budget cuts. In Miami-Dade County, for instance, the average number of felony cases per lawyer rose to almost 500, up from 367. And the number of misdemeanor cases, well over a thousand per lawyer, has almost doubled. Virtually the sole role of public defenders is to convince their client to accept a plea bargain, which is in everyone's interest, often enough, except the client's. For it has been generally acknowledged that should defendants widely insist on their constitutional right to a trial, the entire system would collapse. So the vast majority of cases never get that far. But if they do, the defendant faces what a Boston federal judge called "savage sentences" that can be five times as long as those of defendants who take a plea.

While the plea bargain is presented to the defendant as a reward for cooperating with the system, the reality is that a defendant is being penalized for simply asserting his fundamental rights. In the great scheme of things, the primary purpose of lawyers defending the indigent is not to ensure justice, as law students are taught, but to create the appearance of justice, to play their part in maintaining the fiction of a system that is fair and impartial.

Though there are horror stories enough of defense attorneys sleeping or being drunk at trial, of their incompetence and/or indifference, the fundamental problem does not lie in the deficiencies of individual lawyers but in an unjust system. More will be required to cure the problem than higher pay for defense attorneys or their better screening. Of course, one can find conscientious defenders of the poor, lawyers who give of themselves beyond the call of duty, accepting a lower standard of living because they are dedicated to the underdog. However, while the motivation of such people is admirable, they are still objectively contributing to the credibility of a system that deserves no credibility.

The Jury

The jury system, it is claimed, is still another jewel in the crown of the American justice system. Juries, it is said, stand as a bulwark against government arbitrariness and despotism, ensuring that justice is dispensed not from on high but by ordinary citizens who bring with them their valuable life experience and their common sense. In real life, however, only a tiny fraction of all cases end up before juries. But even where they do, juries, in addition to bringing their common sense, also bring their prejudices and the effects of brainwashing by the corporate media and the politicians-for-hire. All-white juries were an integral part of the notorious Southern justice system. But Northern juries have often dispensed the same kind of Southern justice.

In the good old days there was little problem about Blacks on juries. In the South they were simply barred, while in the North, grossly underrepresented. With the Black freedom movement, the situation dramatically changed. But the system, both North and South, has ways of getting around the inconvenience of Supreme Court rulings. Take the federal court in the Eastern District of New York, comprising Brooklyn, a borough with a large Black population, and Long Island, heavily white and one of the most segregated areas in the country. Jury pools have routinely been brought in from Long Island to serve in the Brooklyn courthouse. But people from New York City have not been brought out to serve in Long Island's courthouses. In the Southern District, covering Manhattan, people of color have also been grossly underrepresented in the jury pool. Often there is little need to take formal measures to ensure that Blacks and Latinos are underrepresented. For example, a study in Houston, Texas, found that residents of the predominantly white, affluent neighborhoods were up to seven times more likely to show up for jury duty than persons from low-income neighborhoods of color.

On the other hand, there is no talk of jury nullification in the South and elsewhere when juries continue to dispense white supremacist justice in the best Jim Crow tradition. (See the case of Marcus Dixon, for example, a black Georgia high school student, just turned 18, who was sentenced to 10 years for having consensual sex with his white girlfriend about to turn 16. Eventually, this travesty was overturned, but only as a result of mass protests.)

At any rate, for a time following the O.J. Simpson verdict there was a spate of demands to dilute the power of Black jurors, to change the requirement for conviction from unanimity to a majority verdict. And there has been agitation to lower the barriers to the peremptory challenge of potential Black jurors, supported by an increasingly sympathetic Supreme Court. They finally did get O.J., throwing the book at him on ludicrous charges. Both prosecutor and judge made sure there would be no slip-up this time, seeing to it that the jury was not contaminated with an African-American presence.

The Judiciary

We now move on to the highest reaches of the criminal justice system: the judiciary. While the public pretty generally views politicians as corrupt, judges have managed to maintain an image of disinterestedness, remote from money-grubbing considerations. We shall skip the lowly small town courts, where defendants are routinely denied their basic legal rights and where money is regularly "misplaced," or stolen. Many state court judges have been heavily implicated in garden-variety corruption. A New York State Supreme Court Justice while under investigation revealed that judgeships in Brooklyn were up for sale by Democratic Party officials. That contributions to the political parties are made in return for a judgeship plum is a routine practice nationwide, and well known to the legal profession.

In New York State, for almost a century judges were undemocratically handpicked by party leaders. Now courts have ruled that the judges must run in open primaries. Before, they were *corruptly selected*; henceforth they will be *corruptly elected* through big money financing their campaigns, as witness an investigative piece by a *New York Times* story by Ralph Blumenthal at the end of 2005 on the Texas state court system:

"'Judges in Texas swing the gavel with one hand and take money with the other,' said Craig McDonald, director of Texans for Public Justice, a non-partisan group that tracks the influence of money and corporate power in the state." And the story continued, "In 1987, *60 minutes*, in a program called 'Justice for Sale,' showed Texas Supreme

Court Justices taking hundreds of thousands of dollars in campaign donations from lawyers appearing before them. Eleven years later *60 minutes* found that little had changed.

"In 1998, Texans for Public Justice issued its own report finding that the seven Texas Supreme Court Justices elected since 1994 had raised $9.2 million, of which 40 percent came from interests with cases before the court. A survey taken for the court itself, the group said, found that nearly half of the judges themselves thought that campaign contributions significantly affected their decisions.

"Federal judges [appointed] go on an extraordinary number of junkets paid for by corporations and organizations with an interest in their rulings....have gone on more than 1,000 junkets in the last 15 years, sometimes with their spouses and often at lavish resorts. Judges refuse even to report the trips honestly...The judiciary has also been lax about uncovering financial conflicts in judges' rulings -- and it has refused to crack down on judges who fail to obey the law by taking themselves off cases in which they hold financial interests."[33]

Across the nation a large number of judges and their wives have been given all-expenses paid trips to Miami by conservative foundations where they receive formal lectures on the virtues of unregulated capitalism. A particularly notorious incident involved United States Supreme Court Justice Anthony Scalia who, after golfing with Vice President Cheney, would not recuse himself from a case involving a corporation in which Cheney had a personal stake.

Judicial elections are becoming ever more expensive. In 2002, campaign spending for judgeships, financed by corporate interests, totaled $29 million. Just two years later it had reached $42 million and is rapidly rising.

Above all, judges are vetted for their reliability in safeguarding the status quo. When slavery was the foundation of Southern (and to a large extent Northern) wealth, the Supreme Court ruled in the *Dred Scott* decision of 1857 that a Black man had no rights that a white man need respect. After the Civil War, 40 years later, in *Plessy v. Ferguson* the Supreme Court decided that Black men did indeed have rights -- which the white man could safely ignore. Now that's progress. Learned Southern judges didn't blush in carrying out the vilest miscarriages of justice, including their routine railroading of Black defendants and their equally routine protection of white lynch mobs. Judges, North and South, right up to the Supreme Court, put their legal stamp of approval on US apartheid and Black disenfranchisement, all the Constitutional amendments notwithstanding.

But resentment of Jim Crow was festering in Black veterans returning from World War II and later the Korean War, and they and others in their generation increasingly began to challenge it. At the same time, US-style apartheid was becoming increasingly untenable for the United States in its Cold War competition for the "hearts and minds" of the peoples of the world, overwhelmingly of color. So the courts slowly, ever so tentatively, began reversing 200 years of judicial precedent, 200 years of indisputable judicial logic.

Then the freedom movement burst forth with mass

demonstrations, passive resistance, civil disobedience, fiery rebellions. The Supreme Court put its ear to the ground, heard and responded to the persuasive argument of marching feet. Turning its law books upside down it decided that the humanity of African-Americans should be recognized, with all de-lib-er-ate speed.

African-Americans have not been the only group that the courts have systematically victimized. Labor, too, has suffered from the lawlessness of the bench. Thus Matthew Josephson in his classic work, *The Robber Barons*:

"In 1886 and 1887, the courts began to interfere actively with the movement to organize labor; and in 1888, the first celebrated 'injunction' was issued by a federal court in connection with a Western railway strike, and was justified on the ground of the Interstate Commerce Act, which forbade 'conspiracy in restraint of trade.' Thus the very laws which for long years it was found impossible to enforce against collusive combination or conspiracy among the industrialists were invoked with remarkable promptness and effectiveness against the associations of laborers."[34]

For most of its history the Supreme Court sanctioned the imprisonment of labor leaders for the crime of organizing unions.

When an aroused public forced Congress to pass the Interstate Commerce Act against the predatory railroad trusts, the Supreme Court sabotaged the law for almost 20 years, running interference for the robber barons as they ripped off farmers, workers, and the general public.

Between 1899 and 1937, the Supreme Court struck

down 212 state laws because they violated the basic rights of persons. In 194 of these 212 cases, corporations were the "persons" whose rights were deemed violated.

Early New Deal laws, which-made some modest attempts to aid the working people, were repeatedly struck down by the Supreme Court as unconstitutional. But the Court reversed itself when public outrage against those rulings reached a boiling point. So while its function is to be an anchor against radical currents, the Supreme Court tacks to and fro in the political seas. If it does not take those currents into account, then there is the danger of the whole ship of state going down, and the courts along with it.

The Supreme Court is surrounded with an aura of learnedness and devotion to legal principle. Its important doctrine of *stare decisis*, that is, relying on precedent, supposedly ensures consistency and continuity of its judgments. Actually, it has overruled itself at least 150 times. Concerning one principle alone, it has changed its mind 12 times. The fact is that the court is a political instrument no less than the other branches of government. But it strives to convey the impression that it is above politics, for its credibility requires that illusion. If there was ever any doubt, however, that the Supreme Court was political, that doubt was erased in 2000 with *Bush v. Gore*, when the Court went even beyond upholding the general interests of the elite and, engaging in the most extraordinary legal gymnastics for the sake of ensuring a Republican presidential victory, simply disregarded two centuries of established legal principles.

During World War II, the Supreme Court

determined that there was nothing unconstitutional about putting Japanese-Americans into concentration camps for the crime of their ethnicity. And at the height of the Cold War, the Court saw no constitutional impediment to effectively outlawing a Communist Party that was engaged in purely legal activities, saw no problem with loyalty oaths, blacklists, and the other repressive acts shredding the Bill of Rights that came to be known as McCarthyism. Later, in some instances, the Court reversed itself, but only after Cold War hysteria had subsided, and long after repression had successfully silenced the voices of opposition.

Nor has the Supreme Court held the government accountable for its violations of hundreds of treaties with the native peoples. It has, rather, validated their shameful plunder and genocide. Nor has it ever declared illegal Washington's endless wars of aggression, its repeated actions in contravention of the UN Charter and other international treaties.

The Court's indifference to the Constitution is most glaring in the persecution of political radicals. To obtain convictions, prosecutors pull out all the stops, no conduct being too outrageous, no trick too dirty. And the Supreme Court almost invariably legitimizes those travesties. Like the second set of books kept by crooked corporations, in the case of political defendants the courts operate with a second set of judicial procedures.

Today the courts are complicit in tenderly protecting the "rights" of today's robber barons. And the growing number of "strict constructionists" on the bench are steadily and strictly constructing a police state.

Thanks to the Court it is getting ever easier for police to get warrants based on anonymous tips, to use illegally seized material as evidence if they are acting in "good faith," to raid homes of those on probation without a warrant, to allow millions of people, overwhelmingly of color, to be stopped on the street without cause and searched, again without cause. It has upheld the racially-biased death penalty, endorsed the chokehold and the use of the taser, has approved the search of vehicles under the pretext of stopping motorists for routine traffic infractions. And it has declared constitutional the egregiously unconstitutional torrent of laws and executive actions associated with the "war on terror."

There is also a whiff of corruption in the US Supreme Court Justices being allowed to own stocks. Not only does such ownership promote a corporate bias generally, but from time to time the judges even insist on hearing cases where as a result of such ownership they have a direct conflict of interest.

Prison

Having been shepherded through the labyrinth of the criminal justice system, the "offender" is finally ushered into prison to "pay his debt to society." Incidentally, we wonder how much wealthier this society would be if the 700,000 prison and jail guards, administrators, service workers and assorted personnel were employed in some kind of productive labor. We raise the same question about the million people employed in official law enforcement and another million who work in the private security industry. *Finally, we wonder what kind of society we have which requires so much protection.*

Correction Officers

A few words about "Corrections Officers." Many of those entering that career, as many of those who pursue a career in the police department, have an appropriately authoritarian personality. Coming from the working class, and therefore considered a nullity according to the dominant values of society, they are given a rare opportunity to exercise power, power which is equated with brutality. It does not take long to convince them that treating inmates with dignity is dangerous and a manifestation of weakness. In addition, operating safely outside the view of society and encouraged by their superiors, white prison guards are given free rein to vent their racism, committing crimes against inmates which, if done outside the walls, would warrant long prison sentences or even land them on Death Row. In the case of African-American guards, there is enormous pressure to ingratiate themselves with their white colleagues by demonstrating that they are "team players."

Finally, since prisoners routinely have access to drugs as well as other contraband, particularly those prisoners that are "connected," it is clear that there exist among correction officers corrupt networks which the institution's higher-ups either wink at or in which they are themselves implicated. We have already alluded to their widespread rape of female prisoners.

PUNISHMENT

Let us pause to consider the question of punishment in general. For thousands of years, a crime committed against an individual was redressed by a family member of the injured party, often with assistance from fellow clan members. Justice was equated with revenge. Modern ideas about punishment have gradually but only partially replaced the old idea of vendetta. The distance between the concept of vengeance and justice is a measure of the level of society's evolution.

The notion of justice as revenge has in this country been making a comeback. This is seen with particular force in the new judicial procedure of the "victim impact statement" whereby, for example, family members of crime victims are allowed to pour out their anger and suffering at the trial's sentencing phase. Consumed with hatred, they demand an eye for an eye. The message of the so-called victims' rights movement is that to protect the rights of alleged criminals is to deny the rights of their victims. (Again, keep in mind this idea is applied only in the case of street crime.)

In modern times, we have come to accept that the primary aim of the state with regard to crime is not vengeance but deterrence. In determining the fate of criminals, it is therefore the interest of *society* that is paramount, not that of the victim or victim's family. This means that all the circumstances of a case must be considered, including the life circumstances of the perpetrator, the chances of that perpetrator committing further crimes, and the effect of punishment on the perpetrator as well as on other potential crime perpetrators.

In a just society, punishment would be only one component of the state's response to crime. It would also be obliged to look into the social conditions which play a role in the commission of crime. Thus, there are times when not only the defendant but society itself should be in the dock.

DEATH PENALTY

This country, whose government presumes to lecture the rest of the world on human rights, ranks near the top in the number of state executions. At present, there are some 3,300 prisoners languishing on Death Row. Given that it has been demonstrated through state-by-state analysis that no correlation exists between the murder rate and the execution rate, it would seem that death sentences are handed out for reasons having nothing to do with the professed desire to curb heinous crimes. Canada has executed no one for almost half a century, yet the murder rates in both Canada and the U.S. have moved in parallel during that time.

While there is a growing national movement against capital punishment, there still remain powerful forces trying to restore the death penalty in states where it does not currently exist, and to expedite its execution where it does. Meanwhile, ample proof that capital punishment is permeated with racism (no coincidence that it is the old

Confederate states which have the greatest number of executions) has not prevented the Supreme Court from restoring it after a brief suspension. With the twisted logic in which it specializes, it has once again given executions the green light, ruling that "patterns of statistical racial disparities were meaningless unless one could show specific evidence of discrimination based on race." In other words, absent the smoking gun of a confession of racist intent, which today's sophisticated officials take care not to provide, proving racism is a virtually hopeless task. The Court's majority let the cat out of the bag when it acknowledged that by admitting racial bias in death penalty cases, it would open up a Pandora's Box regarding convictions for other types of crime. As Supreme Court Justice Brennan acidly remarked, the Court's decision seemed to suggest "a fear of too much justice."[35] Indeed it does. For the Supreme Court knows all too well that/racism is part and parcel of prosecutions numbering in the hundreds of thousands. What the Supreme Court has demonstrated here and elsewhere is that *all that is demanded is enough justice to keep the system at an even keel, avoiding stirring up a hornet's nest of popular indignation, while at the same time not permitting so much justice that it would undermine the foundations of a fundamentally unjust legal (and social) system.*

A handful of people of conscience, using new DNA techniques, have devoted themselves to rescuing innocent inmates on Death Row as well as those who have been condemned to long prison terms. So far, they have succeeded in freeing over 200, whose period of unjustified incarceration taken together has added up to 6000 years.

With results such as these, obtained with meager resources, it is clear that this is just the tip of the iceberg. This year, for example, Texan Charles Chatman was released after 27 years in prison for a rape he did not commit, the fifteenth wrongly convicted prisoner in the past seven years in Dallas County alone, with other dubious cases in that county still pending. Incidentally, Chatman's release had been refused on three occasions by his parole board, each time because he maintained his innocence -- standard operating procedure for parole boards everywhere.

Those who equate justice with retribution demand a murderer's execution -- as long as we are talking retail, that is. We do not mean to deny the horror of murder but, again, things must be put in perspective. For if one were to add together all the heinous murders committed in this country in the past 40 years, it would not equal the toll of life caused by the US Government's invasion of Iraq alone. Moreover, the murders of Iraqis were committed not in some frenzy, not under the influence of some mind-impairing substance or uncontrollable passion, were not the unplanned outcome of crimes against property gone sour. They were committed with cold and sober calculation. What punishment then suffices for such outrages for which the vast majority of the US oligarchy is responsible? The same voices demanding ever harsher penalties for retail murder cry treason against those who denounce wholesale slaughter. And if there is opposition to a war by elements of the elite, it is not to the slaughter but to the bungling of the slaughter, to the slaughter's being badly planned and executed. The oligarchy still defends the nuclear annihilation of hundreds of thousands of innocent Japanese civilians in Hiroshima and Nagasaki. Important elements of the oligarchy still justify the murder of millions of Vietnamese and Koreans, their regret being only that the US did not have the will to stay the course and perpetrate still more murder and destruction.

There is nothing new in pointing out this double-standard. But it never becomes part of mainstream discussion, which is only pursued in some lonely corner of radical political discourse, as are so many other truths unacceptable to the champions of the status quo.

But even beyond objections to capital punishment, is not a life sentence also a death sentence, cruel even if usual punishment, contributing nothing to society's protection, and dehumanizing not only those kept behind bars but a society that finds such punishment acceptable?

THE PRISON POPULATION

There are three key facts concerning the present prison population:

First, in the last 40 years the numbers of the incarcerated have soared at an unprecedented rate to an unprecedented level. While in 1970 there were 200,000 state and federal prisoners, and 500,000 in 1985, by 1990 the figure had reached one million. At present, it has doubled again. Today, the number of those under the control of the criminal justice system (in jails and prisons, on probation and parole) has *tripled* since 1980, rising to 7 million. By 2006, there were five times more inmates per capita in the United States than in Britain, 7 times more than in Germany, 10 times more than in France, and 12 times more than in Japan.

Second, there has been a dramatic change in the prison population's ethnic make-up. Back in 1930, three-quarters of the inmates were white and less than one-quarter African-American. Today, 50 percent of the prison population is African-American, although they make up only a little more than 10 percent of the general population. In 1991, about 20 percent of Black men could expect to be imprisoned during the course of their lives. That figure has now risen to about one-third, compared to only 4 percent of white men. Latinos make up 25 percent of the prison population, although they only constitute slightly more than 10 percent of the general population. Whites now comprise about a quarter of the prison population while constituting over half of the general population. Surely, if these disproportions stem from genetic make-up, the criminality and/or violence genes could not have mutated in so short a time.

In some cities, such as Washington, D.C. and Baltimore, more than half of all young Black men are under the control of the criminal justice system. In 2002, the incarceration rate was 450 per 100,000 whites, 1,176 per 100,000 Latinos, and 3,437 per 100,000 African-Americans. For every 20 African-American men there is one in prison; for every 180 white men there is one in prison. The three states with the highest incarceration rates are, of course, the former Deep South slave states of Louisiana, Mississippi and Texas. In 1980, while more than three times the number of African-American men were in colleges and universities than in jail or prison, twenty years later there were more African-American men incarcerated than in -institutions of higher learning. Latinos-are beginning to catch up to African-Americans. They have become the fastest-growing ethnic component of the male prison population.

Third, not only has there been a sharp change in the ethnic composition of the prison population, there has likewise been a substantial shift in the nature of the crimes for which they are being incarcerated. Thus, in 1980, nonviolent offenses accounted for 33 percent of the new prisoners, while in 1988 the percentage had almost doubled. Today, half of all state and federal prisoners are serving time for nonviolent offenses, a great portion of whom having been swept up in the "War on Drugs."

INCARCERATION AND CRIME

While the prison population has been soaring, the crime rate has dropped dramatically. This would seem to confirm the conventional notion that imprisonment deters crime. Rudolph Giuliani and his admirers take credit for the spectacular downturn in New York City's violent crime under his mayoral watch. Some of his tactics have been copied across the country. What has not been publicized, however, is that the so-called New York Miracle occurred at the same time that New York State had the second slowest-growing prison population in the nation and when New York City's jail system was actually downsized. Moreover, New York had a much greater percentage drop in homicides than that of California, despite, the fact that California added nine times more inmates per week than did New York.

POLITICAL PRISONERS
AND OTHER MARTYRS

All imprisonment has a political aspect. "The particular form that punishment takes and the severity of punishment accorded specific offenses is a matter of political policy and varies considerably among political systems..."[36]

By way of illustration, for the same types of crime, sentences are five times heavier in the United States than in Canada and Australia, and seven times heavier than those of most European countries. Over and above this disproportion between the US and other countries, Blacks *within* the United States suffer disproportionate punishment, disproportionate arrest rates, and unequal and inadequate representation. On such grounds, therefore, all African-Americans behind bars can be classified as political prisoners. But there is another sense in which African-Americans are political prisoners. For in large part, the crimes they commit are a reaction to crimes and injustices perpetrated *against them*, crimes which invariably go unpunished: the crime of mis-education, the crime of job discrimination, the crime of wages which cannot sustain a family, the crime of substandard housing or no housing at all, of inferior health care, of unrelenting police abuse – in short, the crime of being barred (no pun intended) by a political and economic system from living a life worthy of human beings.

Putting all that aside, as well, there exist political prisoners in the most direct sense. *Officially*, the United

States does not now nor has it ever had political prisoners. *Officially*, we have freedom of speech and assembly. *Officially*, people are not prosecuted for engaging in peaceful political activities because, as our schoolbooks tell us, such activities are guaranteed under our democracy. After all, the Constitution provides the legal means to change laws and policies, and therefore there is no justification for defiance of the law. *All absolutely irrefutable, as long as one does not consult personal experience or a history book.* Actually, the first political prisoners were the indigenous peoples herded into internment camps called reservations.

We mentioned that only a few years after the American Revolution, under the upper-class Administration of John Adams, people were thrown in prison simply for publishing views critical of the government or sympathetic to the French Revolution. Ever since then, those who have spoken and acted in the interests of the laboring people, the oppressed, and especially African-Americans, those who struggled to end apartheid in the American South, those who fought for decent wages and humane working conditions, for the right to unionize – that is, those who were conspirators in restraint of profits – and those who opposed unjust wars, hot or cold, were repeatedly arrested, sometimes imprisoned, occasionally executed, but routinely clubbed, gassed, deported if they weren't citizens, put under constant surveillance, their meetings raided, their phones tapped, organizational premises broken into, files stolen, literature seized, and in the case of African-Americans, whipsawed between the terror of the state and that of the lynch mob.

If with respect to African-Americans charged with street crime, the criminal justice system operates with particular harshness, trampling on due process and the requirements of equal justice, there is an absolutely fierce vindictiveness toward Blacks engaged in political resistance. Here the greatest terror must be visited upon those who would make no bargain with white supremacy. This special vengeance began even before the modern Black freedom movement. We skip the horrors visited upon slaves who resisted their bondage through attempted escape or rebellion. The slaveholder's gruesome and barbaric punishments, even for petty insubordination, had behind it not only the armed might of the Southern states, but the sanction and full military power of the federal government. And we know the fate of African-Americans in the period after Reconstruction when the white elite, North and South, buried the hatchet, first between themselves and then together on the skull of African-Americans, when the full fury of official as well as vigilante terror came down upon Blacks claiming no more than the citizenship guaranteed in the 14th Amendment to the Constitution.

But to be terrorized is not to be paralyzed. From the West Indies came Marcus Garvey, a man with a message of pride, calling on his people to get off their knees. And the government's response was swift: "The niggers will stay on their knees and Garvey is going down with them." Framed, imprisoned, deported.

There was the incarceration and torture of the hero of the Puerto Rican independence movement, Albizu Campos, another dangerous "nigger" in the eyes

299

of the Establishment. Accusing the prison authorities of poisoning him by radiation (he eventually died of cancer), he was labeled insane, until the government finally admitted radiating not only him but other prisoners, as well. Here was another of our government's biological and psychological warfare experiments carried out to advance the science of oppression.

Puerto Rico, fast forward to the present. The case of another fighter for Puerto Rican freedom, Filiberto Ojeda Rios. Captured after having carried out an operation to advance the cause, he escaped the vengeance of the colonizer's court, whose authority he did not recognize. In hiding for many years, he continued the struggle with his pen. At age 72, just "coincidentally" on the anniversary of the first blow by Puerto Rican patriots against Spanish rule, his house was surrounded by the FBI and a fusilade followed. One bullet hit its mark. Lying wounded, blood oozing out under the door to his home in plain view of the agents waiting outside, for 12 hours the FBI refused to allow him medical attention as he slowly bled to death.

Back to the 1930s and the Great Depression. There was Angelo Herndon, Black Communist labor organizer, convicted of insurrection against the State of Georgia, his crime being to have led hunger marches. Sentenced to 18 to 20 years, a five-year national campaign finally gained his release.

1949. Paul Robeson, magnificent African-American artist of international renown, uncompromising fighter for racial justice, for social justice generally, and for peace, a triple threat. With state connivance, an attempt was made to murder him during his outdoor concert in Peekskill, New York. The attempt having been foiled by thousands of progressive war veterans, Black and white, who surrounded him with love as well as some hardware, the government did the next best thing and cut off all his means of support, took away his passport, saw to his being barred from US concert halls, made sure his recordings were banned from the airwaves. Eventually, Robeson broke through the quarantine, to the cheers of the world.

W.E.B. DuBois, great African-American scholar, pioneer sociologist, gathering a rich harvest from the barely tilled field of authentic Black history. He was 83 years old when they brought him into a courtroom in manacles, charged with being an "agent of a foreign power." (In the days of the Cold War, to agitate for peace was equated with treason.) That battle won, he emigrated to Ghana where he could continue his truth-telling unmuzzled.

Black *and* Communist, Henry Winston was imprisoned with fellow party leaders. His repeated requests for medical attention refused, he eventually went blind. Cause of blindness, omitted from the prison medical report: political vindictiveness.

Robert Williams, head of the Monroe, North Carolina chapter of the NAACP during the height of the civil rights movement. Battling racist terror, he called for Black people to arm themselves in self-defense. Rescuing a white couple who had stumbled into a life-threatening situation during a riot, he was subsequently charged with their kidnapping. Rather than submit himself to Southern "justice" and a lifetime behind bars, he fled the country and spent long years in exile.

Especially relentless were government attacks on the Black Panthers. The FBI set up the infamous covert operations known as COINTELPRO, originally designed against the Left, but turned into a weapon whose primary target was the Black freedom movement. Even before COINTELPRO, the FBI had a long record of hostility to Black equality. (For an in-depth account, see Kenneth O'Reilly's *Racial Matters*). It spent most of its time investigating and trying to discredit civil rights activists, and sat on its hands when it came to protecting the victims of segregationist terror. The Southern offices of the FBI worked closely with the local law, who were either in the Ku Klux Klan or who worked hand in glove with them. Through its network of informants and infiltrators, the FBI had advance knowledge of the murderous hate crimes perpetrated by white supremacist groups and did nothing to prevent them.

In its drive to "neutralize" the Panthers, the FBI with other police agencies, violently attacked Panther offices, gunning down many Panther members. Chicago Black Panther leader Fred Hampton was shot in his bed, his home blasted with 98 bullets, only one outgoing round being found in the "shootout." In that same raid, Panther leader Mark Clark was also killed, as was, in the space of a year, almost 30 other party members. Black Panther Geronimo Pratt was framed for murder, spent 27 years in prison, eight of which after his innocence had been conclusively established. Black Panther Dhoruba Bin Wahad, also framed for murder, spent 19 years in prison until exonerated. _____

302

The Panthers were subjected to constant harassment. As described by Rodger Streitmatter in *Voices of Revolution*, "A mind-numbing series of arrests [and constant re-arrests] trials, convictions, [acquittals], imprisonments, overturned convictions, escapes to foreign countries, and violent deaths, took a devastating toll" in lives and treasure (more than $5 million spent in defense fees) -- the public side of persecution. The covert side: instigating violence among Panthers members, and between Panthers and other freedom organizations, spreading false accusations about Panther leaders being government agents through forged documents, and promoting whispering campaigns by infiltrators to sow suspicion.[37] All good. The Panther Party ultimately tore itself apart, that is, whatever was left which the government had not already destroyed.

George Jackson. Convicted at the age of 18 of robbing a gas station of $70 and sentenced to 1 to 70 years. As incarceration dragged on year after year, Jackson became radicalized, joined the Black Panther Party, and became a potent political force inside the walls. Not to be tolerated. There were constant threats to his life, he was subjected to years of isolation, and he was charged with crimes in which he had taken no part. Meanwhile, his outraged teenage brother Jonathan became entrapped in a COINTELPRO operation, losing his life in a failed attempt to rescue George by force. As part of that same COINTELPRO operation, George Jackson was himself soon gunned down "trying to escape."

Leonard Peltier, native activist, victim of still another

shameful episode at the Wounded Knee reservation, convicted of murdering two FBI agents. Two Courts of Appeals condemned the government for gross misconduct in suppressing and fabricating evidence and in coercing testimony. Mere trifles. Peltier remains in prison after 30 years, appeals denied, clemency denied, justice denied. (See Ward Churchill's *Agents of Repression* for a good summary of COINTELPRO activities as well as the true history of COINTELPRO's savage attacks on the American Indian Movement.)

Given the violence and lawlessness of the state against those seeking liberation through legal channels, a group of freedom-fighters took the path of armed struggle. As in the case of members of the Irish Republican Army, they were tried as common criminals. And if African-Americans engaging in legal resistance were given long sentences, it was to be expected that for members of the Black Liberation Army, prison would be their tomb. As with other freedom-fighters, they were condemned to endless stretches of solitary confinement, refused proper medical treatment, and subjected to a campaign of persecution, including harassment of those who dared visit them. To this day, about 90 aging fighters for Black freedom are rotting behind bars. (For their names and biographies, look up the New York City Jericho Movement, nycjericho@gmail.com). They remain in prison for no other reason than to serve as an object lesson, a warning of the dire consequences of militancy in the cause of freedom and social justice. (Right-wingers like David Horowitz, not content with the physical extermination of the Black Panthers and alarmed that they might serve as an inspiration to future generations of social activists, have been at great pains to prove they were nothing but a criminal gang masquerading as revolutionaries. The truth is that it is Horowitz who is part of a criminal gang masquerading as historians.) Recently, as a result of .a long campaign on their behalf, two former Black Panthers were taken out of the solitary in which they had been buried for 36 years, the charge of their killing a prison guard exposed as pure fabrication.

At least equal in savagery was the persecution of the Philadelphia Black radical group, MOVE, which holds a terrifying belief in the sacred character of all of nature, all forms of life -- animal, human, even humans of African ancestry, the latter proving to be the last straw. Its members were subjected to repeated police raids, attempts to take their children from them, beatings when they ventured out on the street, not excluding the clubbing of pregnant women and their subsequent miscarriages. In one case a baby's skull was crushed in his mother's arms. In 1978, in a military-style operation, MOVE's communal house was surrounded and flooded, as its occupants, including children, huddled in the basement. Then the cops let the bullets fly, one being killed by their own, for which a group of MOVE members were framed and are now serving 30 to 100 years. Thirty years later they remain behind bars, repeatedly turned down for parole for refusing to express remorse for crimes of which they are innocent.

The campaign against MOVE reached a crescendo in another military-style operation when once again their communal house was surrounded. Refusing orders to come out, fearing what indeed proved to be in store for them, 10,000 rounds were poured into their home. Still the families refused to budge. So an incendiary bomb was dropped on their roof, the second occasion since the Civil War that a bomb was dropped on a domestic target (others being dropped in 1921 on the aggravatingly prosperous Black neighborhood of Greenwood in Tulsa, Oklahoma). Trying to flee the inferno, six adults and five children burned to death, were shot to death, or both. Meanwhile the arriving firemen were ordered not to extinguish the flames, resulting in 60 neighborhood homes being likewise incinerated.

While public opinion against MOVE was being whipped up to the necessary hysteria, a heroic Philadelphia journalist, Mumia Abu-Jamal, tried to set the record straight. For this and for exposing the police department's reign of terror against African-Americans generally, he became another Black victim of state vengeance, arrested on the false charge of murdering a policeman. The trial was conducted in the manner typical of such cases. Presiding Pennsylvania Supreme Court Justice Albert Sabo, known as the "hanging judge," overheard by a court reporter to say he was going to help the prosecutor "fry the nigger," prevented Mumia from defending himself. Since his conviction, key prosecution witnesses have recanted their testimony. A mountain of evidence has been uncovered revealing, as in the case of Peltier, suborned perjury and other police and prosecutorial misconduct. But the courts have found Mumia's conviction too important to be overturned by facts. He languished on Death Row for over 20 years, which did not prevent him from broadcasting and writing with unique eloquence the truth about the nature of US society and still remains in prison.

Heading the list of political martyrs, Malcolm X and Martin Luther King. Uncompromising in struggle, Malcolm exposed white liberals as treacherous hypocrites. Nor did he bite his tongue in denouncing Black leaders who sold out their people. Compounding all this, he linked the struggle of African-Americans with colonial struggles worldwide. He had to be silenced, of course. His assassination was arranged on orders from the very highest circles of government, carried out by US intelligence agents and local police, whatever secondary culpability may be ascribed to the Nation of Islam.

As for Martin Luther King, his message became increasingly radical and dangerous to the rulers of America. Denouncing the Vietnam War, supporting the strike of Memphis sanitation workers, organizing a Poor People's March, increasingly speaking in class terms, linking the issues of racism, militarism and capitalism, beginning to wonder out loud about the futility of integrating "into a burning house," he, too, had to go. Same orders, same actors behind the scene, who set up a patsy to take the fall.

PRISON CONDITIONS

The prison experience, one would think, should be an educational one, and we are not just speaking of formal schooling. Given that it is said that inmates have committed morally repugnant offenses, then it would seem to be just common sense that prison would provide inmates with a morally elevating environment, would teach moral behavior by example. What we find, however, is the very opposite, namely, conduct by the prison authorities that in its viciousness and cruelty is more repugnant than the criminal acts that brought the vast majority of inmates to the institution. For example, Special Housing Units (or Sadistic Housing Units, as they should be called) are an integral part of every institution. Used for the most unmanageable and violent of the prison population, such lockdowns are considered indispensable in preventing institutional chaos. The unremitting tension and violence of the prison environment is real enough, but it is not the inmates who are its source. It is a prison regime which treats human beings like wild dogs, isolating, goading and tormenting inmates to the breaking point. As the prison authorities well know, nothing is more destructive of the prisoner's health, mental as well as physical, than isolation, and many already have mental problems when they arrive.

SHU's are used not only against those considered discipline problems, but against political militants -- Black nationalists, Puerto Rican independence fighters, even jailhouse lawyers and doctors -- that is, people who in one way or another maintain a spirit of resistance to what they recognize as oppression both inside *and* outside the walls.

The problem of prison overcrowding grows ever more critical. Provided with too little space in the best of cases (cells typically measuring four feet wide, 10 feet deep and seven feet high, not wide enough for a man to fully stretch his arms apart), they are more like caskets than an environment for the living. Further, inmates are often forced to double-bunk, which is not just doubly but exponentially inhumane. It is more than a little ironic that the modern science of zoo-keeping recommends that animals, even the most dangerous, be provided with a spacious environment, reproducing as nearly as possible their original habitat, rather than the cramped and barred spaces of the past. In the matter of human keeping, however, instead of trying to create as normal an environment as possible, the trend is just the reverse: ever smaller cages, solitary confinement, incessant snapping of the disciplinary whip, cruel restrictions on family visitation, humiliating strip searches, including body cavity searches, as well as a steady stream of other indignities. And so while beasts are increasingly treated with humaneness, humans are increasingly treated as beasts.

Prison rape is routine. A young person's chances of avoiding sexual assault is almost nil, despite a Supreme Court ruling in 1994 that prison officials are responsible for inmate sexually predatory behavior. At best, the officials look the other way. And there is a reason for their permissiveness. Enabling predatory sexual behavior is something that bolsters their control. Those who do not "cooperate" with the administration may find the way opened by prison guards for sexual assault by fellow inmates. Officials even make arrangements to facilitate liaisons, which naturally requires something back in return. Of course, rape is particularly dangerous, along with unsafe sex generally, given that the rate of HIV/AIDS, in prison is nearly three times greater than that in the general population. Nevertheless, prison wardens refuse to make condoms available.

State prisons are generally located at great distances from the prisoners' homes. In New York State, for example, two-thirds of the prisons are located more than three hours away from New York City, the home of 70 percent of the state's prison population. Unreasonable obstacles are placed in the way of visitation, making the maintenance of family relationships extremely difficult. And the situation is compounded by the growing practice of transferring prisoners to distant states.

Particularly tragic is the incarceration of women. They are pouring into prison at a rate nine times that of 30 years ago. Growing at twice the pace of the male inmates, they now constitute 10 percent of the prison population. Here is another layer of victimization, for in many instances they have been incarcerated for defending themselves against domestic battering or have been hooked on drugs by male partners who ensnare them in illegal drug operations. Three-quarters are mothers, two-thirds of whose children are under 18. Half their children have never visited them, mainly because of hardships caused by the great distance from their homes. It is not unusual for pregnant women to be put in shackles as they give birth in prison infirmaries, to be pressured to give up their babies, and in an increasing number of cases to have their children taken away from them by the courts for being "unfit" on the testimony of "social service workers." In terms of the percentage of their communities, about four times as many Black women as white are incarcerated. Regularly traded, sold, loaned and pimped, many are raped with impunity by prison guards. At this writing, a human rights organization has just published a report on such prison rapes by guards in Alabama.

The political upsurge of the 1960s and '70s, which brought progressive changes in society generally, also resulted in a number of enlightened prison reforms. But in these past several decades of political reaction and social regression, prison conditions have also worsened. In 1994, federal grants for prison college courses were ended, and many states followed suit shortly afterward. By 1995, only eight of the thousands of educational programs for inmates nationwide remained, despite the fact that they have been shown to be an effective tool in reducing, recidivism. Solitary confinement has been expanding, strip searches stepped up, and tasers (hand-held instruments of torture) are becoming standard issue. Touted by the police and prison authorities as being less lethal than conventional weapons, more than 200 inmates have died at the hands of these "humane" devices. Prison libraries have been eliminated or access curbed; hot meals have been reduced; visiting hours curtailed; exercise gear and cable TV removed. The infamous chain gangs are making a comeback a half-century after a Hollywood film exposing their horrors stirred the nation's conscience and forced their abolition. Reinstituted in Alabama in 1995, Florida and Arizona quickly followed.

Prison authorities are sowing discord by stoking racial antagonisms -- the age-old technique of divide-and-conquer. Not only do correction officers treat Blacks more severely than whites for similar rule infractions, or punish Blacks for infractions not committed, they actively incite ethnic groups against one another, especially encouraging white prisoners to engage in racist violence.

The vindictive prison regime is justified by the philosophy that incarceration is not punishment enough. Former Massachusetts Governor William F. Wald proclaimed that prisons should be a "tour through the circles of hell". Gary Gerbitz, a Tennessee District Attorney, complained that the conditions of the ghetto dweller were such that imprisonment resulted in an actual improvement in his quality of life. One might have thought Mr. Gerbitz was calling for serious social reform. But his conclusion and that of other social deviants of his ilk is that rather than improve conditions outside the walls it is necessary to make life inside still more hellish.

Various states are now *charging* prisoners rent for their palacial accommodations and five star catering, as well as fees for what passes as medical care. Deductions are made from what is humorously referred to as wages from prison industry. Actually, inmates are lucky to be paid anything at all, for the 13th Amendment outlawing slavery specifically exempts those behind bars. Always in the forefront of social engineering, California charges parolees between 50 and 100 dollars for costs incurred in harassing -- excuse me, "supervising" them after discharge.

The degrading and brutal treatment of prisoners is defended on the grounds that it is required for the security of the institution. We are told that prison is by nature violent, given that it gathers together in one place society's most violent individuals. One finds in *Politics of Punishment*, another explanation: The roots of prison violence "reaches deeply into the prison system itself. It is a system which renders a man impotent, denies his individuality, destroys his identity, and grinds him ceaselessly under a heavy yoke of uncertainty and injustice. Such a system generates rage and bitterness which in some men will be turned upon others, whether tormentors or brothers. Prisons, then, are generating the very behavior which they are ostensibly designed to eliminate. They are destroying rather than rehabilitating men. They are promoting violence rather than controlling it."[38]

Is it then surprising that half the prison population will be back behind bars within three years of .release? Surely it takes no Einstein to see that all this is a recipe for disaster as each year the prisons disgorge back into society hundreds of thousands of their brutalized and embittered graduates. Liberal sociologists and criminologists recognize that the harsh prison regime is counter-productive and therefore "mistaken." However, that is as far as they will go -- dare go. But surely there is something more at work here on the part of prison authorities than mere error or short-sightedness. We shall return to this later.

Of those in prison today, some 400,000 are mentally ill, as are 60 percent of. those in jail. Two-thirds of inmates report mental health problems. Truly has American society made great strides. In the 19th century, mental institutions were virtual prisons. Today, jails and prisons are virtual mental institutions, which are far less expensive to the state than providing effective psychiatric care. Nearly one-quarter of those in prison lockdown are mentally ill, almost half of whom have attempted suicide and a third self-mutilation. Not only is it outrageous that the mentally ill are in prison at all, but worse still, their abnormal behavior is interpreted as being willfully disruptive, requiring still harsher punishment. Is it any wonder that their condition deteriorates in prison or, for that matter, that many become mentally ill who enter prison relatively stable?

Almost 40 percent of the inmates have tuberculosis, a condition further spread by overcrowded conditions, and almost 30 percent have hepatitis C, an epidemic exacerbated by refusal of the authorities to provide appropriate health care.

TORTURE

Exposure of the systematic torture of detainees in Iraq and Afghanistan came as a thunderbolt to millions of Americans who grew up believing in the good-guy image of Uncle Sam. Actually, torture has always been part of the prison regime here at home, providing good practice for Guantanamo, Abu Gharaib and Bagram.

More than a decade ago, *New York Times* columnist Anthony Lewis exposed the existence of torture in the Atlanta federal prison. At least 100 cases were documented of inmates being held for five days in four-point restraint, spread-eagled, and forced to urinate and defecate on themselves. The Atlanta experience was not unique. Torture was similarly exposed in Florida, Texas, and in other state prisons by investigators for the BBC and Human Rights Watch, exposing the use of dogs, cattle prods, and toxic chemicals, all videotaped.

Along with physical abuse and intimidation, professional psychologists, whose training, the public will be happy to learn, has not gone to waste, have developed what they believe to be the most effective method for dealing with "terrorists." This involves inflicting not only pain but *humiliation*. The theory is that the path to breaking a prisoner's will is through undermining his self-respect. Hence, at Abu-Gharaib, prisoners were forced to pose for nude, sexually suggestive, and other humiliating photographs. So, too, in our domestic prisons, everything is designed to shatter the prisoner's self-respect, it being well understood that nothing is more subversive of the established order, either inside or outside the walls, than the *dignity* of the oppressed.

But beyond what is conventionally understood as torture, should we not include the endless tedium and long years of isolation -- not only the isolation of 23- and 24-hour lockdown, but isolation even in the company of other inmates?

"PRIVILEGES": PRISON AND "WHITE SKIN"

Prison management involves the use of both carrot and stick. The carrot is the "privileges" offered to the prisoner for obedient behavior. This encourages the inmate to view as a favor that which he should be receiving as a matter of right, reducing him to dependence on the jailer's good will and rewarding a slavish mentality. The system of privileges is also a means of playing prisoners against one another.

There are those within Left and Black Nationalist circles who subscribe to the theory of "white skin privilege," that is, to the idea that the vast majority of whites, including white workers and the white poor, have a stake in the system of white supremacy. This idea is supposed to be militantly anti-racist. But just as the prison trusty is privileged and yet remains a prisoner, so many European-Americans can be considered as trusties outside the walls. It is true that to a greater or lesser degree, the majority of white working people believe it is in their interest to uphold and support institutional racism. But the *reality* is that white working people are themselves exploited and powerless victims of the same oppressive system. The "privilege" they enjoy is that of not being as exploited and oppressed as African-Americans. The chains they wear are lighter, but they are still chains. *Most important, their chains are fastened to those of African-Americans and can only be broken if those of the African-Americans are broken, as well.* The history of the South is the most vivid illustration of this. There, where the overwhelming majority of African-Americans have lived until relatively recently, where racist oppression has taken its most extreme forms – from slavery to semi-feudal oppression, peonage and legal Jim Crow – where the lot of African-Americans was a devastating pauperdom, perpetual debt, squalor, illiteracy – precisely there one also found the depths of white degradation. One would have expected, if the theory of the opposition of interests between the masses of whites and African-Americans were correct, to find in that region of greatest Black exploitation the greatest white *affluence*. But what one found instead was a cesspool of white benightedness, illiteracy, and abject poverty, where the condition of southern white workers and farmers was far inferior by every measure to that of whites in other regions.

PRISON DISCIPLINE: A PRESCRIPTION

Finding a solution to the problem of prison discipline is not rocket science: Let the prison administration stop treating inmates as wild animals, recognize their humanity, and stop trying to crush their spirit. Let them fill prison days with meaningful and personally satisfying activity and provide work that pays real wages, facilitate access to family and loved ones, including conjugal visits. Also, allow inmates to share in the planning and implementation of the prison regime, including matters of discipline.

The state's adamant refusal to consider such an approach stems not from certainty of its inevitable failure but from fear of its potential success. It is said that inmates to some degree already do set rules. Thus, for example, they maintain among themselves a rigid racial segregation to which the prison authorities are supposedly forced to acquiesce. In some matters, prisoners do devise and enforce internal discipline. But this is not an authentic self-determination and often only amounts to prisoners carrying out for the administration what it would be illegal or inconvenient for them to do directly. The authorities, for example, stoke racial and ethnic hostility and then helplessly throw up their hands as the prisoners adopt "their own" code of segregation. On the other hand, inmate rules do help to reduce conflicts among prisoners and, in sometimes twisted form, do represent a kind of assertion of their humanity, a demand for respect to be observed among the prisoners themselves. And the more they are treated with contempt by their jailers, the more fiercely within their own ranks is this demand for respect asserted.

In today's circumstances it appears ludicrous to turn prison discipline over to the inmates -- "inmates running the asylum." But if the threat of violence hangs like a pall over prison institutions it is largely because prison conditions endlessly provoke it. Actually, competent, self-confident, well-organized, and disciplined inmates with a strong sense of solidarity is the last thing wanted by prison authorities. The Attica rebellion was a magnificent example of what is possible when for a moment inmates take charge of their surroundings. During that uprising, order reigned. Impartial observers allowed inside the walls were amazed at the absence of chaos, at the prisoners' self-discipline and the reasonableness of their demands, which simply called for humane treatment. In stark contrast were the hysterical and inflammatory calls by the media and the politicians that the rebellion be drowned in blood. And, indeed, the uprising ended with the tragic and wanton slaughter of inmates and guards alike, thanks to Nelson Rockefeller, the New York "law-and-order" Governor who had decided to sacrifice however many lives on the altar of his presidential ambition. After the gunfire came the merciless beatings, inmates forced to run a gauntlet of club-swinging guards despite the promise that there would be no retribution (another broken treaty with the "natives"). The slaughter was wildly cheered by the entire Establishment claque as well as a large, venomously racist segment of the public. That episode threw a piercing light on just who the real barbarians are, the real dregs of society. And it was the Attica Rebellion which brought home to me what had previously been only a gnawing suspicion, that while prisons are still needed, for the most part it is the *wrong* people who are in them.

PRISONER RIGHTS

Appealing to the courts is one of the few tools available to prisoners to fight their cruel and unjust conditions. But a thoroughly deceitful media campaign, instigated at the behest of the politicians, has convinced the public that the courts are being deluged with inmate complaints that are trivial and even absurd. Concealing the typical and genuine inmate grievances, the media has held up to ridicule the few which were not representative, such as one supposed demand to be furnished with Converse shoes rather than Reebok. That media campaign paved the way for Congress to severely limit the ability of prisoners to gain access to the courts. One law barred public defenders from assisting prisoners to receive federal funds. Another law set the fee for their services so low that few private lawyers could afford to take such cases. In 1996, the Prison Litigation Reform Act required inmates to exhaust administrative remedies before they could sue, forcing them to wander through a bureaucratic maze and making it almost impossible for them to ever get their day in court. Recently, the Supreme Court lowered some of those hurdles, but the process remains difficult. All this has the support of a large portion of public opinion which is indignant at the very idea that a prisoner has or should have any rights at all.

The campaign against the prisoner's right to sue is similar to the one against "frivolous lawsuits" outside the walls, which are supposedly generated by greedy trial lawyers. In the overwhelming majority of cases such suits are undertaken against real corporate or government malfeasance. Here is another illustration of the fact that the same forces behind the "war on crime" are also engaging in a war against the poor, against people of modest means, against people of color, against the interests of the vast majority of the people, and on behalf of a handful of parasites.

PRISONER MOVEMENT

The gross injustices in the penal system point to the burning need for a prisoner movement – not so much an *advocacy* movement that speaks *on behalf of* prisoners, not a missionary movement with the goal of prisoner moral uplift, not a movement based on "rehabilitation theory," but on "empowerment theory," as former political prisoner Eddie Ellis has called it, a movement "designed to produce structural and systematic transformation in the community as well as in the prison."

It must be a movement in the prisoner's own voice, a movement led by current and past inmates, actively supported by their family members and loved ones, as well as by the progressive community generally, dealing not alone with issues of the criminal justice system but with virtually all social justice issues, for they are intimately intertwined. Such a movement has the potential to become a truly powerful force for change, a force for fundamental social change. Conversely, a key component of social justice movements must be the demand for a fundamental overhaul of the criminal justice system.

FELONY DISENFRANCHISEMENT

Being behind bars means losing most of one's rights, including the right to vote. Convicted felons are automatically disenfranchised, as are in many states even those on probation or parole. Often they remain disenfranchised even when they have served their time in full and are no longer under the criminal justice system's jurisdiction. Of course, since the Black community is the criminal justice system's special target, it is the Black community that is hit particularly hard. To see what lies behind this disenfranchisement, which claims to be color-blind, it needs to be put in historical context.

BLACK DISENFRANCHISEMENT; SOME HISTORY

We shall show that since the Civil War, the well-being not only of the South but also of the country as a whole has been inextricably linked to the political strength of African-Americans.

After their Civil War victory, the Republicans at first imposed upon the southern rebels terms that were extraordinarily lenient. To regain their previous place in the Union, all that was required of the secessionists was that they formally accept the end of slavery. Of course, having no other choice, they agreed. But as soon as they were allowed to get back in the saddle through a bloody reigh of terror, they proceeded to enact a series of Black Codes that re-established slavery in all but name

Meanwhile, the Republican Party was losing elections in the North. And so it rushed to pass the Fifteenth Amendment, giving Blacks the right to vote, backed up by the Union Army -- not out of any concern for the plight of the former slaves but alarmed at the prospect of their own loss of power. For an ever stronger alliance was developing between the southern Confederates, now re-empowered, and the Democratic Party in the North. So the Republican Party was revived in the South as the freedmen came out and voted in huge numbers, together with a small number of poor whites who before the war had lived a miserable existence in the hills, unable to compete with the large plantations worked by slave labor. Though opposing secession, they had been powerless to prevent it.

Thus began the brief period of Reconstruction, the sweeping away of the Black Codes and all official racial discrimination. Thanks to the Black vote the South's first public school system was created, which gave educational opportunities not only to Black children but to the children of poor whites, as well. Thanks to the Black vote the rights of all women were expanded. Throughout the former Confederacy the right of a married woman to her own property was recognized for the first time, no longer subject to being taken from her to pay her husband's debts. In South Carolina, the state where Black political influence was greatest, the right of divorce was newly recognized, and in other states the grounds for divorce were expanded. Thanks to the Black vote public services, were introduced and public hospitals built, along with orphanages and institutions for the mentally ill, serving all. South Carolina paid for medical care for the poor, while other kinds of aid to the indigent were set up in a number of states and localities. Thanks to the Black vote, imprisonment for debt was ended, a measure primarily benefiting debt-ridden white farmers. Confiscation of crops, homes or tools by creditors was outlawed. Laws were passed ensuring that wages were paid, against a history of the swindling of the worker. Crop liens were outlawed and other measures passed protecting tenant farmers, Black and white, from landlord confiscations. Thanks to the Black vote the big landowners were no longer able to evade taxation, as they had before, through unjust laws or unjust application of the law. Previously, it was on the shoulders of poor whites that the main tax burden had been placed. Idle portions of plantation land were confiscated and made available for the first time both to landless Blacks and land-poor whites, as were large landholdings in tax arrears. Major improvements in infrastructure were begun, intended to benefit the entire population, rather than as in the past, only the plantation elite. Judges were now elected rather than being the planters' appointed stooges. Penal codes were drawn up to reflect the requirements of justice rather than the elite's economic interests. The number of capital crimes was reduced. In Alabama, free legal counsel was for the first time supplied to indigent defendants. For the first time democratic local government and law enforcement bodies were set up that were responsive to their constituencies. Property qualifications for voting and for holding office were eliminated.

It was precisely in states where the Black vote was the strongest that democratic and progressive measures were most thoroughgoing.

The progressive nature of Reconstruction measures presented a stark choice for whites seeking a way out of the grim backwardness and poverty of the past. Eric Foner, in his extremely valuable *A Short History of Reconstruction*, cites a white North Carolina newspaper observation that the choice for masses of whites was "between salvation at the hand of the Negro or destruction at the hands of the rebels."[39] (Foner and all historians presenting the truth of that much maligned period stand on the shoulders of W.E.B. DuBois' pioneering *Black Reconstruction*.)

With the violent overthrow of Reconstruction and the suppression of the Black vote, public schools were dismantled ,or gutted -- for white children as well as Black. In Louisiana, state services virtually disappeared, and spending on public schools was cut so much it was the only. state into the 20th century to see a decline in white literacy. In Florida, a nearly constructed agricultural college was abandoned, the only institution of higher learning in that state. Public hospitals were closed in Alabama.

A reign of terror overthrew Reconstruction as tens of thousands were murdered, lynched and beaten, predominantly African-Americans, but also whites who stood in the way of restoring the old order. Whole communities of Black people were burned out of their homes. That terror lasted for almost a century. And with Blacks disenfranchised, it was assured that the South would remain a cesspool of economic and social backwardness.

Thanks to Black disenfranchisement and the seniority system in Washington, the politicians of the "Solid South" ruled Congressional committees and key leadership positions for decades, acting as a bulwark against progressive legislation, bulwark against social reform, against the rights of labor, against civil liberties and militarism.

Outside the South, the Black vote has often been the factor tilting the scales in favor of democratic reforms, for peace and against foreign adventures, against McCarthyite and police state repression, and for social and economic measures that have widely benefited the masses of every ethnicity.

One mechanism for suppressing the Black vote in the South, and later throughout the country, were laws disenfranchising those who committed certain types of crime. And the Southern elite made no secret of their motive. The crimes were those supposedly most frequently committed by Blacks. Murder and armed robbery were not on that list. The Chief Justice of the Louisiana Supreme Court stated publicly that the passage of a criminal disenfranchisement law was necessary to establish the supremacy of the white race.

Other mechanisms of disenfranchisement, crafted to get around the 14th and 15th Amendments, were disguised as aimed at illiterates *of all races*, at those *of all races* who could not "reasonably" interpret their state constitution, at those *of all races* who could not pay a poll tax, etc. So today, disenfranchisement is a penalty for felons *of all races*, There could be no racial motivation, it is argued, wink, wink, since the Supreme. Court has ruled racial disenfranchisement to be clearly unconstitutional.

Today, 46 states and Washington, D.C. disenfranchise those behind bars; 32 states disenfranchise felons on parole; 29 states disenfranchise those on probation; 14 states disenfranchise felons who have fully served their sentence. In some states, one may lose one's vote for life for a single sale of marijuana or for shoplifting. Even where in theory the vote has been restored, in practice getting it back is a very difficult process.

As a result, in some states almost a third of Black men have lost their right to vote, and in many others almost a quarter. It is estimated that across the nation there are more than 5 million men disenfranchised, three-quarters of whom are no longer serving time, about a third of whom are Black. In some states, such as Mississippi, Virginia, Wyoming and Iowa, a quarter of the Black male population have permanently lost their right to vote. In Florida and Alabama, that number is one-third. Given current trends, between 30 and 40 percent of African-American men nationwide will lose their right to vote for some or all of their adult lives.

In Alabama, they are now expanding the list of offenses subject to disenfranchisement, most of them nonviolent, including the sale of marijuana.

The most dramatic situation involves Florida, where the number of disenfranchised has now risen to 950,000, the vast majority of whom are Black. Still not sufficient for their purposes, the Republicans in 2000 stole the election in Florida and thereby the national election by hiring a private company to compile a list of felons that was bogus, resulting in many being barred from the ballot box who, although not felons, had a criminal propensity for voting for the Democratic Party. Added to that were other devices, exposed in detail by Juan Gonzalez of the *New York Daily News*, resulting in the illegal suppression of tens of thousands of additional Black votes.

In Ohio, in the 2004 election, other voting suppression tactics were used -- again, mainly targeting Black voters -- resulting in the Republicans stealing another presidential election. In both cases the Democratic Party preferred to roll over and cede the election rather than make an issue of. Black voting rights -- reminiscent of the practice of the supposedly dovish, Israeli Labor Party which over the years refused to count the votes of the few "Arab" deputies when those votes would give Labor a legislative victory or maintain a Labor government in power.

Florida has recently eased restrictions for many ex-felons, in theory, but they will be allowed to vote ,among other conditions, only after having paid full restitution to their victims -- not very likely.

While there is a growing movement to restore the vote to ex-felons, the rabid racists push back. For instance, not too long ago in Pennsylvania, after a state court ruled that probationers and parolees had the right to vote, the legislature tried to nullify the decision.

But even among those pressing for reform, only a tiny minority support voting rights for those behind bars., Again, the corporate criminals, the political criminals, and the media criminals not only are allowed to vote but, generally speaking, it is only their "vote" that really counts.

"PRISON INDUSTRIAL COMPLEX'

It is fashionable today for the more conscious critics of the criminal justice system, those who are aware of its underlying inequities, to talk about a "prison-industrial complex." And by that term is usually meant that there is a significant commercial interest in incarceration, that prisons have become primarily profit centers. According to this theory, it is the profit motive which lies behind the huge increase in the prison population. While those who subscribe to this theory sometimes acknowledge that social control is also a function of the criminal justice system, they nevertheless place their main emphasis on the profits generated through prison construction, the sale of prison supplies, and the commercial exploitation of prison labor.

Indeed, in the 1980s, Congress authorized prison

administrators as well as private companies to use inmates for commercial purposes. By 1996, more than 70,000 were so employed. And during the years of unprecedented prison expansion, construction companies did indeed receive lucrative contracts worth over $5 billion. By way of comparison, however, the Pentagon *annually* spends $140 billion just on weapons procurement. In other words, in the boom period of prison construction, Pentagon weapons contractors were receiving six to seven *trillion* dollars, or over a *thousand* times more than prison construction contractors. In the great profit scheme of things, prison construction has been small potatoes indeed.

A lot is made of prison expansion as a jobs creation program for poor whites in rural and depressed communities. But historically, the oligarchy has never been concerned about workers' jobs, not even the jobs of white workers. In fact, as is well known, in the last several decades it has encouraged the country's deindustrialization with its massive transfer of jobs abroad. True, a few rural legislators saw prison construction as a boon to their economically devastated communities. But the boon has turned into a bust. Prisons have not provided the hoped-for stimulus to local economies, for most prison purchases of goods and services have bypassed local businesses and are made regionally or nationally. Moreover, prison expansion in rural communities has caused a strain on their housing, schools, and other local services. In addition, many prison employees commute and pay their taxes elsewhere, forcing the state to bail out with subsidies those communities hosting prisons. As for the anticipated bonanza of prison jobs, pay is low (nationwide averaging about $23,000) and working conditions highly stressful. As a matter of fact, corrections officers have a 10-year-lower life expectancy than the civilian population, and among the highest rates of heart disease, divorce, and suicide. In Midwestern and Southern states, the turnover rate is heavy. In fact, there is a nationwide shortage of prison guards.

Also cited as evidence of a prison-industrial complex is the new and until recently growing phenomenon of prison privatization. But if one looks at the number of prisoners under private supervision, they are puny indeed, representing only about 5 percent of the prison population and now leveling off. Incidentally, the guards in many of the private facilities are paid the munificent sum of $8 an hour. Contracts of the twenty-odd firms supervising prisons total $250 million, or an average of about $10 million per company, a mere drop in the bucket compared to the revenues of major corporations. Finally, a number of scandals involving privatized prisons have aroused public indignation as well as embarrassment of the state authorities.

Much is made of the use of prison labor, with its seemingly enormous profit potential, given that the inmates can be pressured to work for practically nothing and without the standard benefits of free labor. In practice, however, corporations find prison labor generally unattractive. To begin with, there are legal limits to the use of prison labor in regions where free labor is readily available. Such limits were imposed in response to the demands of both organized labor and business interests concerned with unfair competition. Most state-owned prison industries are only allowed to sell their products to other state agencies, and the percentage of inmates engaged in such production is quite small and has been declining over the last several decades. Furthermore, most state-run prison industries actually lose money, or at best break even, despite the fact that they receive hidden state subsidies and preferential treatment. UNICOR, which makes federal office furniture, is an economic basket case. Engaging in some work for the Pentagon, its products are more costly than comparable ones supplied by private firms and are of inferior quality.

Few corporations are interested in prison labor. Forced labor is not efficient. The president of a firm supplying goods to the federal government testified before Congress that it took at least four prison workers to match the work of one person in the private sector. Moreover, the extra staff and guards needed to monitor the inmates more than offset any advantage of lower wages. And the vast majority of private companies shun the stigma, a public relations problem.

We do not mean to altogether exclude commercial motivations. We live in a capitalist society where there is a tendency to convert every social activity into a profit-driven one. Thus, one can speak of a science-industrial complex, a university-industrial complex, an arts-industrial complex, and a charity or social-welfare-industrial complex. In our "free enterprise" society, even the efforts of individuals and groups to pursue high-minded social goals become increasingly prostituted. In that sense one can speak of a prison-industrial complex, where business interests seek every opportunity to batten on inmate misery.

If one could speak of a prison-industrial complex anywhere, it would have been in connection with the horrors of the old convict lease system, when Southern states regularly rented out to farm, factory and mine owners their mostly Black victims of Jim Crow justice, including "vagrants" rounded up for just the purpose. Often, being put at the disposal of such employers meant an early death. While profitable both to the states and the employers, the convict lease system produced only a fraction of what was extracted from "free" Southern Black labor. The most widespread form of exploitation was the sharecropping system and the peonage that went with it. One can make a case that the principal purpose of the convict lease system was to terrorize the sharecroppers who, if they did not accept the landlord's terms, including being cheated, would face eviction, charges of vagrancy, and the threat of a fate far worse than sharecropping.

The main objection to the theory of the prison-industrial complex is that it masks or underestimates the *politics* which lies behind the huge upsurge of the prison population, the fact that this has been part and parcel of the process of rolling back the gains of the Black freedom movement. That movement not only boldly confronted the system of white supremacy, but as indicated previously, triggered and inspired most of the other social movements of its time – the anti-war, free speech, women's liberation, gay liberation, the movements of other oppressed national and ethnic groups, including the Native peoples, Chicanos, Puerto Ricans, Asian-Americans, the environmental movement, the movement to defend civil liberties, and the movements on behalf of children and the elderly. And it set in motion a great counter-cultural movement, a reaction against the era's socially repressive conservatism. The political ferment of the 1960s, sparked by the Black freedom movement, forced the government to reluctantly institute a variety of anti-poverty programs, massively expand health protections, including Medicare and Medicaid, and address a host of other popular concerns with the creation of the Environmental Protection Agency, the Occupational Safety and Health Administration, the Consumer Safety Administration, and the Mine Enforcement and Safety Administration, among others. Important new rights were won for those ensnared in the criminal justice system – the Miranda rights, extension of the right to counsel, expansion of prisoners' rights, etc.

The Black freedom movement also dealt the first serious blow to McCarthyism. It stimulated such disaffection among Black (and some white troops) in Vietnam, many units being in a state of virtual insurrection, that the army ceased to be a reliable instrument in prosecuting the war. It was this, together with the resistance of the Vietnamese people, of course, that led to the peace that all the anti-war demonstrations had not succeeded in achieving, one of history's most closely guarded secrets.

In sum, the African-American freedom movement has been a catalyst for a host of democratic movements which have transformed both American politics and culture. Moreover, the freedom movement was beginning to challenge the very roots of oppression, exemplified by the increasingly overt radicalism of Martin Luther King and the growing influence of Malcolm X.

After making some initial concessions, after putting an end to the Southern, legal Jim Crow system (as opposed to de facto Northern Jim Crow, which continues to thrive throughout the country), the US oligarchy saw that things were getting out of hand. So the course toward democracy began to be reversed, picking up speed with the implosion of the socialist states and the emergence of the US as the sole superpower, ending the competition for the hearts and minds of the people of color in the Third World. The gains of the 1960s and '70s were rolled back, assisted by a propaganda campaign tarring Blacks as criminals, predators, rapists, murderers, drug dealers, and parasites generally. While Republicans took the lead in the racist smears, the Democrats were not far behind. Many in the white population were brainwashed into believing that the reforms of the 1960s and '70s had produced nothing but anarchy, permissiveness, and self-indulgence, resulting in the sapping of the nation's moral fiber, in the destruction of "family values," not only among Blacks but spilling over into the white community, as well.

Today, the Right wing has succeeded in demonizing all protest against racial injustice, which they label "playing the race card" or engaging in "the politics of racial grievance." The Obama Presidential victory, hailed as proof of the emergence of the post-racial society, was, of course, nothing of the sort, when to earn that victory Obama found it necessary to campaign not as a

Black man but as a man who just happened to be Black, found it necessary to repudiate his "mentor" Rev. Jeremiah Wright around whom a hysteria was whipped up for merely telling some home truths about the reality of white supremacy in America, and even had to keep his supporter old Jesse Jackson out of sight. Obama has subsequently demonstrated that he is "color blind," meaning blind and indifferent to the continued oppression of people of color.

IMPACT OF MASS INCARCERATION

The racist counterattack begun with Richard Nixon and his "Southern Strategy" went into high gear with Ronald Reagan, of which the mass incarceration of Blacks was a key part. It continued to be pursued in each subsequent administration, including that of the "first Black President" Bill Clinton, greatly contributing to the profound crisis of a large segment of the African-American community. That crisis is masked, to some degree, by the success, extremely tenuous, of modest numbers of African-Americans who have entered the middle class, including a sliver of beneficiaries of the crumbs of political office.

The incarceration of a million mostly young Black men has gravely damaged the Black family, about which the white power structure has shed so many crocodile tears, has ripped apart the fabric of community' life, and further undermined the community's economic viability.

Mass incarceration is part and parcel of the scourge of police brutality, harassment and abuse. Unfortunately, this has not been widely understood, for in the endless campaigns against police brutality the related issue of the criminalization of an entire generation is rarely raised. It is much easier to generate indignation around police brutality because it is understood to be totally unjustified, while the incarcerated are often viewed, even within the community, as guilty and receiving their just deserts.

Mass incarceration is linked to the fact that the powers-that-be have no place in today's economy for large numbers of African-Americans, who they now consider obsolete. There is no place for them even on the bottom rungs of the economy, for in this era of corporate globalization those rungs have been cut off. Economically valueless to the elite, they are looked upon as a permanent political danger, "social dynamite."

With this country's growing internal repression and international aggressiveness, with the ever tightening stranglehold over every facet of our lives by a handful of economic behemoths, with the growing dehumanization of our culture, mass incarceration is, as historian John Hope Franklin has aptly said, a "metaphor for our society."

REHABILITATION

Theories about the causes of street crime quite naturally shape attitudes toward rehabilitation. Whether prisoners can be "reformed" is an endlessly raging debate. To the reactionaries, street criminals are incorrigible. Efforts at rehabilitation have been a failure, they say, and as proof they point to the high recidivism rate despite countless rehabilitation programs. They therefore conclude that prison time should be made as painful as possible, passing over in silence the fact that this policy has long been in effect and has also failed miserably. (Concern about recidivism only extends to the street criminal. It does not apply to the corporate criminal, who typically perpetrates crimes not only repeatedly but uninterruptedly, concerning which the ever-forgiving state constantly wipes the slate clean.)

Liberals are more optimistic. They believe in rehabilitation, stress more humane treatment within prison, and the need for supportive services upon release. Since they believe that most people who commit crimes (street crimes) have been damaged by social deprivation, then it follows that those who have gone astray can be weaned away from crime by social intervention -- the provision of psychological counseling, education, and job and skills training programs which they believe should be undertaken both inside prison walls and after the prisoner's release. They acknowledge that prison rehabilitation programs have not always been successful, but they blame inadequate resources and a lack of creativity.

There is still another point of view, however, a radical one, that is never allowed into the debate. It condemns the conservatives as iron-fisted defenders of the status quo whose cynical view of the prison population expresses the fear and contempt by the elite of the poor and people of color generally. But it also criticizes the liberals for a superficial analysis and for offering no real solution.

A real solution would require tackling the problem of street crime at its roots, something which the liberals for various reasons, some ideological, some, self-interested, are unwilling or unable to do.

Take the question of education, for example. Undoubtedly, prisoners on average are far behind the general population in educational attainment. In fact, a large proportion are functionally illiterate. Obviously, there is need for further schooling which should be made available in prison, right up through the college level. But the public education system in the *general* population is itself a disaster, especially for African-Americans and Latinos. So the public school system is constantly reproducing the functional illiteracy of the prison population.

Certainly job training should be part of a prison and post-prison program. But the general population from which the prison population comes, especially Black men, are suffering disastrous rates of unemployment, comparable to the worst period of the Great Depression of the 1930s. What chance is there, then, of great numbers of prisoners obtaining family-sustaining jobs when they are not available to those without a prison record?

Yes, decent and affordable housing is desperately needed for those re-entering society. But how is this need to be met when, for example, there is a waiting list of several hundred thousand for New York City public housing, when gentrification is displacing hundreds of thousands of the poor and those of modest means, and when the housing crisis is becoming acute even for the middle class?

The point is that the solution to the problems of

those released from prison is tied to the solution if the problems of society generally, just as the solution to the problem of street crime is tied to the solution of social inequities.

Both conservatives and liberals agree that street criminals are deficient, not only in education, not only in employability, but also in moral character. For them the main "character defect" which must be cured is disrespect for authority. And deference to authority is considered by conservatives and liberals alike the chief measure of the prisoner's rehabilitation. While the conservative heaps scorn on criminals as vicious and hopelessly degraded, as sub-human types, the liberal has a more patronizing view of them and believes they can be "redeemed," at least some of them.

What is the definition of rehabilitation, according to both liberals and right-wingers? It is learning to "fit in," to be satisfied with a low-paying, menial job, to live out one's existence without making waves, and to sink into the likely premature grave silently, without fuss. Both Right-wingers and liberals agree that special encouragement should be given to those rare individuals of exceptional ability to help them "make it," and thereby become a role model for children. But be sure not to teach those children enough mathematics to figure out what their own real odds are.

The liberal solutions are truly feeble, for while acknowledging the social roots of street crime, their main focus is on individual, rather than social rehabilitation. For social rehabilitation can only come about through political struggle. Even personal rehabilitation, if we are speaking of significant numbers, can only come about through political struggle. And here we are speaking of the kind of personal rehabilitation that lies along the road taken by Malcolm X. That kind of rehabilitation requires a political understanding of the nature of our society, an ability to identify the real victims and the real victimizers. This is the kind of personal rehabilitation that is contagious, that spreads among the incarcerated and beyond. The first step in this rehabilitation process involves the stripping away of self-hate. It involves waking up to the fact that those who engage in street crime are not morally inferior, but rather that it is those at the top, the eminently successful and respectable, who are the real degenerates.

The second step in genuine rehabilitation, again using Malcolm X as a model, is to *act* on one's new awareness, to help spread that awareness and to work to destroy those anti-human forces which, while oppressing Black people in ways that are particularly vicious, are standing on the necks of the great majority of *all* people.

The struggle to completely overhaul society does not mean ignoring the need for immediate reforms. We do not deny the importance of demanding that all who come out of prison be furnished with paid training that leads to a guaranteed living wage job, be given affordable housing, free high-quality health care, etc. But for such demands to be more than just pious wishes, they must be backed by a mass movement whose goal is real people power.

PAROLE/RELEASE

Since the entire process of the criminal justice system is racist and vindictive, it would be strange if at the end of the process, the procedures for parole that fasten two million ex-prisoners with another set of chains, would be any different. Whites are disproportionately awarded and Blacks disproportionately denied both probation and parole.

California is on the cutting edge of prison policy nationally -- cutting indeed. The particular harshness of California's criminal justice system carries right through to parole. California was the first state to end discretionary parole and parole boards. 16 states soon followed. In California, even after completing their full sentence, former inmates must serve three years under supervision. In Texas, one may be subject to parole restrictions for up to 20 years. Nationwide, there has been a steady decline in the percentage of people released on parole, from almost 70 percent in the late 1970s to less than 25 percent today. In California, 90 percent of parolees return to prison not for a new crime but for parole violations. Around half of those in prison are there only for technical violations of their conditions of parole, not because of new criminal acts. And parole revocation hearings take place without the parolee having benefit of counsel. While in 1977, only about 8,000 parolees were sent back to prison, by 1999 that figure had reached 90,000. The situation is similar in prisons around the country. Yet the fact is that parolees and probationers are responsible for commission of only 4 percent of the most serious crimes.

As the National Criminal Justice Commission describes the shift in philosophy: "In the 1960s and 1970s, probation officers believed that their mission was to rehabilitate offenders, whom they regarded as clients. The goal was to increase community safety by helping them adjust to community life. Probation officers assisted them in finding work, overcoming drug problems, and accepting family responsibility. In the 1960s, parole systems reacted to the harsher political climate and changed their role toward one of punishment. The focus became catching offenders for violations and largely abandoned efforts to help the offender solve the problems that may have led to the offense."[40]

Parole officers now carry firearms, search homes and workplaces in clear violation of the Fourth Amendment (although the Supreme Court has ruled otherwise), can order arrests without probable cause and confine parolees without bail. This is why some inmates prefer to serve out their time than live under the yoke of parole supervision.

The change of parole philosophy just happened to coincide with the shift of the prison's ethnic composition from predominantly white to overwhelmingly of color. While back in the 1960s, approximately half of the parolees found full-time employment, today 70 percent of parolees -- and they are pouring out at the rate of over half a million a year -- remain unemployed a year after their release. 20 percent are homeless.

As a result of ever harsher sentences and parole policies, the prison population is substantially aging. From 1995 to 2003, middle-aged men accounted for more than half of the growth of the inmate population, despite the fact that for men 45 and over, recidivism rates for burglary and robbery are sharply reduced. For aggravated assault, the rate rapidly declines after age 21. Obviously, there is no purpose in retaining older inmates except to carry out a vindictive political agenda.

Nowhere is the hypocrisy of the government's war on crime more abundantly clear than in the treatment of those who have re-entered society. For example, the law allows employers to refuse to hire those who have served time, even though they have "paid their debt to society." In fact, in the great majority of states, prospective employers and all state licensing agencies have the legal right to take into consideration in their hiring decisions not only the applicant's prison record, but even arrests where the charges were dismissed. Obviously, this is a heavy burden for Black youth. Routinely rounded up, half become saddled with an arrest record.

When former inmates are able to find jobs, they earn only half the pay of those who were never incarcerated. And since African-Americans are imprisoned disproportionately, they face still more disproportionate discrimination on the job market. But it goes beyond that. In New York City, for example, white men with prison records receive far more offers for entry-level jobs than Black men with identical records. In fact, white ex-cons are offered jobs as often, if not more often, than Black men who have never been convicted of a crime but who are, as the title of a volume of Black prison verse puts it, "born into a felony."

One would think that in its war on crime the state would recognize a duty to provide family-sustaining jobs for former prisoners. One would think that the state would recognize its obligation to help them fill in the gaps in their education and assist in their meeting the competition of an ever more educated workforce. One would think it would be in society's interest to help them re-enter society successfully -- common sense. But common sense has nothing to do with the matter. On the contrary, former felons are actually legally barred from working in many occupations -- including law, real estate, medicine, nursing, physical therapy, and education. Those merely convicted of drug use cannot have a driver's license, cannot, therefore, drive to work, much less get a job as a cab or truck driver. (On the other hand, there was no legal barrier to the felon Ted Stevens continuing to serve as Senator of Alaska, which, on reflection, makes perfect sense, since being a crook has never disqualified anyone from holding political office.)

Liberals point to these restrictions by the state as misguided, counterproductive, and they call for reform. What they do not do is point out the political logic of such seeming irrationality, as well as all the other irrationalities of the criminal justice system. The liberals assume that the policy-makers are truly interested in reducing crime, assume that all the instances of inequity that run through the entire system are the result of mere blunders, lack of comprehension, short-sightedness, etc. The naive sociologists, criminologists and liberal lay people who urge their laundry list of reforms do not understand that for the supporters of the status quo, everything is going swimmingly, thank you.

Recently, there has been a shift in thinking in some Establishment quarters and within the "correctional" system itself. Some states are experimenting with re-entry programs to help former prisoners integrate into their communities to avoid "re-offending." Even a number of politicians are getting on board. It would be wonderful to believe that all this is the result of a new-found humanity. Alas, humanity has nothing to do with it. The fact is that the federal government is running up huge deficits and the state governments are awash in red ink. The prisons are filled and there's no money to build more. So, for example, there was the Bush Administration plan to contribute $165 million annually for rehabilitation: schooling, drug treatment programs, employment and housing assistance, family and community reintegration. With 650,000 exiting the prisons each year, that comes to the grand sum of $275 per person, $550 counting state matching grants. Not quite on the scale of the millions of dollars of subsidies given to each oil company. But it's the thought that counts.

"EX-OFFENDER"

A term often used to describe perpetrators of street crime is "offenders," and of course upon completion of their prison terms they are referred to as "ex-offenders." But just who is it that has been offended? Society? Well, to the extent they have offended society, they have equally been offended *by* society. In fact, society is the main offender or, rather, those who rule society.

346

But what about the criminals' victims? Have they not been offended? Yes, and those victims should direct their indignation principally at those who control this society, those who have the power to greatly reduce street crime by dealing with the conditions that produce street crime. Of course, those in power will do no such thing, because street crime is a small price for them to pay to maintain things as they are, a small price for maintaining their privileges. And, anyway, it is not they who generally are street crime's victims. Actually, the fat cats find street crime quite useful. It distracts the public from the elite's much more serious crime, helps fan racism, which is indispensable in maintaining elite rule, causes divisions *within* the oppressed communities, and is used to justify both crackdowns on civil liberties and cutbacks on vital social programs.

The ones we should be offended by are those who engage in crimes on a truly grand scale, committed not because they were forced to in order to survive, but out of greed and lust for power, crimes committed by the corporate elite, the venal politicians and the media moguls. Not only are those criminals not called offenders, they are even hailed as our most upstanding citizens. What is most offensive is that some of the worst crimes against humanity are perfectly legal, crimes that only the elite are in a position to perpetrate.

Of course it is deplorable that street criminals victimize innocent people, including members of their own communities. But the misery of those communities is not caused by street criminals. It is not the street criminals who are responsible for the abysmal health care, the disastrous schools, the jobs that do not exist and the jobs that exist but do not pay a living wage, the slum housing and exorbitant rents, police brutality and endless harassment.

Not surprisingly, many victims of oppression internalize the value system that supports their oppression. Hence, what passes for street wisdom is the saying, "If you can't do the time, don't do the crime," thereby conceding that incarceration, the conditions in prison, as well as the length of prison sentences, are entirely justified. But 99.9 percent of the worst offenders, together with their huge network of co-conspirators, confederates, apologists, all those who serve them in one capacity or another for a slice of the loot or for just a few crumbs, never "do the time."

Those screaming from the rooftops about street crime in reality couldn't care less about such crime. For, as we have said, if they did care, they would use their power to rid society of those social inequities which are responsible for street crime. That much is easy. What is far more difficult is rooting out the kind of crime which goes hand in hand with positions of power and privilege. And this can only be done through social change, fundamental social change.

HATE CRIMES

The great majority of states have added to their penal law the category of "hate crime," to which the Right objects, arguing that whatever a criminal's motivation, the damage is the same: a murder is a murder, an assault is an assault. Moreover, it is contended that since Blacks commit more crimes against whites than whites against Blacks, Blacks have no right to claim special victimization.

But there is a huge difference between a crime committed for economic gain and a crime motivated by racism. The latter is not only a blow against the individual victim but has the effect of terrorizing an entire community, and in periods of racial crisis, carries the threat of genocide. The murder of a white man by an African-American, say, during the commission of a robbery, carries no such threat.

Thus, lynching, for example, was not so much an act of violence to exact vengeance upon a particular victim as a periodic ritual intended to warn the entire African-American community to "stay in their place."

The pick-up mob assembled to administer beatings, lynchings, and other racist terror has now been replaced by the Men in Blue, night riders with sirens. Today, the most common form of hate crime is police brutality. It is not merely an expression of the individual cop's bigotry, to be addressed by the liberal milksop prescription of "sensitivity training." For police brutality is fully sanctioned, covered up and protected ,in other words encouraged, by the police brass, who receive their orders from their political superiors. Police brutality, as we have noted earlier, is essential to the system of white supremacy which, in turn, anchors our entire system of property relations. Ultimately, one might say that the present organization of society is itself a hate crime.

AFFIRMATIVE ACTION

One of the most successful strategies of the Right has been the stirring up of white resentment against affirmative action, which is, after all, only a very modest tool to redress historic inequities. Nevertheless, affirmative action for African-Americans is condemned as reverse discrimination, a grab by unqualified and undeserving Blacks who have shamelessly repudiated Martin Luther King's dream of the day when everyone "will be judged not by the color of their skin but by the content of their character." Apparently, that glorious day has arrived, so the ever-rightward-moving Supreme Court has in one arena after another ruled affirmative action unnecessary and therefore unconstitutional.

But the informal networks of family connections, social connections, business connections, alumni connections, fraternity connections, and political connections, all giving whites an inside track thanks to the legacy of slavery, Jim Crow, and hundreds of years of white advantage, constitute an unending affirmative action program. The huge racial disparities in wealth and income from which many white children benefit, including the benefits of inheritance, although they have done nothing to earn those benefits, is another affirmative action program which, like all the other forms of affirmative action for whites, is deemed natural, just, and so very constitutional.

CONCLUSION

The penal system is but a replica, in more brutal form because hidden from public view,, of the larger society outside the walls. Each day, correction officials commit untold numbers of crimes against inmates. And the perpetrators of such crimes are, from a moral standpoint, far inferior to those who are being "corrected."

Our justice system, both criminal and civil, is an *injustice* system. But this understanding is not sufficient. What is key is the realization that it is a *class* justice system, designed to protect the lives, property and rule of the oligarchy, who consider its racist character and other inequities not shameful but *invaluable*. The criminal *justice* system props up the criminal *social* system. Oppression of the poor, of people of color, and especially of African-Americans, is vital to the maintenance of elite power, and the inequities of the criminal justice system can neither be understood nor addressed without understanding and addressing the social structure as a whole. Therefore, efforts at criminal justice reform will prove ultimately futile if they are not part of larger efforts at fundamental social change.

And such change is coming. For when people become aware of their real interests, then the very idea of a small gang owning and controlling the vast resources of the country (and those of the rest of the world), including the people's labor, the very idea of that gang having the right to appropriate for themselves what is produced by the physical and mental efforts of others, will be seen as the moral obscenity that it is. And so when the people are in charge, this barbaric state of affairs will come to an end. And all the corporate elite and their henchmen, all the media owners who themselves are part of the corporate elite, all the politicians who are simply the tools of the corporate elite and whose main job it is to throw sand in the eyes of the people, in a word, who are nothing but glorified con men, along with the whole army of professors and pundits, the well-fed clergy, all the ideologues whose job it is to demonstrate through learned books or else just the one Good Book that black is white and white black, that slavery is freedom and freedom slavery, all the hordes of government officials and bureaucrats who administer unjust laws or who administer just laws in an unjust way – all these parasites will have to go out and find an honest living. And when the people are in charge, it will not simply mean casting a vote every so many years. Rather, the people will be actively involved in planning their own future and then helping to execute those plans, from the neighborhood up to the national level.

In short, one day all the things we now can only lament as a "crying shame" will be dealt with as a shameful crime. And when that great day arrives, then the gates will swing open for the vast majority of the "degenerates," "animals," the "criminal element" now languishing in our dungeons. Then a truly people's government will work to meet the needs and aspirations of the imprisoned, formerly imprisoned, and those who would ordinarily be heading for prison, needs which are, after all, only the normal needs and aspirations of all people.

Unfortunately, a prison population will remain, but

this population will be largely composed of our formerly esteemed members of society, the leeches battening on the labor of others, the pathological liars known as politicians, and the higher-ups of "law enforcement." In other words, the "upper crust" will be toast. But being optimistic by nature, I believe it will be possible to rehabilitate such anti-social deviants, in spite of the fact that most of them are hardened career criminals. I believe these offenders can be reclaimed through education, a program of honest labor, and proper socialization.

When we say that the wrong people are in prison, it is not that all current prisoners are innocent, although because of their poverty and color many have been falsely convicted, or at least given more time than would have been the case had they greater resources and a white skin. The wrong people are in prison because while the crimes committed by street criminals are for the most part perpetrated out of the need to survive, or out of a righteous resentment and a keen sense of the social injustice which they see no way of overcoming, the crimes of the privileged are perpetrated with a sense of entitlement and expectation of impunity.

We have frequently referred to the elite's insatiable greed. In a certain sense we have been unfair. Their greed, while indisputable, does not stem from some moral defect. For their predatory behavior is dictated by their social and economic position. In the fiercely competitive, dog-eat-dog, shark-eat-sardine world that is this system, to allow sentiments of humanity, compassion, fairness, etc., to enter into business decisions would be suicidal. For example, in order to stay in business every company not only does but *must* rob its workers. For its profits are derived from paying its workers less than the value that those workers produce. If this were not so, there would not be any purpose in hiring them in the first place. A famous French thinker once said that "property is theft," and it is in the above sense that he is absolutely correct. Thus, larceny is at the very heart of our system, is what makes the system tick.

MY "EXAGGERATION"

Many will dismiss my judgments concerning the elite's criminality as preposterous. Having lived in an upside-down society their entire life, the view that society should be turned right-side up can be quite disorienting. Some may admit that while there is a grain of truth in a few of my observations concerning the "business community" or our "public servants" or the media, everything has been wildly exaggerated. Again, perfectly natural, for veneration of the wealthy and powerful is this country's most popular religious cult. I will be accused of tarring business people and politicians with too broad a brush. It will be said that in every occupation there are a few "bad apples," and even if there are more than a few, there are significant numbers who are quite honorable. But my point is that there is a kind of gravitational field that pulls down even well-meaning individuals toward the principles, or rather, lack of them, by which society is governed. Honorable people are thus forced to do dishonorable things if they are to achieve any measure of material success and social acceptance. The moral recipes preached by parents to their small children have to be discarded as soon as the young ones leave the bosom of their family. And most parents would be alarmed if their children did not set them aside when they entered the "real world" -- the instruction never to lie, for example. In the real world, the ethical boundaries which individuals *refuse* to cross are generally the measure of the limits to their success. If this is true of the average individual, it is infinitely truer of people who are entrusted with the fortunes of large enterprises, where humane sentiment, generosity and compassion are absolute liabilities. And certainly this is true of politicians, whose job it is to serve the elite, as well as all those running interference for the elite and whose livelihood depends on that service.

As for my claim that the crimes of the elite go unpunished, it will be countered that almost every day one hears of politicians put away for corruption, of corporations being heavily fined, and even of an occasional corporate executive being sent to prison. True. But the legal actions taken against the elite do not even scratch the surface of their criminal deeds. To the extent certain members of the elite are prosecuted, they are the sacrificial lambs who must suffer for the sake of the *preservation* of the crooked system as a whole, the interests of the oligarchy as a whole. Of course, there are certain kinds of misdeeds by corporate executives and politicians that are frowned upon because they damage the interests of other corporations and politicians. For there is a rivalry among the elite, and the law is meant to regulate that rivalry and keep it within orderly bounds. There are rules to which even the elite must adhere in order to maintain the system's stability. The powers-that-be cannot permit sheer anarchy.

Further, the smooth operation of the system requires that the masses have some measure of confidence in the law's supposed even-handedness. The elite needs to keep up appearances. They are prepared to accept a certain amount of cynicism among the masses about the fairness of the law and the dispensation of justice -- that can't be helped. But they cannot afford to so rub the public's nose in it that the people lose all illusions about the system and arrive at the conclusion that what's good for the goose is good for the gander and that they, too, have every right to flout the law.

MY UNJUST VIEWS

It is also difficult for many to accept my judgment that the million men and women working in the criminal justice system, the cops on the beat, the prosecuting attorneys and the defense bar, the judges, corrections officers, parole officers, and all the others working in the system, all simply trying to do their best, working to take care of their families, are collaborators in a criminal enterprise.

Of course, there are varying degrees of culpability, depending on one's behavior and position within the structure. Obviously, it would not be fair to put on the same plane the Nazi hierarchy and the lowly German soldier drafted into Hitler's army. On the other hand, even soldiers in the lowest ranks cannot be completely exonerated of war crimes. True, many who develop misgivings about their role often feel trapped in their jobs and for economic reasons may not see any way out. Still, even they can do things from the inside that work against the system. And segments of the general public, with their reactionary and virulently racist attitudes, must also share blame for the justice system's criminal nature.

AM I TRIVIALIZING STREET CRIME?

I will likewise be criticized for supposedly trivializing street crime, for implying that murder and other violent crimes are petty. I do not regard such crimes as petty. But I do demand that such crimes be judged according to a single standard alongside the crimes of the elite, proportionate to the social damage inflicted.

The perpetrator of street crime often harms himself as well as those he victimizes. His crimes are usually self-defeating and harmful also to his family and his community. This in contrast to the elite criminals, for whom there is little prospect of punishment. Not only do their crimes build up their personal wealth but they add to that of their families, their associates, and their communities. And in the end, one of the fruits of their criminal acts is a bountiful estate claimed as a matter of right by their posterity. Crime doesn't pay? With the rarest of exceptions it *always* pays, if it is committed on a grand enough scale.

While we do not justify street crime, we refuse to moralize about it, to speak of street criminals as "offenders" or "ex-offenders," to urge that they make the "right choices," to preach the need for them to pursue a more upright life and follow a spiritual compass, etc. The alienation, rage and rebelliousness which is widespread among the oppressed, particularly among the youth, and which in part manifests itself in street crime, is a perfectly natural response to their cruel and humiliating conditions. Certain psychological qualities to be found in the "hood," qualities feared and hated by many whites and even sections of the Black middle class, are actually *indispensable* for resisting the injustice of their lives. What is required, however, is the *harnessing* of those qualities in the service of the struggle for social change.

This oppressive system is built on an ideology of rugged individualism. But genuine liberation cannot be attained by "personal redemption," by stepping over the community. This may lead to the rare, and necessarily rare, individual success but it leaves the community mired in the same wretched condition. Again, the only road to freedom is through collective struggle. But the struggle for the advancement of communities of color and for their empowerment, especially of the African-American community, is inseparable from the struggle for democracy for all, for a secure and prosperous life for the vast majority in all communities, for an end to the destructive domination by a handful over *all* communities.

It is not an easy road, often frustrating, requiring great sacrifice. And while there are many drawbacks to traveling this road, it has but one advantage: It is the *only* road that will lead to freedom, not a freedom on paper, but real freedom, a road that will lead to a society that is truly fit for human beings.

ON THE CENTRALITY OF RACISM

In a book devoted to crime and punishment, why has racism been so much its centerpiece? First, because racism is this country's *key crime*. And second, because racism is at the heart of the criminal justice system.

We need not revisit the horrors of the slave past. These are usually dismissed as "ancient history." But it should be noted that slavery existed 100 years longer than the period since its abolition. In fact, if we include the semi-slavery imposed on African-Americans following the very brief interlude of Reconstruction, it has only been two generations since Black people have managed to soar to their present status of second-class citizenship, North as well as South (Barack Obama notwithstanding). 400 years of humiliation and still counting.

One constantly hears the liberal refrain, "While much progress has been made, much remains to be done," as opposed to the conservative one that "While much remains to be done, much progress has been made." What is closer to the truth is that "The more things change, the more they remain the same." Yes, thanks to the Black freedom movement that peaked in the 1960s, US apartheid is less terror-driven. Progress has been made, but what is not mentioned is that regress has been made, as well.

Though "White" and "Colored" signs have been taken down, segregation in the area of housing is greater than ever, but now proceeding on the honor system. Jim Crow statutes and racial covenants are a thing of the past, replaced by "color-blind" zoning regulations and the knowing wink. In real life, Blacks and whites are steered "by custom" to what has been ordained as their respective neighborhoods, a scheme in which real estate agents, landlords, developers, banks and the local politicians all work hand in glove. There are now at least *four million* housing discrimination violations pending.

After World War II, millions of whites moved to the suburbs, thanks to the construction on a huge scale of tracts of inexpensive houses with white-only covenants, which in turn were made possible by government-financed white-only mortgages. Then more whites took flight to the suburbs when public schools in the cities "tipped," that is when more than a token number of Blacks began attending them. Sparing these suburban whites from the nasty and frightening experience of having to drive through the ghettos on their way to work was one of the reasons behind the massive program of "urban renewal" (also known as Negro removal). Black neighborhoods were chopped up and tens of thousands of African-Americans were uprooted to areas remote from economic activity, while those who remained found themselves stranded in what became zones of economic desolation. Today the "inner city" has become desirable real estate and is being gentrified. Black and Latino dispersal is the master plan (or the master's plan). The most efficient technique is simply blowing up the public housing projects, a la Chicago and Newark, while gentrification proceeds in more genteel fashion in Harlem, Brooklyn, and elsewhere, as rents are raised beyond affordability both in private sector housing as well as in the projects. The most dramatic example of gentrification and ethnic cleansing is New Orleans in the wake of Hurricane Katrina. We are not at the stage of the Final Solution just yet. It remains just a "thought experiment" of former Secretary of Education William Bennett, among others. So while we are not at the stage of extermination, dispersal may well represent the penultimate.

A half-century after *Brown v. Board of Education*, schools in the South, having been (very partially) integrated, are being re-segregated, while in the North they have become even more segregated than those in the former Confederacy. No longer do educators or politicians proclaim the need to keep Black "bucks" in schools separate from innocent white maidens, nor is it any longer asserted (openly) that Blacks are innately stupid. They just happen to be overwhelmingly placed in non-college tracks, in the slower classes, and in special education classes reserved for the emotionally disturbed and the intellectually "challenged." No longer are African-Americans barred formally by institutions of higher learning. Their huge and growing under-representation is simply the natural outcome of the "color-blind" policy mandated by the Supreme Court. And according to Right-wing ideologists, Martin Luther King would have been delighted to see Black people sinking under the weight of "color blindness." *Color blindness here, as elsewhere, simply means blindness to 400 years of oppression based on color.* To be color- blind is to be history-blind. Against reparations and affirmative action, the ideal is held aloft of "equal treatment under the law." But *equal treatment accorded to people in unequal circumstances is not equal treatment.*

No one talks about a "white man's job" any more. Black job applicants are now received with a gracious smile and then rejected with a smile equally gracious. While African-American unemployment rates have historically been high, usually two to three times white unemployment, the magnitude of the present disparity is unprecedented, officially covered up by the statistical sleight-of-hand to which we have previously alluded. In Chicago, for example, only one-tenth of Black teenagers find jobs, and if one doesn't find employment by age 21, one likely never will. Black women, especially immigrants, are once again seen pushing carriages with white babies, a type of "mammy" work previously shunned for years in favor of occupations that paid a living wage and were not associated with the demeaning images of slavery. Many jobs traditionally filled by African-Americans have evaporated because of mechanization and automation, while outsourcing has decimated better-paying jobs in manufacturing where Blacks had previously managed to secure an important foothold.

Laws which make certain types of racial discrimination illegal are generally honored in the breach. Regarding those laws one never hears the words "zero tolerance." They are treated only as minor infractions for which it would be absurd to demand prison time. Racial oppression does not rise, you see, even to the level of "quality-of-life offenses such as fare-beating or the spraying of graffiti.

GRAFFITI

Our good burghers indignantly
Curse the children
Graffitiing the subways, schools,
and other torture chambers.

Well, if you arraign the kids,
Let it be for gilding the lily.
For the city's ugliness
needs no embellishing.

But how about those kids' graffitied lives,
Their hopes besmeared,
Their future trashed?
Our burghers watch unperturbed
As methodically the system
carries out *its* vandalism.

The wealth disparity between Black and white is enormous. While Black household wealth is 10 percent of whites, after subtracting (rapidly sinking) home equity it is less than 1 percent, or a grand total of $300 compared to $36,000 for whites. And

-beyond large segments of the Black community having to cope with their growing obsolescence in this "information age," their shrinking place in the nation's economy;

- beyond being pushed out of the country's major cities through gentrification;

- beyond disproportionately losing their homes as a result of the sub-prime racket;

- beyond the growing crisis in health care that is wreaking particular havoc on African-Americans, with vast racial disparities in infant mortality, cancer outcomes, and premature death caused by high blood pressure, diabetes and AIDS, striking African-American women with particular vengeance;

- beyond the growing shredding of the social safety net, which has been particularly devastating for the Black community;

- beyond the prospect of a bleak future for an increasing number of Black children due, among other things, to an educational system over whom hangs the traditional pall of racist *contempt* and low expectations, the transformation of teachers into drill sergeants, and the further crushing of creativity and the desire to learn;

- beyond all the material privations and inequities...

there finally remain the daily "small" humiliations, the habitual stabs of racist insult, the ever-present harassment and brutality of the police, the media's insulting portrayals, the hidden and not so hidden signifying of the politicians, and the condescension of well-meaning liberals.

That racism is described here not simply as misguided and shameful but criminal will certainly puzzle many, so routine is it, so institutionalized, so taken for granted, oozing out of every pore of US society. And if there is still *little* appreciation by the great majority of white people of the suffering and humiliation associated with 400 years of being Black in America, there is absolutely *no* understanding of how *they themselves have been victimized* by the system of white supremacy.

Why is racism the key crime of this society? Because racist ideology was constructed to justify the theft of this continent from the native peoples and the genocidal wars against them, as well as justification for the kidnapping and enslavement of African peoples, whose labor and thus wealth was whipped out of them by a southern plantation elite. And because the plunder was shared in the North by the manufacturer, merchant, ship-builder and banker. Thus, the *foundation* of the American economy was laid through the colossal crimes against native and African peoples.

Throughout US history, racism has been enormously profitable: to capitalists, large and small, in extracting super-profits from Black labor, and exteraordinarily useful in dividing white worker from Black, indispensable to strike-breaking and union busting. Institutional racism enriched and continues to enrich merchants who charge African-Americans inflated prices for inferior products; enriched and continues to enrich landlords charging extortionate rents to Blacks trapped by residential apartheid while collecting a premium from whites living in "good" Black-free neighborhoods. Racism is a great source of super-profit to banks and finance companies charging African-Americans usurious interest rates as well as getting its cut from the enrichment through racist practices of the other business sectors.

Racism is central to the *criminal justice system* which, in turn, is one of the elite's most powerful tool of social control. The mass incarceration of African-Americans, the criminalization of Black youth, the relentless police sweeps in the ghettos, stop-and-frisks, brutality and harassment, are indispensable measures aimed at a population viewed as dangerous by the oligarchy -- not dangerous in the sense of being a menace to life and property, but *politically* dangerous. For far beyond their numbers, the African-American people have demonstrated their power to alter history.

Such power was shown during the Civil War when in the darkest days of the Union, the tide was turned by a quarter of a million Black soldiers, reluctantly allowed to put on uniforms after a long delay. Incidentally, Lincoln did not free the slaves; the slaves liberated themselves, as large numbers first escaped to Northern lines, then played a crucial role in freeing those still in chains. As a matter of fact, it was the former slaves who freed Lincoln, freed him from the fate of a likely Southern noose. And it was the Union victory to which Blacks had contributed so decisively that freed the North to surge ahead in economic development and enable the United States to become a world power.

The power of African-Americans to advance progressive change was shown again during Reconstruction, when African-Americans were for the first time given a modest voice in government. It was that bit of Black power that made it possible for poor whites as well as Blacks to win important battles against the plantation and merchant aristocracy, including, as previously mentioned, the creation for the first time in southern history of a public school system, a system that was gutted as soon as the white supremacists took over once again.

The potential of Black power was again demonstrated during the 1950s and '60s with its enormous progressive consequences for the entire nation. Conversely, the rollback of the gains of the freedom movement during the past several decades has brought with it a deterioration of the standard of living of most whites, as well as Blacks, has contributed to an increasing concentration of power in the hands of an ever more arrogant and aggressive elite, a growing assault on our liberties, acceleration of the destruction of our environment, and unleashing of wars of aggression, along with the open proclamation of Washington's intention to rule the world.

Racism is central to the maintenance of this criminal social system. And what makes it central is not that it oppresses people of color alone, but that it is damaging to the masses of the people, whatever their national or ethnic background. We pointed out, for example, that slavery not only oppressed Blacks but impoverished millions of southern white farmers who, unable to compete with slave labor, were driven into barren hills and destitution. The terrible price poor whites paid for slavery was nowhere more clearly laid out than in Hinton Helper's devastating pre-Civil War pamphlet, *The Impending Crisis*. A white farmer himself, no friend of the slave, he was perhaps the first to suggest that Blacks were entitled to reparations.

It was racism which broke up the Black-poor white alliance and destroyed Reconstruction, plunging the South, Black and white, still further into a century of poverty, illiteracy, and backwardness, making it a region which led the nation in all the indices of social misery, a region which racism ensured would be free of labor unions.

In the 1880s and '90s, Populism swept the South, a movement of resistance to the oligarchy. For a brief, moment, poor whites joined hands with poor Blacks against their common enemy. But once more, racism torpedoed that alliance, guaranteeing that the region would remain mired in backwardness.

It was racism that kept the AFL weak, at one time the main organization of labor. Because it would organize only skilled, white, native-born workers, it proved helpless to deal with the emerging modern industries such as steel, automobiles, and rubber. Only with the creation of the CIO, which actively combated racism and embraced all workers, was a breakthrough made, paving the way for a surge in union membership, higher wages and improved working conditions. And it was the political muscle of the CIO that was most responsible for the flood of progressive social and economic legislation known as the New Deal, and which put a leash on the rapacity of Big Business, bringing hope and relief to tens of millions of white working people, as well as Black -- in fact, to white even more than Black.

The central role of African-Americans in US

history was revealed again in the 1960s when the Black freedom movement began to shake the underpinnings of elite rule, transforming the political landscape of the nation, serving as a catalyst for the other movements for social justice inspired by its example: the women's movement; the movement of Puerto Ricans, Chicanos, native people, other oppressed national an ethnic groups; movements on behalf of children, the elderly, the disabled, the environment, the movement to defend and expand civil liberties, including the rights of the accused and the imprisoned. Many leaders in the anti-Vietnam War movement were first roused to political activity and became trained in the civil rights movement. It was the Black freedom movement which first stood up to McCarthyism, which had paralyzed all attempts to oppose the Right-wing, anti-labor, anti-democratic offensive at home and the belligerent policy of world domination abroad

The 1960s, with the Black freedom movement in the lead, further alarmed the Establishment because it inspired masses of disaffected youth to adopt what became known as the counter-culture, ripping off the straitjacket of cultural as well as political conformity and challenging the older generation's narrow-minded values.

That progressive upsurge was brought to an end with the Nixon Administration, backed by a "silent majority." The Reagan Administration came in on the platform, not explicit but understood by all, that this was still a "white man's country" and that America would not be pushed around anymore, neither by Blacks at home nor by nations of color abroad. A thirty-year period followed, rolling back many of the gains of the '60s, targeting the working class generally, but African-Americans especially.

It is racism which has been responsible for the reactionary political attitudes of so many whites, who equate poverty with African-Americans and who therefore can be counted on to oppose efforts to improve the conditions of the poor as giveaways to African-American parasites, even though whites make up the poor's majority, leaving the United States with the most close-fisted social protections among all the industrialized nations.

It is racism which has contributed to the broad approval among European- Americans of police state measures, often aimed against African-Americans, now also targeting Muslims, Arabs and South Asians, but paving the way for a Fascism in which those with white skins will not be spared.

And it is racism which has fostered the substantial measure of popular acceptance of US aggressive wars abroad, almost always aimed at peoples of color. The ideology of the "White Man's Burden" is alive and well, although the terminology has been updated.

In sum, it is racism which continues to blind the masses of whites to their common interests with African-Americans, preventing them from joining forces in the struggle against their common enemy.

The problem of racism can never be solved as long as its very presentation is itself racist. As conventionally laid out, it is not racism that is the issue but "race relations," a problem existing between the white and Black communities involving mutual suspicion, mutual-misunderstanding, both sides having legitimate grievances.

(See Barack Obama's "brilliant" and enthusiastically received speech on race during his run for the presidential nomination. Of course, in order to be elected president he could speak no other way.)

Racism, institutional racism, is not mindless, not pathological, as some liberals suggest, but a *rational strategy* that pays huge economic dividends to the elite. Racism is spawned spontaneously by an economic system based on ruthless competition, permanent insecurity, and a hierarchical system that by its very nature promotes and enforces inequality But the elite does not rely simply on the system's inherent tendencies. The "permanent government" knows it must engage in systematic racist indoctrination. For the bigotry of those of European descent is extraordinarily useful in diverting legitimate anger toward those even more victimized than themselves and away from those of their own "race" who are truly responsible for their problems. It is vital to the ruling class that the masses of whites be convinced (as so many are) that *more* for African-Americans means *less* for themselves, that any advance by Black people is obtained at the expense of European-Americans.

There is no greater proof of the depth of racism in this country than the widespread belief that it is basically a thing of the past, magically erased by this or that civil rights law or court decision. Pointing to the existence of an expanding Black middle class, most of whom are only a couple of paychecks from bankruptcy, and the success of a few Black high-profile personalities, many whites are convinced that any further Black demands for equality are nothing but "special pleading," a con game aimed at cashing in on "white liberal guilt."

I have presented but a few illustrations of the central role racism as played in US history, its use as the chief ideological and political means of control by the white elite, and, conversely, the tremendously liberating effects on the majority of society at each forward movement in the anti-racist struggle. The lesson for progressives should be that the anti-racist struggle cannot be relegated to one of a shopping list of concerns but must be recognized as central to every struggle for meaningful reform, including the reform of the criminal justice system, and central, as well, to achieving the ultimate goal, because we can and we will have a *society worthy of human beings.*

P.S.: THE LAST STRAW

The world has now plunged into unprecedented crisis. The mightiest financial institutions are in headlong descent, dragging down with them not only tens of millions of stock market investors, but a large portion of the middle class and the better situated workers who see their retirement savings disappearing into a black hole. Meanwhile, despite being showered with trillions of dollars of the people's money, as well as all kinds of lavish government guarantees, the bankers have gone on strike, refusing to supply desperately needed capital and other funds, and threatening to bring the economy to a grinding halt. While a transit workers strike in New York got its leader jail time, the strike of the bankers has got them one huge handout after another.

We are witnessing the crime of the century, perhaps the greatest robbery in history, and carried out in broad daylight. No guns used, Prof. Jensen will again be relieved to hear. A note was passed to the Secretary of the Treasury, "Give us your money or we all perish!" Turned out to be a hoax. But the money dished out to save the country is being used by the banks to buy out their competitors and give still more bonuses to their top executives, already quite well bonused-up.

Turned out also to be an inside job. The Secretary of the Treasury just happened to be the former CEO of the dominant banking house Goldman Sachs, and the man in charge of dispensing the bailout also just happens to be formerly with Goldman Sachs. Meanwhile, the trembling

Democrats and Republicans, ordered to lie down on the floor of Congress and keep their eyes closed, after some initial grandstanding for their hometown constituencies, quietly lay down, closed their eyes and kept them closed as another $140 billion was ripped off in a tax code giveaway that it was hoped nobody would notice. But still not enough. (When is it ever?) The Federal Reserve further "lent" a couple of trillion dollars to – nobody knows who. For Fed chairman Bernanke is a gentleman of the old school, not a cad who will kiss and tell.

The farce has just begun. The gang makes its getaway, the Congresspeople get up, shake themselves off, and some of them begin to yell that they were victims of a stick-up, that they were forced to give the banks the money, that there was a gun pointed to their head. But the gun turned out to be only Secretary of the Treasury Paulson's little finger.

The farce continues. The Wall Street Treasury Secretary under the Right-wing Bush Administration has been replaced by the Wall Street Treasury Secretary under the "Change we can believe in" Obama Administration, which will cede nothing in its generosity to Captain J.P. Morgan (haven't they named a rum after him?) and the other pirates. All this transpires to the universal outrage of a public powerless to oppose it. But cheer up, we live in a democracy that is the envy of the world, and especially of the terrorists who because of that envy, engage in suicide bombings.

Whipsawed between the worst banking crisis in history and the growing recession that also threatens to be the worst in history, the great mass of the people are facing a stark future: sharply declining living standards, unemployment, homelessness, and the specter of hunger, which is already a reality for millions of Americans, including the 30 million qualified for food stamps but not receiving them.

While the roots of the present financial collapse are usually traced to the sub-prime mortgage scandal, the groundwork was laid during long years of Wall Street's chase after easier and more seductive profits from high risk financial operations and crooked manipulations rather than the normal gain from supporting the country's productive backbone. What we are describing is a capitalism increasingly irrelevant to the needs of the people, increasingly parasitic. And in all this, the financial high-rollers have been abetted by a government eager to do whatever it can to pimp Wall Street's speculative orgies.

The carnage of home foreclosure is steadily spreading well beyond the bloodbath of the sub-prime mortgages. For the bursting of the housing bubble with its fictitiously inflated values has also burst the consumer spending bubble. The foundation of American prosperity during the past few decades has been built on quicksand. While the economic pundits have been quick to blame the people for living beyond their means, the fact is that the people were sucked in by financial institutions egging them on to assume unsustainable debt, luring them into home refinancing ventures, pushing them to become addicted to plastic, using some of the same bait-and-switch tactics with credit cards that were used in the sub-prime swindles. Now consumer debt is maxed out, of savings there are none, family budget strains are growing, particularly after decades of wage stagnation and rising inflation (officially understated), aggravated by a steady rise in unemployment (also officially understated). Thus, the economy is being buffeted by a perfect storm. Wall Street's joyride has ended in a crash that has totaled the financial institutions and wiped out all those in the passenger seats. At the same time, we are experiencing a slow motion disaster that is just part of the ordinary capitalist cycle of boom and bust. That cycle was stretched out, the bust averted for a time, but at the cost of the much more devastating one we are now entering.

In case you were wondering, we are still on the subject of crime. In the early part of this book we detailed the routine nature of the elite's criminal deeds. But the operations of our financial Mafia bear additional examination.

We begin with the mortgage companies who, riding atop the housing bubble, figured out that a lot more money was to be made if one could rope in those traditionally excluded from home ownership, particularly those who had been redlined by the banks in the past, that is, who had been denied loans because of their skin color. So African-Americans and Latinos were suddenly welcomed with open arms. However, instead of getting the normal mortgages for which 65 percent of them were qualified, they were forced into sub-prime contracts with their much harsher terms and trick stipulations. Criminal.

Further, even those who lacked the resources to buy a home were targeted with bait-and-switch offers -- tantalizingly low initial interest rates, to be shortly followed by unaffordably high ones. And once hooked, just to make sure the victims couldn't back out, they were saddled with stiff prepayment penalties. Inexperienced and naive, the borrowers were either unaware of the consequences awaiting them or were reassured that given the rising state of housing values they could always refinance their mortgage down the road. Criminal.

Jackals, also known as loan officers, falsified the lenders' applications, including employment status and earnings, passing them on to their superiors with a wink and picking up a hefty fee with each deal. And the *wolves* for whom they worked, with the alpha male, Countrywide, in the lead (about whom more later), in turn, chewed off fancy profits. Criminal.

Just the beginning. The mortgages were then sold to the Wall Street *vultures*, who then proceeded to "bundle" (in this case a term of art for adulterate) those worthless mortgages with others of more or less dubious value, on the theory that while you can't make a silk purse out of a sow's ear, you could if you stick 100 sows' ears together. These bundles were then "securitized" -- truly an ironic term since it was insecurity they brought to the markets, to the economy, and to the American people. In the process, they helped themselves to a nice financial return. Truly this was a Jesus-like operation, as seven *loaves* taken from people of modest and less than modest means were now feeding the entire world of *sharks*.

All this was part of Wall Street's general *modus operandi* -- creating all kinds of novel investment gimmicks: collateralized debt obligations, derivatives of collateralized debt obligations, derivatives of derivatives, credit default swaps, structured investment vehicles, and other weird and murky devices -- casino games that only the casino House understood, and sometimes not even the House -- all fantastically leveraged deals, also known as flying by the seat of one's pants, high-risk deals put together with borrowed money. Criminality in spades.

More skullduggery: To make these schemes fly, the banks turned to the holy men for their blessings, the ratings companies, Standard & Poor, Moody's and Fitch. It is their vital function to make sure values are what are claimed and that investors aren't buying a pig in a poke. But sure enough, not being so stupid as to bite the hand that fed them, they proceeded to rate all the exquisitely crafted junk "AAA." (No higher is possible.) And to earn their handsome fees they would have given their clients three times AAA.

Meanwhile, the housing bubble burst. Real estate values began to tumble. Sub-prime mortgages were being foreclosed, beginning with a trickle and becoming a mighty flood, spreading to standard mortgages, drowning the real estate market and the economy. Now the financial high flyers, including banks worldwide, found that they themselves were stuck with worthless paper. And with all that "bundling," no one could figure out which stuff was good and which wasn't. So all the buying and selling and all the lending and leveraging -- in short, all the activities that constituted the bread and butter of Wall Street, came to a screeching halt. The banks wouldn't lend to one another, didn't trust one another. In fact, they had been regularly lying to one another, for example, about the interest rates on the money they themselves were borrowing. Apparently, contrary to the old saying, there is *no* honor among thieves.

The pyramid of clever transactions, built on the slender reed of ripping off the poor, has come crashing down. The financial superstars, hoisted on their own petard, are forced to write off hundreds of billions, soon to be trillions, which the government is rushing to make good with the people's money in the biggest bailout in history. You see, the banks are "too big to fail." Their collapse would send the entire economy into a tailspin. On the other hand, the ruin of millions upon millions evicted from their homes presumably will not send the economy into a tailspin and is a matter of no urgency. Still, the trillion dollars initially offered just whetted Wall Street's appetite. The Federal Reserve Bank has according to the latest box score been shoveling some 14 trillion down the drain into the cesspool of the *world* banking system.

Just the beginning. The Federal Reserve has instituted a policy of making available unlimited amounts of money to the banks at *zero* rate of interest and has promised to continue doing so for years to come. This has driven down the earnings of the upper middle class as well as a large segment of the middle class generally, who depend on normal interest rates to help maintain their retirement or future retirement. This shoveling of free money to the banks is called "stimulating the economy." In theory, there is supposed to be a trickle-down benefit of low interest rates for those borrowing from the banks, including those who wish to finance the purchase of a home. But a funny thing happened on the way to the forum: the banks ain't lending

After all this, in spite of the disaster in part caused by the lack of transparency of their maneuvers, the leading banks are now coming together in a vast enterprise called "dark liquidity pool trading," where they will continue to engage in anonymous and still more murky transactions, preparing the way for the next great calamity (if we ever recover from this one).

Getting back to the mortgage swindles. As we have said, there has been no bailout for those threatened with foreclosure. Actually, their bones had not quite been picked clean yet. So descending on them were the *buzzards*, the predatory lenders promising to solve their problems by refinancing their mortgage on terms, as it turns out, that have only thrust them into a morass from which there can be no exit. Criminal.

Finally, not content with their pound of flesh, the *hounds of hell* are biting the dispossessed all the way to bankruptcy court, with false foreclosure charges and all manner of fees, legal and illegal, including late fees, "demand fees," "overnight delivery" fees, fax fees, and "payoff statement charges." The *Times* reports, "Bankruptcy specialists say lenders and loan servicers often do not comply with even the most basic legal requirements." The nation's largest mortgage company, Countrywide Financial, for example, continuing to pursue its debtors through to bankruptcy court had somehow "lost" or destroyed checks totaling more than half a million dollars. It even admitted in court to the fabrication of documents. Countrywide, as well as its individual executives, are now the target of a dozen or more investigations by the Securities and Exchange Commission, California and Illinois federal prosecutors, and a U.S. bankruptcy trustee. Yet amidst a rising chorus of complaints about its criminal practices, it received $11 billion in loans. And finally, Bank of America was happy to welcome Countrywide into its bosom, not deterred by its stink. As for Countrywide's CEO, he was forced to resign in shame with a $142 million severance package.

Then the major banks, too, were caught falsifying mortgage documents -- "robo-signing" it was called -- which put a halt (only temporary) to the stream of evictions.

It is clear from studying the corporate rap sheets that we are not dealing with a few "bad apples" but a culture of criminality, where the law is not only flouted repeatedly but uninterruptedly -- raising the question whether the crimes of Big Business are abuses of our "free enterprise" system or their typical expression.

Adding insult to injury, the Right-wingers are blaming the victims for the present economic debacle. The crisis is being laid at the doorstep of the poor because they acted "irresponsibly" in taking on obligations they could not afford. Moreover, they were encouraged to act irresponsibly by a "politically correct" government which twisted the arms of honorable mortgage companies, scrupulous to a fault, to act contrary to their sound business principles. It follows that the people of color, who make up the great majority of those victimized by the sub-prime racket, forced the mortgage companies to sell their practically worthless paper to Wall Street, twisted Wall Street's arms and made them engage in mortgage bundling, credit default swaps, leveraged transactions, and all the other outrageous manipulations.

The greed that led to the collapse of the financial structure cannot be laid to one, a few, several, or even many financial institutions, one, several or many Wall Street executives. It is universal. The present crisis is only the latest in a series of scandals stretching back to the birth of our financial institutions. In other words, scandals are the norm, and the ruin that results is part of what is now elegantly referred to by the apologists of capitalism as "creative destruction," meaning that millions of people must periodically go under and be crushed in order that capitalism may continue its triumphal march.

Such is capitalism's bitter harvest. How much longer will we tolerate its crimes?

HOSPITAL CRIES

Yes, let her rip, little one,
Open up your lungs
And pour out your rage.
With criticism you enter the world,
With criticism I am going out.
So holler away, little one,
And I'll join along.
They may not hear *me*,
But I'm betting on *you*.

NOTES TO PART 1-
THE CRIME OF IMPUNITY

1. Christopher Jencks, *New York Review of Books* February 1, 1987
2. *Ibid.*
3. The President's Commission on Enforcement and Administration of Justice, Task Force Report: Crime and Its Impact and Assessment. Chapter 8. White Collar Crime, 1967.
4. Jencks, *Supra*
5. *NY Times,* September 20, 2005
6. *NYT,* August 18, 2006
7. *NYT,* January 3, 2007
8. *NYT,* January 23, 2007
9. *New England Journal of Medicine,* May 21, 2007
10. Richard Horton, *Lancet,* March 2004
11. *JAMA,* April 16, 2008
12. *NYT,* September 27, 2007
13. Gustavus Myers, History of the Great American Fortunes. 1936 ed,. 399
14. *NYT,* February 2, 2006
15. *NYT,* June 12, 2007
16. *NYT,* December 1, 2006
17. *NYT,* March 11, 2008
18. Minnie Fisher Cunningham: A Suffragist's Life in Politics. Judith McArthur and Harold Smith (eds.) 2003, 187
19. Jeannine Swift, Dream and Reality: The Modern Black Struggle for Freedom and Equality. 1991, 132
20. *Wall Street Journal,* September 9, 2005
21. Edwin Black, IBM and the Holocaust. 2001, 338

22. *NYT,* July 18, 2007
23. *NYT,* July 21, 2007
24. Paul Cimbala and Randall Miller (eds.), An Uncommon Time: The Northern Home Front During the Civil War. 2002, 104
25. Matthew Josephson, The Robber Barons: The Great American Capitalist 1861-1901. 2011 edition, 50
26. Robert F.. Kennedy, Jr., Crimes Against Nature. 2004, 7
27. *Natural News,* January 16, 2007
28. Spitzer interview with *Financial Times,* November 3, 2003
29. Gary Weiss, Wall Street Versus America, 2007,46
30. Kennedy, 6
31. *Ibid,* 7
32. James Wilson, The Earth Shall Weep; A History of Native America, 1998, 165
33. Ward Churchill and Jim Vander Wall, Agents of Repression, 1988, 114
34. L.B. Moses, Wild West Shows and the Images of American Indians. 1996, 61
35. Myers, 511
36. Ferdinand Lundberg, The Rich and the Super-Rich. 1968, 115
37. *Ibid.,* 113
38. *Ibid.,* 126
39. House of Representatives, 95th Congress, June 1978 report of the Committee on the Judiciary, White Collar Crime: The Problem and the Federal Response. 45
40. *NYT,* May 11, 2006

41. Robert Pear in *NYT,* December 8, 2006
42. Monica Davey in *NYT*, May 1, 2006
43. C. Vann Woodward, Origins of the New South 1877-1913. 1972, 105
44. *Ibid.*
45. History News Network, George Mason University
46. Milton Friedman, Capitalism and Freedom. 1962, 133
47. Thomas Schoonover, Uncle Sam's War of 1898 and the Origins of Globalization. 2003, 99
48. *Ibid.,* 83
49. *Ibid.,* 77
50. William Appleman Williams, The Tragedy of American Diplomacy. 1984, 63
51. Smedley Butler, Common Sense. 1935
52. Quoted in Gabriel Kolko paper presented to Congressional Conference on War and National Responsibility. February 20-21, 1970
53. *NYT,* March 4, 2007
54. Ben Bagdikian, The Media Monopoly. 2004, 236
55. Gary Weiss, Wall Street Versus America. 2006, 27
56. Karl Menninger, The Crime of Punishment, 2007, 33
57. C.L.R. James, The Black Jacobins. 1989, 88-89

NOTES TO PART 2-
THE CRIME OF PUNISHMENT

1. Keith Medley, We As Freemen: Plessy v. Ferguson. 2003, 208
2. W. Royce Adams, Viewpoints. 2010, 171
3. Karen E. Rosenblum, The Meaning of Difference: American Construction of Race, Sex and Gender, Social Class and Sexual Orientation. 2008, 22
4. Paula Giddings, When and Where I Enter. 1984, 87
5. Gad Heuman, The Slavery Reader. 2003, 257
6. Herbert G. Gutman, The Black Family in Slavery and Freedom 1750-1925. 1976, 213
7. *Ibid.*, 225
8. *Ibid.*, 226
9. *Ibid.*, 456
10. *Ibid.*
11. James M. McPherson, Negro's Civil War. 1971, 113
12. Kenneth Cooper, *Washington Post*, June 215, 2000
13. New York Civil Liberties Union newsletter, September 10, 2007
14. David Horowitz, Hating Whitey and other progressive causes. 1999, 44
15. Richard Schickel, D.W. Griffith: An American Life. 1996, 269
16. Ulrich B. Phillips, "The Plantation as a Civilizing Factor," in *Swanee Review*, July 1904, 263
17. Thomas F. Gossett, Race: The History of an Idea in America. 1997, 271
18. Richard C. Cortner, A "Scottsboro"; Case in Mississippi: The Supreme Court and Brown vs. Mississippi. 1996, 48

19. Deborah Gray, Ar'n't I a Woman? 1999, 30
20. *Ibid.,* 47
21. *Ibid.,* 63
22. Gutman, 437
23. Cornel West, Jr. and Eddie Glaude (eds.), African Religious Thought. 2003, 438
24. *NYT,* November 23, 2007
25. Woodward, 160
26. Frederick Douglass, Narratives of the Life of Frederick Douglass (1845) 2004, 67
27. *NYT,* July 18, 1990
28. Alexander Cockburn and Jeffrey St. Clair, Whiteout: The CIA, Drugs, and the Press. 1998, 245
29. *Ibid.,* 260
30. Kristian Williams, Our Enemies in Blue. 2004, 144
31. *NYT,* June 26, 2007
32. *NYT,* November 8, 2005
33. Josephson, 367
34. *NYT,* April 23, 1987
35. Erik Olin Wright (Ed.), The Politics of Punishment. 1973, 24
36. Roger Streitmatter, Voices of Revolution: The Dissident Press in America. 2001, 233
37. Frank L. Rundle, "The Roots of Violence at Soledad," in The Politics of Punishment. 1973, 172
38. Eric Foner, A Short History of Reconstruction. 1988, 133
39. Steven R. Denziger (ed.), The Real War on Crime: The Report if the National Criminal Justice Commission. 1996, 190

Selected Bibliography

Arnold, Thurman, <u>The Folklore of Capitalism</u>, Yale Univ. Press, 1937

Bagdikian, Ben H., <u>The Media Monopoly</u>, 4th ed., Beacon Press, 1992

Barry, John M., <u>Rising Tide, The Great Mississippi Flood of 1927. And How It Changed America</u>, Simon & Schuster, 1997

Black, Edwin, <u>IBM and the Holocaust</u>, Crown, 2001

Bloom, Jack M., <u>Class, Race & The Civil Rights Movvement</u>, Indiana U. Press, 1987

Brawley, Benjamin, <u>A Social History of the American Negro</u>, Collier Books, 1970

Carroll, Peter N., and David W. Noble, <u>The Free and the Unfree: New History of the United States</u>, 2nd ed., Penguin Books, 1988

Churchill, Ward and Jim Vander Wall, <u>Agents of Repression</u>, South End Press, 1988

Clinard, Marshall, and Peter Yeager, <u>Corporate Crime</u>, Free Press, 1980

Cockburn, Alexander, and Jeffrey St. Clair, <u>Whiteout</u>, Verso, 1988

Currie, Elliott, <u>Crime and Punishment in America</u>, Henry Holt, 1998

Denziger, Steven, ed., <u>The Real War on Crime</u>, Harper Perennial, 1996

Douglass, Frederick, <u>Narrative of the Life of Frederick Douglass</u>, Prestwick House, 2004 ed.

Downe, Mark, <u>American Foundations</u>, MIT Press, 2001

Dubois, W.E.B., <u>Black Reconstruction</u> in America, Russell & Russel, 1935

Foner, Eric, <u>A Short History of Reconstruction</u>, Harper-Collins, 1989

Franklin, John Hope, and Alfred A. Moss, <u>From Slavery to Freedom</u>, 8th ed., McGraw-Hill, 2000

Friedman, Lawrence M., <u>Crime and Punishment in American History</u>, Basic Books, 1993

Giddings, Paula, <u>When and Where I Enter</u>, Bantam, 1984

Greene, Helen Taylor and Shaun L. Gabbidon (eds.), <u>Encyclopedia of Race and Crime</u>, Sage, 2009

Gutman, Herbert, <u>The Black Family in Slavery and Freedom</u>, 1750-1925. Pantheon Books, 1976

Holbrook, Stewart H., The Age of the Moguls, Doubleday, 1953

Irons, Peter, A People's History of the Supreme Court, Viking, 1995

Jacobson, Michael, Downsizing Prisons, NYU Press, 2005

Josephson, Matthew, Robber Barons, Harcourt Brace, 1934
_____, The Great American Capitalist, Harcourt Brace and Co., 1934

Kennedy, Robert F., Crimes Against Nature, Perennial

LaFeber, Ferdinand, Richard Blenberg and Nancy Walsh, The American Century, 3rd ed., Knopf, 1986

Levinson, David (ed.), Encyclopedia of Crime and Punishment, Sage, 2002

Lundberg Ferdinand The Rich and the Super-Rich, Lyle Stuart 1968

Mauer, Marc, The Race to Incarcerate, The New Press, 2006

Mayer, Jeremy D., Running on Race, Random House, 2001

McCoy Alfred W.. The Politics of Heroin, rev. ed., Lawrence Hill, 2003

Mokhiber, Russell, Corporate Crime and Violence, Sierra Club Books, 1988

Myers, Gustavus, History of the Great American Fortunes, Modern Library, 1936

Nader, Ralph, The Ralph Nader Reader, Seven Stories Press, 2000

NOBO Journal of AfricanAmerican Dialogue, Black Prison Movements USA, Africa World Press, 1995

Parenti, Christian, Lockdown America, Verso, 1999

O'Brien, Robyn, The Unhealthy Truth. How Our Food is Making Us Sick and What We Can Do About It, Harmony, 2009

O'Reilly, Kenneth, Racial Matters: The FBI's Secret File on Black America, Free Press, 1989

Perkins, John, Confessions of an Economic Hit Man, Berrett-Koehler, 2004

Schoonover, Thomas, Uncle Sam's War of 1989 and the Origins of Globalization, Univ. Press of Kentucky, 2003

Streitmatter, Rodger, Voices of Revolution: The Dissident Press in America, Columbia U. Press, 2001

Sutherland, Edwin H., White Collar Crime, The Uncut Version, Yale Univ. Press, 1985

Thomas, Dana, <u>Lords of the Land</u>, G.P. Putnam & Sons, 1977

Webb, Gary, <u>Dark Alliance</u>, Seven Stories Press, 1998

Weiss, Gary, <u>Wall Street Versus America</u>, Portfolio, 2006

White, Deborah Gray, <u>Ar'n't I a Woman?</u>, W.W. Norton, 1999

Wilkinson, J. Harvie, III, <u>From Brown to Bakke</u>, Oxford U. Press, 1979

Williams, Kristian, <u>Our Enemies in Blue</u>, Soft Skull Press, 2004

Williams, William Appleman, <u>The Tragedy of American Diplomacy</u>, W.W. Norton, 1984 ed.

Woodward, C. Vann, <u>Origins of the New South</u>, Louisiana State U. Press, 1971

Wright, Erid Olin, ed., <u>The Politics of Punishment</u>, Harper & Row, 1973

Websites

Justice Policy Institute
The Sentencing Project
The Vera Institute
The Urban Institute
Corporate Crime Reporter